The
Third
Sex

The
Third
Sex

The New
Professional
Woman

Patricia A. McBroom

PARAGON HOUSE

First paperback edition, 1992

Published in the United States by
Paragon House
90 Fifth Avenue
New York, N.Y. 10011

Library of Congress Cataloging-in-Publication Data

McBroom, Patricia.
The third sex : the new professional woman / Patricia A. McBroom. — 1st pbk. ed. p. cm.
Originally published: New York : W. Morrow, c. 1986.
Includes bibliographical references and index.
ISBN 1-55778-405-1
1. Women in the professions–United States. 2. Women in finance–New York (N.Y.)
3. Women in finance–California–San Francisco.
4. Sex role—United States. I. Title.
[HD6054.2.U6M36 1992]   331.4'81'000973—dc20   91-44163   CIP

10 9 8 7 6 5 4 3 2 1

Manufactured in the United States of America

To my family

Preface to the Paragon House Edition

Many people have wondered why I titled this book *The Third Sex.* Some readers have been incensed, believing that I was calling them weird or implying homosexual tendencies. Others felt the title was ill-advised because it could be misinterpreted.

A quite opposite reaction came from people who thought the title captured their sense of having been through an enormous change as women, which forever separated them from their traditional gender roles. They saw the title, as I meant it, to represent change from *The Second Sex,* Simone de Beauvoir's title for her classic work on female subordination.

This split in reaction has been nearly equal and quite strongly felt. I decided, as a result, to devote this preface to exploring the multiple meanings of the words *the third sex,* as they apply to us as women. The meanings are loaded with both positive and negative implications, and this ambivalence is a central feature of the gender changes of the past two decades. I would not change the title if I could do it all over again, but I do apologize for any grief it may have caused among people who felt the struggle was hard enough without having some book call them weird.

The women in this book have walked through a wall separating the two genders. They have taken risks with their sexual identity, not their sexual preference, to learn how to live and work in a world defined by men. The passage has been alternately confusing, frightening, alienating, and exhilarating, and it remains that way for millions of young women just setting out on new careers.

This new path is a third way of being in the world—that is, it borrows from the male and female past but belongs to neither. The result is to alter normal gender behavior for women so dramatically and so thoroughly that a new cultural form is created, identified in historical literature of the twentieth century as the New Woman and identified here as The Third Sex.

Preface

There are so many feelings accompanying this change that any one incident cannot capture the whole of it, but the following story tells a common experience of being in the space between the two genders.

While I was traveling in Morocco in the early 1970's with a friend, we picked up a small boy along a road near the Sahara. He was hitchhiking to his home in the next village. From the back seat of our car, the boy talked avidly, inviting us to his home, all the while calling me *monsieur*. I was wearing jeans and short hair and thought he could have make a mistake, so I laughed and tried to correct him. But he kept on using the word.

When we reached his goatherder's house, his family welcomed us warmly, inviting us upstairs for tea. The small abode room on the second floor was empty of furniture, except for an Oriental carpet spread out on the floor. The owners gestured for us to sit down, which we did, along with all the male members of the family. The women stood in a corner giggling. They served us without ever sitting down.

As the only woman on the carpet, I felt uncomfortable and ambivalent. Glad to have the privilege of sitting down, I also felt different and apart from every other person in the room. I clearly didn't belong to the women's group and I clearly wasn't a man. I was some member of another gender, which I thought of as a third sex.

Senior executive women talk about having similar experiences in social settings where the professional woman may find herself standing as the sole woman among male colleagues, while every other female in the room—all spouses—have gathered somewhere else.

It was equally strange in the 1960s to go to a pool during the day and find only women and children there. Somehow I wasn't part of the same gender, although I was heterosexual. I was doing something different with my life, and that was the split that began among women as so many of us departed from traditional roles over the past three decades.

In spite of the sense of being at times in a no-man's land between the two genders, it has been exhilarating to take on the prerogatives of a fully empowered adult human being. This change from a subordinate female role, enshrined in the gender patterns of the postwar era, was the crucial task of women over the last thirty years—to support their own lives and to develop and defend their own ideas. It has been a magnificent accomplishment.

Knowledge generated by women is now enriching intellectual life throughout the society, its power demonstrated by the degree of male opposition in some academic circles. And women are helping to bring new organizational and leadership skills to business that mitigate some of the more destructive aspects of a work hierarchy.

These things were made possible because individual women everywhere took the heart-stopping step of breaking the mold, over and over again, in personal ambition, family patterns, public persona, gender behavior. We stretched what was allowable for "proper" women. We hungered for the freedom to exercise direct authority rather than to stand behind the scenes. We wanted to affect the course of history in ways other than solely through rocking the cradle. We are doing that.

There was a price to pay for these advances, and that too is part of the story of the third sex. Too frequently the accomplishments have been felt in painful personal loses. In reaching for elite professional roles, women encounter male culture in its most powerful and resistant form. The standard-bearers of that culture often describe a preferred model for female achievement that involves surrendering reproduction. Women hear in multiple ways that they cannot excel and also parent. Moreover, the lengthy training period for many professions leads to perpetual delays in personal life that bear down particularly hard on women.

In addition, some women who may have already surrendered personal options can collude with male culture in setting up an ascetic model for ambitious women in which a kind of female monkhood is seen as a completely equivalent and reasonable alternative to having a family. In a cartoon published in the *New York Times*, a woman is talking to a man at a cocktail party about her daughter. She says "I know what you mean. My daughter doesn't know whether to get married or live alone or just move in with somebody or to quit smoking, except for marijuana, or to become totally drug free or to quit drinking altogether or to have a child or to adopt or just to ignore sex or become celibate and take more sedatives or...."

The point of the cartoon would seem to be that our lives as women are impossibly complicated with choices. From a position of no choice thirty years ago, now we have so many that young women are baffled about how to lead their lives. But hidden among the alterna-

9

tives are choices in which the daughter surrenders sex, children, and marriage. Such an alternative as renouncing sex and living alone would not be offered to a young man unless he were training for the priesthood. Yet this is presented to women and sometimes demanded of them if they expect to have significant careers.

This classic dilemma for women of having to choose between family roles and career roles, which dates back more than a hundred years, erupted into public consciousness during the five years since this book was written. A new chapter traces developments since 1986, as they appeared in the pages of the *Harvard Business Review*. I have used that publication as a window on intellectual leadership in American business.

We are not close to solving the dilemma, most especially at the political level. As the new material demonstrates, a national effort to provide working people with more family time has been stymied, along with efforts to change a workaholic culture. Elite professions still demand body and soul of their practitioners.

Yet a slowly growing number of women do seem to be integrating the two roles. Like the working mothers in this book, they plunge ahead following their own instincts, and many of them find that, contrary to the prophecies of doom, children and careers do mix. There is always more than one way to skin a cat.

Patricia McBroom
Oakland, 1991

Preface

Millions of men and women are struggling with the consequences of collapsing gender worlds, triggered by the mass movement of women into professional roles originally restricted to men. This major cultural change on the part of women affects reproduction, marriage, gender identity and behavior, relationships with parents, relationships with children, and every other corner of personal life. Moreover, it is accompanied by a profound impact on the lives of men and the meaning of masculine identity. Changes like these, which have been in process for 150 years at least, are coming so fast and in such numbers today that social science can hardly do more than snatch an image of the scene before it moves on again.

This book is such a snapshot. It captures a picture of forty-four financial women in New York and San Francisco from the fall of 1981 to the spring of 1982, whom I interviewed with lengthy, in-depth questions such as: In what ways have they changed over the years, how do they feel about being mothers, what do they think of femininity, what were their parents like, and what, if anything, have they surrendered for the sake of their career?

I structured the interviews to yield data that I could analyze for patterns that would throw light on the integrating worlds of men and women. I then placed my data in a historic and cultural framework, drawing on European history as well as information about gender behavior from non-Western, preindustrial cultures. It is my hope that this analysis—which took two and a half years—will give men and women everywhere a better understanding of the stressful cultural changes now going on in their lives.

I selected women working in finance, but the group could have been from medicine, or law, or any one of several other professions. The important point was to limit the sample to one working environment. An anthropologist studies the behavior of individuals within a cultural setting. Each profession can be considered a subculture of American life, with its own special values, beliefs, customs, and practices affecting the ability of professionals to have families. The opportunities for personal life that career men and women deal with are not the same in medicine, teaching, communications, and business, to name only a few. More humanism is encountered in medicine, for instance, than in business. More freedom for personal idiosyncrasies is allowed to people in communications. More flexible time is afforded to faculty members in a university. All of these factors influence the way women adapt to their careers. By limiting my sample to one profession I simplified the sources of environmental variation. More significantly, however, an anthropologist understands human behavior *only* within a cultural setting; it has no meaning otherwise. From my perspective, there is no such thing as a representative sample of American women, but only individual women acting within many different kinds of cultural settings. The problem is to find an environment that is small and well defined—and significant enough to be relevant to the larger society.

A modern, mass society, such as the population of the United States, presents serious problems to an anthropologist who wants to understand cultural forces. To begin with, America is not a single culture but an amalgam of many different traditions, often brought together in a new and ever changing urban setting. Moreover, it is huge, far too big to study with the in-depth, personalized techniques of an anthropologist, whose methods are designed to understand smaller groups linked together by common beliefs and customs. Finally, modern American society seems to have no boundaries. Neighbors may have nothing in common but the fact that they live in the same apartment building. Close friends can come from different parts of the country. When could I stop interviewing people, secure in the knowledge that I found the limits of a commonly shared culture?

Sociologists have resolved this problem by developing large, random samples who supposedly reflect a cross section of all Americans, or an entire class. These techniques allow them to make statistically valid statements about a large group of people; but because these are statements about the masses, they often lack depth. The sociologist still may not know, when he or she is through, *why* people act the way they do. Most of the significant forces motivating individual behavior remain unknown.

Anthropologists have often resolved the problem by focusing on bounded social entities—a small town, an ethnic neighborhood, a school or institution—groups with coherent rules that most of us can understand or at least recognize. In this setting, it is possible to observe and talk with enough people to begin seeing the written and unwritten cultural rules that shape people's lives. Tom Wolfe used this method with the Air Force community that produced America's astronauts, and was able to paint an indelible picture of the Right Stuff which leads these men repeatedly to risk their lives in the air.

My study solves the problem by choosing a network of individuals within one single profession. The group I chose had to meet several criteria: It had to be small enough to be a community or network with significant cultural effects. Second, it had to be representative enough to reflect mainstream culture—not the mass society, but the white, middle- and upper-class Euro-American traditions that still hold sway in the world of public authority. Third, it had to be a profession that was until recently dominated by men, so that I could look at the maximum impact on the gender identity of women. Only in that way could I come to know the confrontation between women's new lives as career professionals and their older roles as wives and mothers. Careers are obviously affecting female reproduction, for instance, but precisely how and why? In past generations, the reproductive rate among achieving women has hovered around zero. With millions of women moving into professional careers, that historical fact raises serious questions about the effects of professionalism on family life. Can the majority of women who achieve public authority in this society do so without sacrificing their rights to parenthood? Do they want to? Professionalism is very different from simply working for a living. Women have always worked, but only recently have they moved fully into the male gender sphere, which is the world of public authority. The cultural forces they confront there affect the entire range of feminine traditions.

Fortunately, the financial communities in New York and San Francisco are coherent culture groups. Many of these people know each other; they speak of their communities as "the Street" (Wall Street in New York and Montgomery Street in San Francisco), which means both a place and a group of people. Gossip and rumors flow through the networks. Many of the women belong to "old girl" networks that help female professionals advance in their careers.

It was from these networks that I chose the female sample. I found the forty-four women through personal referrals; each woman I interviewed gave me the names of one or more other women who might be interviewed. Sometimes they were friends; more often they knew each other only by name or reputation. The women ranged in age from twenty-nine to fifty-seven, with the great majority in their thirties. One woman was forty-five, another was fifty-seven, the rest were under the age of forty-two. Their salaries ranged from $30,000 to $100,000 a year. Half the women were married and half were unmarried (divorced, widowed, or never married). There were seven women with children in New York and eight women with children in San Francisco. These figures do not reflect the actual percentages of married, single, and working mothers in either city, but it was important to keep the numbers more or less comparable to understand the impact of careers on private lives.

I also interviewed twelve men and I gave them a slightly altered questionnaire so as to isolate those areas where men and women experience similar problems. I found these men by referral alone, each one recommending another who would be capable of commenting on their companies and how women were adapting to professional positions. Most of the men were drawn from the senior management of major financial institutions in New York and San Francisco.

Both men and women received the same structured, two-hour interview, in which I asked questions on parenthood, gender concepts, family background, friendships and love affairs in the office, and the effects of work on home life.* My study was exploratory, that is, I began it without a hypothesis, but with a series of questions aimed at tracking the effects of financial careers on family roles and feminine identity. I had no assurance that any of the coded items in my interview would correlate to form patterns. But some did, and the patterns that emerged within individual respondents traced a picture of gender identity change. It also revealed why some women have families and other women do not.

Particularly useful to me was a methodology devised by anthropologist James P. Spradley for analyzing semantic domains. I asked the women I interviewed to name all the words (connotations) they associated with the concepts of "being feminine," "being a woman," and "being a lady."

*The questionnaire used in this study is included at the back of the book.

These words, and the images they provoked in conversation, allowed me to analyze female identity and to see the links between the many different ideas of femininity and the choices these women were making. Their ideas, which tied in with their family background and culture history, told me which women were integrating family and work, and which women were not. Among the women who were mastering both sides of their lives, a concept of feminine strength and power, a redefinition of femininity in the light of integrated gender roles emerged.

At the same time, I observed the legacy of a Euro-American patriarchy that swept the Western world in the nineteenth century, dividing the genders into virtual sexual ghettos. Historically, these patriarchal traditions have acted to keep women at home with precious little economic or political power. Women who ventured into the professional world did so by sacrificing reproduction and that is still largely true today. The majority of these women in corporate executive positions have no children. The forces that inhibit their lives as family women are both internal and external, arising from traditional ideas of femininity combined with corporate practices that make no room for family life. As the gender cultures merge, so must these legacies of patriarchy change, if the middle-class family is to survive.

Acknowledgments

As in the ballad sung by Frank Sinatra, I like to think "I did it my way." But when I sit down to acknowledge my debts to other people, the connective tissue that joins my work to the labor and support of others begins to show.

I could not have written a book like this without years of intellectual dialogue with three anthropologists at the University of Pennsylvania who nurtured my thinking and allowed me to see the common human themes that run through all cultures, no matter how simple or complex. Dr. Peggy Reeves Sanday's analysis of equality and inequality in tribal societies is crucial to the theories advanced in this book. Her work combined with others points up the central cultural effects of bringing men into the childrearing process. The contribution by Dr. Ward Goodenough is deep and diffuse. As my teacher and mentor, he taught me the meaning of culture. His work on identity change in native peoples adapting to westernization provided the paradigm for understanding the processes of change in the lives of these financial women. Dr. William Davenport's global perspective on the social sciences and his creative enthusiasm entertained and informed me for many years.

I owe special thanks to the forty-four women and twelve men who allowed me to probe their minds and hearts on sensitive issues, and I hope they will receive some return benefit from this book.

I would also like to thank Dr. Emily Massara for the use of her sunny writing nook, William Speers and Jane Marie Glodek for sharing their house with me, the Society Hill Health Club in Philadelphia for its Jacuzzi where I wrote through my word blocks, Dr. Bart Knapp and Marye O'Reilly-Knapp for their heartfelt support, my stepdaughter, Valerie Drake, for her loving enthusiasm, my editor, Maria Guarnaschelli, for seeing the promise of this work, Barbara Seaman for giving me a blue, pinstriped suit, and the Arcadia Foundation for giving me a timely grant.

My mother, Mary McBroom, gave me crucial financial support and

17

Acknowledgments

my thanks to her cannot be measured. The book would not have been written without her help.

Finally, I would like to thank Dr. Richard Porterfield, who shared with me his knowledge of European history and who believed in me through the long, dark months of grappling with these issues. His love and moral support kept me going.

Contents

Contents

The
Third
Sex

I
The Gender Cultures

1
The Masculine Professional

At the top of Wall Street, the blackened form of a Gothic cathedral straddles the narrow canyon where millions of dollars are traded daily. The church faces down the street from Broadway, which crosses the canyon like the top line on the letter "T" so that Wall Street gives the visual effect of dead-ending right into the main doors of the church. From there, it falls down rapidly to the Hudson River—short, winding, and narrow, like a water chute through which a human flood flows each day. Toward the middle of the street, you catch the fishy smell of a commercial river port, and at the bottom, from the perspective of the wharf, you can look back and upward to the black spires of the Trinity Church, etched against the New York skyline, as if to say that no amount of modern money and towering glass can daunt the power of the Church.

At eight o'clock on an August morning, the doors of the church were flung wide open, revealing a plush red carpet that swept out from the sanctuary. It looked like a yawning mouth. I watched that morning from a vantage point on Broadway. From the depths of the church, a well-dressed man in a three-piece suit suddenly strode into the sunlight. He was walking fast, exuding a vigorous sense of purpose. I played with the thought that he had just been infused with the spirit of Christianity to wrestle with another day of competitive buying and selling in the capitalist economy. It's hard to ignore the symbols on Wall Street. In one short block lie all the ancient Western connections between religion and commerce. The energy seems to flow in an unbroken stream from church to river and back again. The figure walked quickly off the red carpet, down the steps of the church, and disappeared into the throng below. Power sparkled in the air, which is characteristic of New York. But on Wall Street, the effect seemed to be doubled. Here the men and women represent a distillate of the toughest economic brokers in the country. No one lingers under the sun.

A few years ago, the financial throng would have been mostly male. But on that day in 1981, numbers of women, also dressed in well-cut suits, walked swiftly and proudly among the men, to the same beat and the same purpose. These are the women who have made the leap from a world of female authority to a world of male authority. They not only work full time but their work is done in demanding, competitive careers. They are responsible for managing and investing millions of dollars. They take the same risks the men do. They have similar authority and are held directly accountable for economic outcome. Befitting their roles as professional women in finance, they have also adopted the clothing and many of the behaviors of the men in their male-dominated environments.

When the suit goes on in the morning, it carries with it a set of feelings, attitudes, privileges, and responsibilities that are new to the majority of American women. More than just another piece of clothing, the suit is a new outer shell of the personality. When financial women wear it, they act and feel differently. They are no longer only themselves but a part of something else, with public functions borrowed from a larger sphere. The suit protects vulnerability and hides the self. In the language of transactional analysis, it could be called a frog suit, or psychological armor. A broader name, to take in its public function, is the mask of the professional. Not only does it shield the vulnerable, natural self; it also confers psychological strength and behavior patterns that go along with the job as stockbroker, banker, or investment counselor. In that sense, the suit for a money professional is like the robe of a Supreme Court justice or the white coat of a doctor.

Men who wear the suit learn to take it off at strategic times to demonstrate their personal control over the mask. A Philadelphia banker wears tennis clothes to the office on Saturday "to show that I am a human being." A senior executive, especially, is not a man to be trapped behind the suit. He is, above all, an individual, and he demonstrates his personal power by his ability to put himself above the role. One New York executive, now president of an international financial organization, took a job in his early years where, according to custom,

26

the professionals always wore suit jackets behind the desk, even in sweltering summer heat without air conditioning. He refused to make himself uncomfortable and got the rule changed in twenty-four hours. "I couldn't afford to have my suit cleaned every day," he explained.

Women experience a distinct evolution in their degree of control over the mask. Those just out of MBA school have it firmly in place: navy blue suit, white blouse tied into a bow under the chin, low-heeled shoes, along with the expected attributes of aggressive rationality and a clear work focus, which come under the word "businesslike." Sensitivity and humor, sexuality and vulnerability are not supposed to show; nor do they, since they are part of the self that is hidden behind the mask.

As women gather confidence and years on the job, they begin to modify the suit for their own personal expression. In the words of a Wall Street broker:

> You get to the point where you feel you don't have to wear the full suit anymore. You work your way along, wearing a blue suit and a serious white blouse, and then, after a few years, you say, "Nah. I can stand on my own two feet. I'll wear less serious clothes because I know people take me seriously." So there is an evolution.

This woman, professionally masterful at the age of thirty-seven and soaring personally as a new mother, lets her natural, ebullient self leak out on special occasions. During her pregnancy, she was seized one morning by the desire to wear a bright red dress to work. "I stuck out anyway," she explained. That day she went out to lunch with another pregnant stockbroker, and, arm in arm with a male colleague, they sailed down Wall Street.

Most members of the women's professional and financial organizations in Philadelphia and New York—and to a lesser degree in San Francisco—will not however reveal, even to each other in the company of women, the difficulties they experience at a personal level. Very little shows beyond the mask—the smooth, unruffled, rational exterior which allows them to function in a professional role where human feelings are a nuisance that may interfere with political maneuvering and compromise. No matter the pain, the professional does not cry, does not show anger, does not reveal significant personal feelings. A woman banker in Philadelphia was divorced six months before she told any of her co-workers. She then informed them by calling each one individually into her office and stating the fact, asking if they had any questions. A secretary, not realizing the aloof, rational mode of the professional, threw her arms around the woman and cried, "Are you all right?" The young banker laughed. A financial manager on Wall Street got pregnant, got divorced, and gave birth before she told her boss that she was no longer married.

Even severe physical pain is hidden among women in their own professional organizations. One young woman had spastic colitis, insomnia, and depression, which she traced to her super-drive at work. She feared that she might be killing herself at the age of twenty-seven, but would not tell her female colleagues, even when she left the city to move to an island off the coast of Florida. She told them she had gotten a better job, and they believed her. They had no knowledge of the physical and psychological pain she had endured for two years.

This is how women, as they transform themselves into professional roles, see the world: Control of the self for the sake of the image is the way of the professional.

"It's the way you are perceived that's important," said the president of one of the professional organizations. "If it's power you want, you have to forfeit sexuality." She believes that women should do everything in their power to reduce the awareness of feminine identity and keep a reputation that is as clean as a whistle until some point in the indefinite future when professional women have more freedom to be the way they want to be. "We can't have it all at once," she said.

Men have grappled for generations with the privileges and price of wearing the mask. Its privileges are all too obvious—money, status, and public authority being among them. The price, however, is less concrete. It involves the potential erosion of personal identity into professional roles that are in the end devoid of intimacy and emotional enrichment. For those who rely on the mask too heavily or lose the ability to remove it after hours, the price is paid in sterile relationships and, over time, loss of joy and existential meaning. Much has been written about the effects on men of being trained for work slots: the loss of emotional freedom, the underdevelopment of human sensitivity. It has been commonly observed that most men past the age of forty are not satisfied with their level of work achievement and many turn in toward their families at that point. Women are now facing the very same issues, which raise important questions about what the professional role is doing to a woman's intimate life and personal self.

A female professional in finance faces two major problems that men do not have to contend with. She has far more difficulty achieving a family life than does her male counterpart. Men are protected in many ways from being taken over psychologically by the mask, because women and children have acted as the humanizers at home. A family is easily available to a male professional, and it serves as a source of emotional release and renewal for him. Even if the feelings he releases are negative, they are feelings. Part of the bargain the sexes have made in this culture is that females will be the emotional ones—the ones who do not mask their feelings.

I asked several executive men in these interviews if they could have achieved what they did at work without a family. They all said no without hesitation. Yet many women today are trying to achieve the same alone, having received a clear message that children and career do not mix; they cannot do both.

In the lives of these women, it is clear to me, as it has never been with men, what price people can unwittingly pay for career roles and public achievement. It is also clear to me, from these interviews, that women who do preserve their personal, intimate lives, usually by having children, or who otherwise manage to retain and develop the nurturant, relational aspects of themselves, have experienced a transformation in feminine identity. They were able to drop outmoded feminine attitudes and—behind the mask of professional behavior—to find new strengths as females. Or else they started from a position of feminine strength that was rooted in positive identification with a strong mother.

It is possible, although difficult, for women to mix family life and careers—a task rendered more difficult than it should be by the inadequate social arrangements for child care. Yet it needs to be done. The alternative for us strivers is either to give up the struggle for equality, or to allow our human juices to be drained away behind the professional mask, in lives stripped of family connections.

The second problem is as noxious to women as the first, and to some extent, contributes to it. The roles we are moving into were shaped by men. They offer us a poisonous confusion between the things that belong to the role and are therefore a necessary part of doing business (or journalism or medicine), and the things that belong to masculine behavior and can be changed to fit our own gender identity.

I was on Wall Street to begin an exploratory series of interviews with financial men and women that would last six months. Hopefully, it would reveal what women were doing with their private lives and gender identity as they transformed themselves into professionals, in roles made by and for men. Generations of cultural history have shaped the professional role in the masculine image; no one really knows, not even we professional women, how we will change those roles to fit our lives and minds.

Cultures that make a major distinction between men's and women's work, as American society has done, also develop very prominent gender cultures. Both men and women see the sexes as being temperamentally different by nature. Separate masculine and feminine cultures, complete with different ideologies and different sets of personality traits, emerge to support and perpetuate the division of labor.

Margaret Mead, who pioneered the study of sex cultures, saw that primitive groups could split up sexual behavior in all sorts of ways—ways that bore no similarity whatsoever to the divisions we make between masculine and feminine behavior. In one Philippine culture, for instance, it was believed that no man could keep a secret. The Manus of the Admiralty Islands assumed that only men enjoy playing with babies. The Toda of southwest India thought that domestic work was too sacred for women. The Arapesh of New Guinea insisted that women's heads were stronger than men's. The Dakota Indians believed that the ability to withstand danger and hardship were masculine characteristics; they deliberately meted out emotional hardship to the boys.

Not every culture studied by anthropologists has made such distinctions. In some cultures, men and women do similar work and are perceived as essentially the same kind of people. Peggy Reeves Sanday, in a recent cross-cultural analysis of 150 primitive groups, found that cultures with a high degree of integration in labor also made fewer sexual distinctions in the rest of social life. Fathers, for instance, were closely involved with the care of children. Moreover, the ethos of these cultures was different: People emphasized cooperation over competition.

But in none of the primitive cultures have anthropologists seen such massive switching of sex roles as is going on in contemporary America. What remains as distinctly masculine and feminine behavior when we do the same work is still very much a mystery.

Typically, although not exclusively, the direct exercise of public authority in this society has belonged to the world of men; it has been their work. The feminine world, by contrast, has been geared to the exercise of indirect public power and the nurturance of intimates. For women to switch gears within one, or, at the most, two generations means that they must drop and relearn whole sets of behaviors, having to do with the balance between egoism and altruism, rationality and emotionality, assertiveness and compliance, among other personal changes that cut across sexual behavior, love relationships, and child rearing. I had already experienced in my own life the difficulties of coping in a professional world defined by men and knew of its impact on my private life. I wanted to know how these women were doing it.

As I mingled with the proud, striding figures on Wall Street, I was reminded of a scene described by anthropologist Gregory Bateson. On special ceremonial occasions, the women of the Iatmul tribe of New Guinea put on the clothes of men. They painted their faces white, wore ornaments used by the men on headhunting expeditions, and carried lime sticks with which they made loud grating noises. The change in clothes was paralleled by a change in personality. While they wore the male costume, the women dropped their usual jolly behavior and marched with the same proud bearing and loud aggressiveness typical of Iatmul men.

I didn't know then what I would discover later—that the suit for financial women, and probably for men as well, is also a mask with a set of more or less common behavioral traits. For women, however, the mask is mingled with masculine identity, and that sets up a potentially serious conflict. It means that at some level, for many women, feminine identity has been split off or submerged because it conflicts with the roles required at work. The earlier, and in some senses, more organic feminine identity has not been abolished; it has simply been pushed behind a door, kept at home, or encapsulated beneath the shell of the new woman. That has happened, in part, because many of us have had no idea how to modify the roles to suit ourselves as females. We haven't even known what feminine means, beyond the images that drove us from home in the first place—images of women trapped in suburban homes with squalling children.

Many of us junked femininity in our hearts, if not from our faces. The lipstick and eye makeup continued, as did the illusory search for a man who was stronger than we were. But the fear of "dwindling into a wife"—the phrase sociologist Jesse Bernard used in her book *The Future of Marriage*—set up a hidden barrier against marriage and motherhood. In the 1950s, before the feminist movement of the 1960s expanded women's options into careers, those roles carried some awful images: dirty dishes. Stultified minds. Empty conversations. Pretense and face paint. Simpering and sacrifice. Economic control. Subordination. Stories of devastated housewives and depressed mothers. That was the stuff of being feminine to thousands of middle-class women with college educations, the women Betty Friedan wrote about.

The stuff of the male world, by contrast, looked very attractive: money, status, social authority, sexual power, exciting jobs. What wasn't apparent to women who saw the things men had was that it was the *role* that held all the power, *not* the individual man. He was powerful *insofar* as he had a good job. The social niche he occupied was more important than he was. Behind the mask of the professional lurked thousands of men with no sense of themselves outside work and little time or freedom to find out. The erosion of personal identity and private options revealed itself to women as an insidious process, a slow change over years, with the dawning realization that they were sacrificing something very profound and very important by the forces operating in the career world. That "something" was somehow related to feminine identity.

Many professional women in finance make a radical division between their work lives and their private lives. Their work friends are separate from their personal friends. They will not date men they work with, or, if they are married, have no desire to socialize with colleagues, beyond lunch and an occasional drink. The division extends into the personality. Those with families describe themselves as becoming different people when they go home. And it includes a division in female identity. A senior investment officer in San Francisco, young, married, and with a newborn child, identifies herself as a "woman" at work and "feminine" at home. With conscious awareness, she literally puts on her "woman" in the morning, along with her suit:

> The things that go with a woman in my definition are just surface traits. They're just your exterior. They don't get into what you really are underneath, and underneath, I'm a feminine person. I'm not ashamed of that, but I'm not going to go around the office being a feminine person. I'm going to go around being a woman. OK?

I associate woman with being professional, competent, efficient, direct and assertive. I don't see woman as a wife or mother. I see her as a professional. It is part of yourself, but it's the exterior. It's what you let people see. You know, it's like putting on a new outfit. It's you, but you take it off when you go home.

If you feel good with the traits of a woman, you can walk into any meeting and pitch anything you want. You can talk to the chairman of the board of any major corporation.

I have my feminine mystique at home, and then, when I come to work, I cover it with my "woman," my three-piece blue suit. That's the way it is. You don't put the feminine in a closet. You don't shrink from it, but you don't expose it to the world. You don't expose your innermost qualities to just anybody.

This young, bright woman, like many others who clearly understand the competitive aggression of the world they work in, protects her feminine identity with everyone but a few selected individuals she can trust:

Occasionally . . . you let a little bit of that out in your weak moments. You can't keep things tucked under your vest all the time. But I only expose my [feminine qualities] on a selected basis, when I want to let my guard down. Because, I don't care what you say. There are people out there who will try to get you. Men or women, they see a weak spot and they'll go after it.

When I first encountered that kind of separation, I thought the women were making a big mistake. Influenced by psychological theory, which says that segmentation of the different parts of one's life leads to pathology, I believed that women might experience a split in psychological reality that could be dangerous. Or else they might lose personal strength at work, if for instance they left gender identity at home. In some cases, those problems seemed to be occurring. But in most, the separation crystallized as necessary and even desirable.

The woman just quoted was happy with her husband and new baby. She's also effective at work. The professional mask she puts on covers her feminine identity but does not hide it from herself. Her vulnerable, feeling self is very much alive behind the mask all the time. As the women with families told me their stories, I realized that taking the work personality home could intrude upon and destroy their intimate relationships. Perhaps the professional roles are unsafe for human beings

33

since they tend to be organized around power. Relationships formed at work tend to be professionally useful. Trust, vulnerability, and loyalty—the things of home—did not even occur in these female descriptions of their working environment. The women had learned to take the mask off, which was just as important as learning to put it on. To do the opposite—to carry private life and vulnerability into the office—is to ask for trouble, as the roles are presently constituted. The workplace is no place like home.

Day had turned into evening. The magnetic pull of Wall Street was beginning to subside as the human flood streamed down the street into the subways. I waited for my first interview with a married woman who had asked for this hour because she wanted complete privacy in a nearly empty building. I wrote my name at the after-hours registration desk and soared to the fiftieth floor. Joyce met me at the door.

She was medium height and sturdily built, with vigorous blond hair that sprang out from her face, lightly brushing the collar of her beige suit. She greeted me and asked me to wait in the outer office while she finished a conference with one of her male co-workers. Through the partly open door, I could hear her ultra-low, powerful voice pushing aggressively at the man. She was angry.

The conference finished on a less than friendly tone, the man left, and Joyce welcomed me into her office. Immediately she began talking about confidentiality: "Would anybody know that I'm in the sample, unless I told them? I mean, I would like complete anonymity. Couldn't you just say, 'One woman I spoke to' . . . or do you have to give more than that? I mean, if anybody reads this book, I'm quite identifiable." She sneezed. "Excuse me. Shit. Am I on tape with that?"

At thirty-nine, Joyce looked much younger than her age. She had no children, a result of numerous small decisions along the way to put work first. For years, she traveled widely and worked until midnight. "I didn't even go home at night. I wasn't even involved in my marriage except on weekends. Did I surrender my home life for work? Yes. I think so. I think so." There was a long silence, after which Joyce said quietly:

> I'm sorry that I don't have a child. The time is quickly going by. I suppose I could do a last-ditch effort and still have one. I'm not going to. And I'm probably sorry that I'm not. But I'm not sorry enough to do it.

Joyce struggles with the tough role she developed for work. It hangs onto her when she goes home. Although she has moved past the stage of wearing a navy blue suit, she still does not feel like herself at work. That has to do with the toughness and her inability to bring forth the natural sweetness that still lies within. This is how she recalls her transformation into a financial professional, and her difficulty now in controlling the mask:

> I was a sweet, lovely little bank officer, the darling of a lot of people. The head of the department used to say to me, "Like a good little girl, run back to your desk and get this." I wasn't offended. I went back to my desk and got it. You know, I was the first woman to be hired and they all really liked me. I was smart. The work ethic wasn't very high there. People used to come to work all dressed up.
>
> But then I came to [an industrial corporation] and truly. . . . Maybe it's the difference between industry and banks. . . . Or maybe it was the time, or my particular situation, but it was unbelievably different. We were getting the product out the door every day. I'd be sitting at my desk and my boss would shout from his office, "Get in here, Joyce. I've got five minutes to do this thing!" So that's why I toughened up. I mean, if somebody yells at you that you've got five minutes, you learn pretty quickly how to get it done in five minutes, if that means telling a guy you're going to kill him. They didn't do this to me because I was a woman. They did it to the best of men.

Joyce knows there is another side of her which in many ways she no longer has access to. It's not that she wants to go back to being a "good little girl," but the tough role is no answer either.

> I believed that I was tougher than I was, not wanting to admit my weaknesses. I think that's part of what goes on with career women. Had I not chosen a career, I would have been a much softer, more forgiving, more tolerant person. I have tolerance for very little. Just don't muck me up and don't get on the wrong side of me.
>
> I used to be much more soft spoken. My voice is . . . uh . . . everybody listens to me. I think there is an authority there. I think I scare most people out of their pants, is what I think. And it's a very unconscious thing. I don't mean to, and I wouldn't have been this way, had I not pursued a career, gotten a little power and authority. It goes to one's head.
>
> You see, I carry it home, too. It all kind of mooshes together. If you've

got a personality in the office, it's very difficult to leave that at six or seven o'clock. I'm tough at home. I mean, if a salesperson gets on the wrong side of me, holy smokes, watch out! But I think down deep I'm not that sort of person. I consider my husband supportive, but he thinks I'm tough, far tougher than anybody needs to be, and he's one of the good guys. He lets me run around the world and I don't come home and it's OK. Then I come home and it's OK. But he doesn't think I'm very feminine. He doesn't use that word, but he talks about toughness and not being very understanding and being boss. "Leave that at the office." That kind of thing. That's more of a problem now, because I think I know how to act in the office. I just don't know how to undo that when I go home.

I've grown a lot in the past few years, where I can be comfortable with somebody saying, "Don't you look nice," or, "I love the way . . ." Ten years ago, I would have decked them. "What the hell do you mean? I'm here to work." Now I'll take a compliment from anyone. So, I've worked through some of this business of being feminine. But still, there are areas . . . not in business, but on the periphery, where I think I am still trying to prove something. Perhaps I really am tough and maybe my reactions aren't as natural as I would like them to be. You know, I think it has something to do with not knowing where you should draw the line between being a woman and just being a person. I'm closer to being a person than I used to be.

Joyce is looking at the fourth decade of life—a time to evaluate the past, to find the meaning in what you've done, the risks, the road taken and the ones passed by, the personal payoff. But it doesn't stack up quite right.

I'm not sorry for what I've done. But I am sorry that I gave up so much. Perhaps, had I been more directed, I would have been further along in my career. Children. A home life. I love children. I truly love kids and I get along well with them. I don't want you to believe that I consciously at age twenty-five, as girls do now, made the decision that I wasn't going to marry or have children. I was not that definite. It just sort of happened that way. And, now that I look back on my thirties and see that I did give up an awful lot in terms of a home life, I'm not very far along in my career for having done that. So, that's what I'm sorry about. The quid pro quo is not enough for me. And when you ask, "Would I have done it over again?" I don't know. I don't know.

Joyce could still have a child, but she won't, the reason being that her husband is not enthusiastic and she herself does not want to give up personal free time.

> I think I can be loving and very understanding with children. The thing I don't want—and this is selfish—is giving up my own time. Something's got to give, and if you can't give up dedication to your job without getting fired or not getting promoted, what do you give up? My own free time, the only time I have to be with myself, and that's what I'm not willing to give up.

She is convinced that a woman of normal energy levels cannot have both. And her husband tells her that. He thinks she must choose between the two and that she has chosen a career. Nevertheless, he's dissatisfied with all the things they've given up over the years for her career. "What the hell was it worth for him to have a wife who's a vice president?"

Midlife presents adults with a challenge. Either they will become rigid and personally stymied, or they can be reinvigorated in a form of adolescent rejuvenation, which involves getting in touch with the parts of the self that were potentials at puberty but never developed in adulthood. For many professional women, that part of the self is the hidden, encapsulated, outdated, neglected feminine. Joyce's description of the feminine fits that of many other New Yorkers I interviewed, with the exception of the women with children. Childbearing, it seems, reconnects women with the feminine parts of themselves—one of the most important results to emerge from this group of professionals. But for those who have not experienced the intense organic, psychological childbearing stage, descriptions of what it means to be feminine hark back to images of the past. Joyce laughed.

> Crinolines, petticoats, hair curlers, stuffed animals. I don't know. Feminine is soft. Feminine is pretty. Feminine is not so strong. I guess my concept is that you sit back and if someone says something you don't like, you might not react to it. But how can you work here and worry about your career without [speaking your mind]? So, I don't understand yet how you can match it all.
>
> The bottom line of it is that men are the judge of who's feminine and who's not. Line ten men up against the wall and 9.9 percent of them would say [of a professional woman with authority], "She's not feminine."

So I think the perception of the world is that if you've got power and authority, you couldn't possibly be supportive and loving or whatever feminine means. Plus, if you have a position of power, you've got to push enough people around to do what you have to do, that all of a sudden, you really aren't whatever feminine means. [Her voice went small and quiet] You know, I don't think I know what it means. Women call me up and ask for my opinion of this or that. I'm not a very good role model, but I'm it. I never wanted to be a pioneer. It's very hard. It's just crazy. This whole issue.

The interview was over. We packed our briefcases and walked down the silent halls to the elevator. On the way, Joyce burst out with a revelation.

"I know this isn't relevant to your study, but I hate men. You know? As a group, I don't like them. I've only felt this way for the past few years. Individually, I love some men, but on the whole. . . ." She waved her arms. "That's a terrible thing to say. It's like saying you don't like Polish people."

I stared at her with sudden insight into my own emotions. What she said was perfectly logical. By her definition, she could not possibly be feminine. The nature of her work ruled it out. If she was not feminine—in her own mind—men would not like her or be attracted. Therefore, she did not like them. From one sweeping conclusion, based on a restrictive definition that feminine women cannot exercise power, all the negative consequences followed in logical order. The interview with Joyce had given me what I had expected to find: a professional woman who had grown tough in the job and who had surrendered not just childbearing but a whole side of the personality having to do with gentleness and nurturance—of herself most of all. It was the portrait of a woman caught in the opposite world of a male–female dichotomy. Rather than being trapped in a small, private sphere taking care of others, with no access to the big world of public authority, she was trapped in a command post, with plenty of public authority, but no access to the private world where emotional nourishment takes place.

There were elements of her story that recalled an anecdote I heard from a male banker on Wall Street who was talking about toughness on the job and burned-out people. He told me that as a lesson in leadership, some corporations show a war film called *Twelve O'Clock High,* starring Gregory Peck. Peck plays a doctor who is suddenly ripped out of his medical role and sent in to take over as the commander of a bomber wing which has been beaten by the enemy to the point of moral and physical collapse. It is Peck's job to put the group together again.

> He drives up to the camp, sitting in the front seat of the jeep, and then there is this marvelous scene. Peck says to the driver, "Stop here, Joe." He gets out, walks around to the back, smokes a cigarette, and gets in, this time in the back seat of the jeep, saying, "Drive on, Sergeant." He adjusts his personality, becoming a tough, driving kind of guy. He isn't that way by nature. He whips the place into shape, but extends his role to the point that he has a nervous breakdown. He went beyond maximum feasible effort. Fortunately, he was able to break down. I mean, he had shunts in his head that just closed down. He tried to get into a plane and he couldn't do it anymore. So the planes went up without him and you see him at the end coming out of it, as the planes return.

The point this executive was trying to make was that displaying toughness in leadership roles doesn't have to be done often—as long as people know it's there. The people who are tough all the time burn out. For him, the issue was leadership style, and his advice to women was that first they have to understand what they are internally, and then find a leadership style which is appropriate for them.

First, they have to understand what they are internally. In those few words lies the struggle of generations of women to integrate the opposing gender cultures. To reach this point, a woman searching for her own feminine strengths within the masculine culture travels a road—sometimes a very long road—through contradictory sets of values, ethics, and behavior. Depending on her background and the kind of feminine ethos she has internalized, the passage can be easy or incredibly strange and confusing. To some extent, all of us are affected by a nineteenth-century Euro-American society that split the masculine and feminine worlds into two segregated camps. The more we know about where we have come from culturally speaking, and what we are getting into, the better able we are to avoid the multiple pitfalls of the age. In that spirit, this book is offered. The women who speak here generously shared sensitive information on their personal passages through the male and female worlds. They want other women to know they are not alone if the integration seems difficult. Although we may come from different points in time, some of these processes are reoccurring—and have been reoccurring for the past 150 years.

As a starting point, I would like to identify my own culture history, a legacy of the 1950s. I knew years ago that there was something wrong with our cultural definitions of the feminine. I didn't use that word. I could barely tolerate the sound of it because it carried for me many weak and sexually used attributes. I don't know where they all came from—the movies, maybe, television, perhaps maturing as a teenager in Southern California during the Marilyn Monroe era, when a woman's body was as close as it's ever been to a commercial product. We were all very sports-minded, so physical activity was not considered unfeminine in California as it was on the East Coast, but it was not good to be intelligent. Supposedly, men liked dumb women, dumb but beautiful. I remember a sense of humiliation at having to compete in a beauty contest for the Rose Bowl queen. Every coed in the college was required to walk through the line for gym credit, so we paraded—two thousand strong—in front of a panel of judges, with numbers on our hips. If we made the first cut, we read our names on a computer print-out tacked up in the dean's office the next day.

I recoiled from the Barbie Doll mold. I owned my own mind and body. I would do what I wanted, taking every risk a man would take and every license, regardless of the rules for feminine behavior. In claiming freedom from the restrictions of feminine life, I followed a masculine model; there didn't seem to be any other. The idea was, if the feminine did not work, try the masculine.

By the mid-seventies, I began to look for a third alternative, through the study of male and female behavior in other cultures and other times. A central motivation behind this search was to find the wellspring of feminine power, because it had become apparent to me that our society was afflicted by an excessive valuation of the masculine ethos. Why, in the quest for equality, did women want to be like men? Why was power so often associated with masculine behavior and not with feminine? Why were women supposed to be nice, good, polite, supportive, giving, not confrontative, not aggressive, not tough, not powerful? There was something suspicious about our cultural distinctions between the masculine and the feminine. They had stripped the feminine of its natural authority. In moderation, feminine qualities represented the best that human beings had to offer, the highest moral good. In excess, those same qualities became weak, passive, and shallow, lacking in backbone. Obviously, women did not lack backbone; the weakness lay in our ideas of the feminine.

I looked in many places for the essential nature of the feminine—a search that female anthropologists have been pursuing on a wide front. I studied one culture where women chase men with knives to extort tribute and another where men drive stakes through the feet of women to keep their wives at home. I learned of one where women dance joyously and one where men throw feasts to win prestige through generosity. There are cultures in which women do the hard physical labor and cultures in which men tend the children. I looked for the precursors of masculine and feminine behavior in chimpanzees, monkeys, modern biology, and human evolution.

In the course of this search, something peculiar happened to my own sense of feminine identity. It reversed itself from negative to positive. I stopped valuing masculine principles, and stopped seeing the world as dominated by men. I began to see the depth and glory of the female spirit, convinced that there is a unique feminine nature—a special way of being in the world—which runs through body, mind, and soul. The overwhelming evidence of biology, evolution, and culture tells me that the sexes are not alike, and that is a blessing. Each sex brings its own comprehension to any issue. We read the message of life differently, and while we can learn the other's codes easily enough, we do better if we also learn to listen to our own internal hunches.

Whenever sexual differences exist, they can be cast in the light of female strengths. True, they have traditionally been cast in the light of male strengths, but that is only because men were doing the thinking and they couldn't help but have a biased perspective. When they looked around, they saw men in charge everywhere and they naturally described the world they knew. It was a world dominated by men. Today that is no longer true. From the boardrooms to the universities to the publishing houses to the churches, women are inexorably moving into positions of authority. And inevitably they will see the world through the eye of the feminine. The two perspectives, running side by side, will broaden human understanding in the same way that two observations upon a star tell us more about the universe.

2
Beneath
the Mask

B ehind the new personality of a professional woman lies an older feminine identity. The frequent lack of fit between the two can cause oppressive conflicts in a woman's self-image. Bumping between the feminine and the professional identities is like trying to walk upright on four legs: the two you evolved on the job and the two you brought with you from the past, built on the accumulated teaching of mothers, fathers, friends, brothers, sisters, and husbands, as well as a wide variety of cultural sources—movies, churches, songs, television, history books, and fairy tales.

These two traditions—the feminine and the professional—clash in some fundamental ways, and quite a few professional women are struggling with the painful possibility that to retain independent strength, they may have to sacrifice the warm and wonderful things that go with men and children. Or they may have the men and children, if they sacrifice independent strength. This is not an inherent conflict. Nothing basic to the male-female condition says that such a conflict should exist. But it is a deep one, which takes us back to the kind of women we have become in order to fulfill our responsibilities as wives and mothers in middle-class American society.

There exist in this culture, as in all cultures, written and unwritten bargains between the sexes, which spell out what each will do for the other in a romantic or family union. These bargains arise from the gender cultures and the division of labor between men and women, being programmed into our conscious or unconscious mind primarily as a series of duties and behaviors. We tell ourselves what we should do for a man if we love him, or what we should do for children if we are good mothers, or how we should behave if we are *really* feminine women. Few ideas are more deeply rooted or emotionally laden. Without knowing why or how, we begin to take care of each other in certain ways, and under the right conditions of marriage and motherhood (or a reasonable facsimile), the bargain surfaces in the form of gifts and expectations. We start acting out the old roles. We start doing for each other the things we are supposed to do. We start fulfilling the terms of the feminine pact.

Many women are lucky. The kind of feminine pact they have developed does not conflict with professional accomplishment. They slide easily between home and work, changing only their clothes and various aspects of behavior, while their basic sense of self remains constant. Half the women I interviewed in New York and better than half in San Francisco seem to have no internal conflicts between feminine and professional personalities, even though they deal with practical problems of child care and sexual prejudice. These are external conflicts, solvable because the women are not divided against themselves.

Others are not so lucky. The feminine and professional stand locked in confrontation at a basic level. I met Marlene waltzing out of her building, headed for a restaurant down the street where she wanted to be interviewed. She seemed to dance with lighthearted assurance and she looked like a sweetheart, even in the navy blue suit and white blouse she was wearing. She had a young, angelic face and long brown hair. Talking with easy command of her professional world, Marlene said that sexual approaches from men at work do not make her angry. She views them as a game, not a threat, and she feels free to share personal confidences with her boss and one female friend. Other people at work she keeps at a friendly distance, which is the common style of a female professional in finance.

I like the social environment at work, not because we're all aloof, but because we think of ourselves as professionals. Professional means that every time you pick up the phone, you are formal and businesslike. You don't have drunken brawls at lunch. Everything is client-centered. You worry about your own bottom line, but you keep the people you're aiming at in mind.

At the beginning of the interview, Marlene seemed to have resolved whatever conflicts she may have experienced between feminine and professional roles.

> I try to be honest and down to earth, which is not always easy in New York. But I basically say, "This is me and I don't care. You like me? Fine." I've discovered that people like you better if you are yourself. I talk to my boss [within limits] the same way I talk to my fiancé. If I have a witty or cutting comment, I will say it. I no longer have the dichotomy that I have had in the past. I can play the game of turning it on and turning it off.

But behind this professional confidence, which Marlene has learned over the years and now finds quite comfortable, a dramatic cultural conflict over gender identity and life choices is being played out. She has no sense of herself as an adult female, *except* in the professional role. She cannot find her identity as a woman because she feels she is not old enough. In her mind, a "woman" is past the age of thirty-five and voluptuous; she's slim, no Sophia Loren, and she's only twenty-nine, so being a woman is out. Nor can she be a "lady" because ladies are associated with class and royalty. And she can't be feminine, because feminine is associated with weakness and Marlene sees herself as strong. She is, after all, a professional woman with the clear and conscious intention of maintaining her economic independence for life.

> I want to work all my life. I protect my own interests. If I ever get divorced, I want to have a job there to support me the day I divorce. I don't want to hang onto anybody out of fear that I can't make it. I don't ever want a guy to tell me, "Oh, I've got another girl, so I'm divorcing you and bullshit on you."

How does she see herself, then, if she is not a woman, not a lady, and not feminine?

> I'm kind of like a girl. A woman is voluptuous, what I try to be with my fiancé, but I don't quite make it. Yea, I'm a woman in the office. I'm a woman for the quota, but I'm not a woman in my mind. I'm a girl. That's not a denigration. If you call me a woman, I think of being over thirty-five.
>
> Being feminine is wearing a dress, maybe even a formal gown, speak-

ing softly, enticing your lover, wearing pearls. Feminine is not—with a capital N—not the office. I really don't think someone who is feminine can be professional. In my personal life, feminine is very much what I want to be. That's more important than my business life. But I don't think of myself as feminine. I really should, but I don't, even though I have diminutive features. I think of myself as masculine. When I am dressing for a ball, I look at myself in the mirror. I have on a gown and a string of beads, but somehow I see myself as a football player. Feminine is definitely non-power. It is weakness. Maybe that's why I think of myself mentally as being masculine. Because I feel strong, I feel masculine.

I had the sensation I was looking at an anorectic who thought she was too fat. How could such a sweet-looking woman, with obviously feminine manners, think of herself as masculine? What could account for that kind of distortion in the mind's self-image?

The conflicts went further. As we reached the questions about motherhood, I learned that Marlene, who was at the time newly engaged, wants children, but the important men in her life were telling her that she should not have them. They will stifle her and interfere with her career.

> Father thinks I should not get married, and if I do, I should not have kids, because marriage and children will stifle me. He thinks I should have a career and go to it. From the time I was nine, I very much liked children. I went into teaching because I love them. I love being a mother. I'm afraid of the restrictions it will put on my life. But I hear everybody telling me what a wonderful experience it is and how they fumble for their keys to get into the house fast enough to see their son or daughter. My fiancé says, "Well, you're going to hang yourself." I know it. Maybe I will—hamper myself too much by deciding to be a mother.

I asked her if other women she knew in financial circles experienced such conflicts between the feminine and professional parts of themselves. She answered:

> No. As a matter of fact, they're very self-confident. I'm not. Not at all. I keep groping for that. I find them being so self-confident, I'm almost minor-leagued by it. I don't know what the hell to do. I keep looking at them and I go home and say, "Something's wrong!"

Marlene works hard at being businesslike and she works hard at being feminine, even though she thinks she's not. At the end of a two-hour interview, she made an astounding prediction. She said she expects to die of cancer in her late forties. My mind reeled. Her conflict seemed complete and total. Every option dead-ended in a catch-22. She had no adult sexual form to grow into. I opened my mouth to say something, but the words were hard to find. Advice would do no good unless it reached the level of image and emotion where the idea of the feminine was formed. There was a way out, but it involved a transformation in feminine identity, from weak to strong. Somehow her feminine self needed permission to be powerful, to be an adult.

A generation ago, Barnard sociologist Mirra Komarovsky pinpointed the deep tensions that were beginning to afflict modern women. They were moving through a culture change so fast that the "modern" role contradicted the "feminine" one. "The goals set by each role are mutually exclusive and the fundamental personality traits each evokes are at points diametrically opposed, so that what are assets for one become liabilities for the other, and the full realization of one role threatens defeat in the other," she wrote in 1946.

A student of that era described the conflicting messages she received from family members. Her statement echoes with the sounds of clashing culture change, like the noise of chaotic water when an outgoing and an incoming tide struggle for dominance:

> How am I to pursue any course singlemindedly when somewhere along the line a person I respect is sure to say, "You're on the wrong track and are wasting your time"? Uncle John telephones every Sunday morning. His first question is, "Did you go out last night?" He would think me a grind if I were to stay home Saturday night to finish a term paper. My father expects me to get an A in every subject and is disappointed by a B. He says I have plenty of time for social life. Mother says, "That A in philosophy is very nice, dear. But please don't become so deep that no man will be good enough for you." And, finally, Aunt Mary's line is careers for women. "Prepare yourself for some profession. This is the only way to ensure yourself independence and an interesting life. You have plenty of time to marry."

The tensions of trying to reconcile these oppositions between the modern and the feminine follow women through every stage of life.

They will persist "until the adult sex roles of women are defined in greater harmony with the . . . character of modern society," Komarovsky said then, and it is no less true now. Until women in their feminine minds can acquire the power and authority traditionally considered a masculine right, they will be at war with themselves.

As I traveled through New York, and to a lesser degree in San Francisco, I picked up a consistent split in female self-concept. To women in finance, the concept of "being feminine" stood for a series of traits associated with being gentle, soft, and weak. The concept of "being a woman" was at times diametrically opposed. It stood for being strong, assertive, and powerful. These were the connotations of the two words from twenty women, selected to reflect the diversity of their expressions. Being feminine meant: weakness, dressing up, pink, curlers, not aggressive, non-power, helplessness, dainty, appealing, conniving, sweet, delicate, gentle, kind, warm, flirtatious, graceful, responsive, sensitive, pretty, accommodating, charming, flattering to men, soft and quiet. A small number of women included the words "strong," "take charge," "successful," and "comfortable with your body" in their definitions. In most cases, they had experienced a change in feminine identity over time.

Being a woman meant: competent, assertive, professional, strong, sensual, proud, tough, superior, mature, sensitive, voluptuous, responsible, sexual, perceptive, nurturing, balanced, adjusted, physical, centered, powerful, aggressive, and motherhood.

The separation between the two concepts was so glaring I thought at first I was dealing with a superficial, media-inspired image of the New Woman. It was as if the word "woman" had ridden in on the wings of the feminist movement to counteract the tendencies of the old feminine. But it meant much more than that. In these two concepts could be found the conflict women feel between the new and the old, the office and the home, the professional and the romantic identities. The words mark the changes in gender identity. They reveal which women have integrated the two roles, which women have rejected the feminine parts of themselves, and which women have fallen into agonizing confusion.

What stood out was not the existence of words like "gentle," "kind," and "sensitive" for feminine, but the presence of a series of "weak" connotations. Half the women in the New York interviews linked the meaning of "feminine" with weakness or similar words, such as "help-less," "silly," "overaccepting," "martyr," and "non-power." Usually they didn't like the word or the idea.

One woman ground to a halt over the word. "Can we go on?" she asked after she blundered around with the definition for a few minutes. "I don't like the word. I don't like it. The word connotes pink to me and that's not the way I would describe myself."

She was petite and black-haired, with startling green eyes the color of a glacial pool. Throughout the interview, she had been incisive, almost fierce with her answers, honest and very powerful. She seemed to know exactly how she felt on most things and made conscious political decisions about her behavior at work. The control lapsed only once, over the word "feminine."

> I don't think I'm very feminine. But I don't think I behave in a masculine way. I . . . I . . . feminine . . . it bothers me to even have to dwell on that. I don't think it means being soft and cushy. It means being able to be what you are—I don't know. So there's some conflict there. I didn't promise I would make this simple.

Another woman linked her distaste for the word to the idea that men are powerful and women follow. She decided in college that she disliked the "female" traits of being "sweet and nice, not very good at business, and having a tendency to cry." I could feel her spirit rise in rebellion at the word when she recalled a friend in college who stood up one day and challenged a Catholic bishop who was teaching a class on marriage and the family. "Your excellency," the young woman had demanded. "Is my *soul* feminine?"

A third woman started out with enthusiasm, saying, "I like the word. I think of a feminine woman . . . I guess appearance, not wearing mannish clothes," and then she ran out of gas. "I guess somebody who . . . [Long pause] . . . I think I'm finished with that." She was bothered throughout the rest of the interview by her discovery that she associated feminine with weakness.

A fourth has started therapy to sort out her confused feelings about herself in relation to men after work. She lives alone at the age of thirty-three and wants access to a part of herself that is not as well developed as the professional side. She thinks "feminine" means weakness and "woman" means strength. She feels constant conflict between her professional and her feminine roles. "I guess I'm a competitive person, with men in particular. I have lots of good women friends, but when it comes to men, I guess I can't let up. I cannot fold my tent and become a shrinking violet."

Who told her she should?

American middle-class women come from a culture with a strong division in labor. The traditional gender cultures trained women to stay home rearing the children, and men to provide complete economic support. Lower-class and black women were less able to follow this pattern, although both emulated white middle-class culture when they could afford it. Such a division of labor between woman the nurturer and man the provider is not typical of primitive cultures, where women supply a high degree of material income. Nor is it a product of human evolution. Increasingly, the division is being seen as a historically limited pattern of the Western middle class, which reached its peak during the nineteenth century with the ethos of the middle-class woman as "emotional, pious, passive, and nurturant."

Attributes of the weak feminine (hysterical, overly emotional, lame-brained, compliant) hail from that recent past in which bourgeois women withdrew from the economic sphere. In an analysis of the nineteenth-century hysterical woman, the historian Carroll Smith-Rosenberg has written that women

> were sharply discouraged from expressing competition or mastery in such "masculine" areas as physical skill, strength and courage, or in academic or commercial pursuits, while at the same time they were encouraged to be coquettish, entertaining, nonthreatening and nurturant. Overt anger and violence were forbidden as unfeminine and vulgar. The effect of this socialization was to teach women to restrict their ego functions to low prestige areas, to depend on others and to altruistically wish not for their own worldly success, but for that of their male supporters.

Cultural traditions die hard. At the end of the twentieth century, one can still see in the personal histories of financial women the threads of the past. Few had mothers who worked while they were growing up; even fewer had mothers with professional occupations. Many remember a restrictive feminine conditioning. Some are still hampered by it, and an alarming number believe they cannot be professionals and family women at the same time. The pact made between the two cultures—that men provide support while women provide child care and domestic services—resulted in a masculine and feminine ethos with opposed traits along many dimensions, including one of power.

A division of labor between the sexes does not necessarily mean low power for women. Anthropologists have known many cultures where men and women do different kinds of work; yet the women are not subordinate, nor do the men attempt to suppress and control them. But the kind of gender division that arose in nineteenth-century European and American society was a severe form of male domination. Rights that women had had in the eighteenth century were lost during the nineteenth. Women, thoroughly suppressed in both their public and their private lives, were held virtually as chattels in the homes of their fathers and later their husbands. A "cult of femininity" arose to justify female subordination on the grounds that women were naturally passive, non-aggressive, and nurturant, with no head for business.

From the mid-nineteenth century, many women fought the spread of these gender ideologies as they struggled for positions in the increasingly segregated male sphere. But the growing prosperity of the middle class allowed women to be kept at home, ruling over a more and more limited domestic sphere composed primarily of children. From the perspective of the child growing up in this system, mothers may seem to have all the power. With fathers absent from the home and mothers overwhelmingly present, a patriarchal system like this can seem to be its opposite: It is mothers who are perceived to dominate, women whose strength must be controlled. As a result, the children of both sexes may develop a phobia concerning female aggression, a phobia that parallels and strengthens the ideology of masculine power.

Left alone in a domestic ghetto, refused access to authority in the public sphere, family women were constantly confronted with the ideology of femininity. For all the power they may or may not have held in their own households, once they stepped beyond those confines, women encountered male power, from bankers, lawyers, doctors, churches, and trade unions. There was no way for family women to succeed in the outside world, nor did they have any alternative but to stay home, reading women's magazines that glorified domesticity and castigated the liberated woman (of whom there were an increasing number).

"Just as a rose comes to its fullest beauty in its own appropriate soil, so does a home woman come to her fairest blooming when her roots are stuck deep in the daily and hourly affairs of her own most dearly beloved," exulted one woman's magazine in 1929, on the eve of the Great Depression. Said another writer of the time: "I know now without any hesitation that [my husband's job] must come first. . . . I am like the invaluable secretary to a big executive. He produces but I make it possible for him to produce efficiently."

A woman might resent at times "the thoughtlessness and omissions" of her husband; but once she "accepted that big biological fact that man was intended to be selfish" and woman self-sacrificing, the way to fulfillment was clear, opined a 1930s issue of the *Ladies Home Journal,* as quoted by historian William H. Chafe in *The American Woman.* In an article entitled "How Not to Get Married," a *Journal* writer declared that "working for a living and financial independence . . . is a fine deterrent to marriage."

Social reality mirrored opinion in the women's magazines. Only slightly more than 12 percent of professional women were married in 1920; 75 percent of the women who earned Ph.D.'s in the half century before 1925 were spinsters. Employers, even school systems, would not hire wives, and most of them dismissed women if they married. The reproduction rate of achieving women hovered around zero. The dichotomy between the male and female spheres was all but complete.

According to the gender ideology that supported this division, if men were to compete well in the outside world, they needed the complete emotional and domestic support of a wife. She was to listen to her husband's problems, give him the limelight, provide emotional guidance, nurture his ego, provide for his well-being, and put his needs and the needs of any children above her own. It is the kind of feminine pact that leaves a human being depleted and secondary—with a large unpaid debt. Over the years, the drain of psychological and social power goes in one direction—out. The image of an isolated, nurturant female at home is that of a fountain. Men and children sip from the fountain at their need. Water is not returned—it is supplied from some underground connection—and the purpose of the fountain is to make the men and children strong. That the bargain doesn't work that way, that it creates dependencies on all sides rather than strengths, is a psychological fact our culture has concealed, because the release of women from the central role of nurturer in the family is still revolutionary, representing a massive cultural change.

As we move toward integrated gender roles, we see more and more clearly where we have come from as a society. As men and women everywhere stretch their capacities to do what the other sex has always done, these notions of innate masculine and feminine behavior collapse into the assumptions they always were. Women learn that they can be aggressive and feminine. Men learn they can be nurturant and masculine. And from this broadened perspective, we can look back at what has been and see the legacy that still affects us. In the 1980s, we continue to struggle with the consequences of the patriarchy that swept the Western world during the nineteenth century, planting in our family and public life the heritage of feminine subordination.

The division of labor prepares women for the role of wife and mother by engendering an overly good and altruistic ethos. Historically, women have been responsible for the moral training of their husbands, including religious training, and that ethos carries on in the notion that women represent the moral conscience of both sexes. Women feel a need to be right rather than effective. They develop deep suspicions, if not outright hostility, toward political negotiations. The corollary is that men are supposedly free of a moral conscience—or so our belief systems tell us. Denial of aggression is part of the feminine ethos, along with an overemphasis on sex and appearance. Women trained to seek social status through a man still look for mates who are more powerful than they are, with more status, more intelligence, more money, or whatever other strengths contribute to worldly success, even when the need is gone and women are themselves the source of their own social position.

All of these traits conflict with the personality required of a professional who assumes responsibility for public authority. The "good" personality has to go, and herein lies a difficult choice for women, as well as the opportunity for personal growth. There is a tendency to believe, in coming to this crossroads, that if a woman gives up her need to be good and altruistic, she will become bad and selfish—as men are—or that if she stops being nice, she will become nasty. None of these things is true. The fears arise from prejudiced thinking about gender cultures. In becoming tough, women do not have to forfeit their kind, warm, and nurturant qualities, because these do not conflict with power and authority. Toughness and warmth are not opposites. What does conflict is the tendency to give power away, to put someone else in charge by serving, and altruistically to channel ego investments through men and children.

It is no wonder that career women who absorb these lessons now find feminine identity incompatible with professional identity. The professional training of women is borrowing heavily from the masculine culture; traits considered part of the masculine domain, such as assertiveness, egotism, and an ethic of achievement, are now part of the New Woman's identity. The dichotomy between the gender cultures has moved inward, to be internalized in the minds of women.

To focus only on women's internal identity conflicts, however, is to misread the reality of their lives in the 1980s. Woman also face in the workplace a culture created out of the masculine ethos with its own priorities, values, and unique history. That world bears the mark of a gender culture that is ignorant of and intolerant of most human needs other than achievement. There is a tendency for some men to feel that if women want the same rewards men have, they should make the same sacrifices. But what sacrifices do men speak of? What dynamics have created the masculine ethos? In the chapter that follows, we see the other side of the male–female dichotomy and the unique role of men in gender-divided cultures.

3

For Men
Only

M arvin, a forty-year-old executive with Citibank, leaned back in his chair, gazed at the sky visible through the window of his office high in a glass tower in Manhattan, and reminisced about the military.

> The thing that really fascinated me about the Army was that you came in there and they just tore you to shreds. Tore down our whole personality, destroyed us, and then built us back up. Once you've been through an experience like that, you are more immune to stress. It's difficult for someone else to come in and cause that kind of stress again.

Men speak of military training as a kind of necessary evil, an encounter with psychological abuse that toughened them up, hardened their emotional arteries, turned them into men; and so it has been for generations. Young American men no longer routinely go through military training (for the moment, at least), but the gender culture they have inherited from the past was dominated by the role of the warrior, and that had deep-seated effects on the masculine ethos that are not immediately apparent. It seems so desirable to be toughened up and resistant to stress that people forget the bottom line and the purpose of all this—which is to create a population of males willing to sacrifice their lives for women and children. Beneath the social and political power of the masculine ethos lie cultural rules, telling men that their own lives rank a poor second compared to their economic and military function. Men are expendable. Women, because they bear children, are not.

Cultural rules like this may seem outdated in a nuclear age, and they are. But nuclear warfare, which obliterates all sexual distinctions, is only forty years old. The gender cultures have had two centuries during which to leave their marks on the social order, ramifying through family tradition and institutional practice. By these rules, a man must give everything he has to support and protect other people, including his own life. His personal development and gratification are not important compared to his performance. His role as a parent is minimal. His method of enacting the masculine ethos (in the absence of war) is to identify so closely with career roles that he has no sense of self outside the professional status. It is only logical that corporate practice and the rules of the professional identity, shaped by this ethos, would leave little space for life outside the boardroom.

The theme of self-sacrifice runs strong in professional life. People give up home, family, play, pleasure, and ultimately self to succeed. Indeed, that is the ethic—to work so hard there is no time left for anything else. By doing so, one becomes a hero. Men pay the price, as they pay with their lives in war, to become superior economic producers capable of supporting women and children in a grand solo performance. It's all right if a man loses sensitivity, heart, and internal life in the struggle—not all right, perhaps, but tolerable—so long as he keeps up his end of the sex bargain. A warrior or a moneybags does not need a heart; a mother does. Nor is it very important what kind of human being a man is, so long as he does his job. In masculine culture, a person is valued for what he can do, not for what he is. He wins love, sex, and appreciation for the products of his labor more than for himself.

Much has been written about the conditioning of boys to this culture, but it bears repeating because too many women bemoan the fact that they didn't have the same conditioning. Boys are not supposed to cry. They should show no weaknesses. Vulnerability and feeling, essential for intimacy, are to be hidden. As they stand on the threshold of adulthood, boys pass through a culturally approved, brutalizing induction process that uses humiliation and abuse as tools for toughening the individual. Capricious and irrational, the abuse rains down on everyone, regardless of his unique state or individual behavior. Because the experience is linked with gender identity and is carried out by an institution of senior men, it is a powerful conditioning device. The young men do not rebel and demand justice; they stand the abuse and become hardened. Like fate, it must be tolerated.

The experience changes personality. One of the executives who recalled his military training thanked the service for turning his liberal beliefs into conservative channels. But—lest it be forgotten—the purpose of all this is to prepare men to sacrifice themselves. An anthropologist, now in his sixties, remembers the sense of betrayal he experienced at a young age when he discovered that as a male, he might have to go to war. His life was less important than the life of a woman, and that lesson has never been lost on him. Most boys, dreaming of glory and conquest, may not understand the sacrificial implications of their role. They see images of medals pinned to their chests and commanders' caps on their heads. They don't see the potential of their own death until a buddy comes home from some distant war lying in a coffin, or until they actually enter the armed services. (These dynamics refer to already grown men. According to psychiatric studies of today's children, most boys and girls of the nuclear age do not believe they will live out their lives, and that is a completely different story.)

In its disregard for the personal lives of men, the role of the provider is not very far from that of the warrior. In neither case is it culturally important what feelings men have, as long as they do their job. A New York psychiatrist, writing about male survival, dreamed up a fanciful origin for the provider role which many men may suspect in their darker moments. At the dawn of humankind, women are the first people on earth; they come up with a Grand Matriarchal Scheme to indenture the gender they are about to create. They need a Provider—someone to bear the brunt of the heavy work—so they create man from a pubic hair. To keep him motivated in his servitude, they give him a penis to glorify himself and a more massive physique so that he can feel powerful. In his world, the more productive he is, the more virtuous he is. Hard work and ambition are good; "unproductive leisure" is bad. A man who works himself to death is a hero. Foolish and neurotic as he may be, the hardworking man is a good man. Like all mythical tales, this reflects on a central theme of life: Men serve with their lives. The body and soul of a man can be sacrificed. The body and soul of a woman cannot.

Men in finance reflect the ethos of their gender culture. One senior executive at a trust bank in New York expressed displeasure at mistakenly hiring a female executive who was pregnant at the time of the interview. She didn't tell him she was about to have a baby; he wouldn't have hired her if he had known. But it was all right in the end, because when the woman developed kidney problems as a result of the pregnancy, she worked from her hospital bed. Hemingway would have approved. A hole in the side of the body should not interfere with function. Another financial woman, knowing the rules for proper professional behavior, tried to work from her hospital bed after a cesarean birth. But the pain overwhelmed her, so she shut the door and said to hell with it.

Several men interviewed for this study mentioned that professional women don't know how to take abuse the way men do. In a centralized hierarchy of power, such as a corporation (or the Army), abuse is inevitable. The point the men were trying to make was that women get bent out of shape emotionally when they have to deal with injustices. One explained the difference by speculating that men are less reactive to the sometimes irrational behavior of the hierarchy because they have been through the military, which was much worse than anything a civilian organization can come up with.

> To be very honest with you, I think women tend to be less tolerant of what I term aberrations from the logic and meritocracy of the institution. They get very upset about them, whereas men don't. Maybe that's a result of having to get up at five-thirty in the morning [at a base in the West] where it's 108 degrees and pick up little pieces of dust off the floor. After going through that exercise, perhaps some of the little shortfalls of the organization don't matter.

This man, a San Francisco banker, and others who spoke about their military training generally think it was valuable in teaching them to take abuse in an organization without losing their rationality. They say it's a shame women haven't gone through the same toughening process; if they had, they might not react so much to the relatively benign injustices of corporate life—benign when compared to the military.

They are probably right. Women, as a class, have not been subjected to abuse by an institution for the purpose of toughening them up. On the contrary, feminine culture encourages women to carry humanistic values that often blind them to the reality of the world men live in. They do tend to react to unfair and insensitive management until they learn something about the nature of organizational politics. But it isn't a lack of toughness that leads women to complain. They are outraged and mystified by the behavior of men in the hierarchy, which makes no sense in their ethical system. They think that bringing things to light will clear the air, believing that stupidity or lack of awareness is the problem. Men, meanwhile, operate on a completely different set of assumptions, and by those rules, open complaining is exactly the wrong thing to do. In fact, direct communication of any kind may be a mistake.

One senior woman in this study who had advanced into the top management of a corporation recounted a common horror story. A new man had recently moved into a superior position in the company and was firing executives right and left, apparently for personal reasons. He didn't seem to like her, either. The night before she was to go on Christmas holiday, she worked late finishing reports to prepare for her absence. He walked in about eight o'clock and told her in an offhanded manner that her bonus check would be less that year. She asked why. Was it because of the economy or her performance? Both, he said, adding that he thought her performance was worse than the year before. Speaking politely and rationally over the lump in her throat, she asked him if he could give her an explanation. He said no, and walked out.

The woman spent the next two weeks agonizing over her poor review and the lost bonus, knowing that there was absolutely nothing she could do to clear the air. If she followed her instincts, she would have gone into his office when she returned and asked him what was wrong. But others had done that and gotten fired anyway. Believing that asking for explanations would make him uncomfortable, she chose instead to ignore this issue, return with a friendly manner, and pretend to like him. That strategy worked (he began to treat her better), but it is not the one she prefers.

> Someday [in the corporate world] we'll get down to the feeling level so that finally we can go in and say, "Hey, we're not getting along. What's the matter? I'm uncomfortable. I feel I could easily be fired overnight no matter how fantastic a job I did, just because you and I don't like each other." I can see that kind of thing happening, eventually, but not right now.

This woman will probably not stay in corporate life much longer. The stresses of swallowing her anger and anxiety, pretending to a geniality she does not feel, have taken their toll over the long run, leading her to consider other employment.

Men who have been subjected to abuse as part of their gender conditioning—in military training as well as in other less obvious ways—act from different premises than women do. Bearing pain without wincing or complaining is a test of how tough they are. The ethic involved is to gain sufficient rank and control to do what a man is supposed to do, namely, protect and support other people, if need be at the expense of himself. The justice of the situation, his immediate comfort with it—these are not particularly relevant issues. Yet for women, who expect a fundamentally sane world that nourishes human potential, justice, fairness, and human comfort are all there is. That is the core of the issue, the heart of the matter.

In an existential and human sense, women—not men—are the privileged gender in American society. Women who defend traditional femininity know that very well. They will argue that they don't want to be men, in spite of the anger they might feel at being dependent upon and controlled by masculine power. They see themselves as being first existentially, privileged by God or nature to carry on the human line. It does not diminish the miracle of the act of birth to point out that a uterus does not give women natural rights to a higher existential plane. Culture gives them that right, by removing men from the nurturant realm and turning them into cannon fodder.

Western culture is not the first or the only one to make these kinds of distinctions. Wherever wars exist as an endemic condition of life so that someone has to be trained for them, men do the fighting; women usually do not. Restriction of war to the male sphere is one of the few gender differences that transcends cultural boundaries. The greater average size, strength, and aggressiveness of men are probably only minimally responsible for this difference because the distinctions are relatively small. In measures of height and strength, men and women differ as a class by a small margin—in the range of 10 percent. Millions of individuals are from a physical standpoint equal, so that if armies were to take the strongest soldiers, they would take many women as well as many men. But there is one absolute difference that sets a man apart from a woman: He cannot give birth. Anthropologist Ernestine Friedl speculates that because women regenerate the population, a culture can more easily tolerate the loss of men than of women. Men are the expendable sex. Other anthropologists comment on the same phenomenon, noting that several activities involving long-distance travel or danger are also typically male tasks in most known cultures.

The arguments make fundamental biological sense. If women fought the wars, they would not be available to repopulate the culture when the war was over. In a massive population, where so many people are expendable, the significance of this simple gender difference is lost. But it quickly becomes apparent in a small band. If 100 people were composed of 75 men and 25 women, the most offspring they could produce would be 250 (assuming 10 children per woman during her lifetime). But if the 100 were composed of 75 women and 25 men, the number of offspring could soar to 750. The size of the female population absolutely limits the size of future generations, which may explain why female infanticide is practiced in regions where protein is scarce. It slows population growth.

According to the work of University of Pennsylvania anthropologist Peggy Reeves Sanday, on the rare occasions when women have been trained as warriors, it has been in the guise of male identity. The historic Amazons of Dahomey are a good example. Given that name by European travelers of the nineteenth century, the Amazons were female soldiers who represented nearly half the standing and reserve armies of Dahomean culture. They were dressed like men, forced to be celibate, and organized, like men, into a military hierarchy made up of an elite corps, a royal guard, and ordinary soldiers. They could not marry until middle age and they were forbidden to bear children. They were stripped of their sexual identity as women, "like powerful nuns who bore arms for their earthly king." Because they were denied childbirth and given arms of destruction instead, they fell into a masculine, not a feminine, mode—a point supported by the Amazons themselves who said, "We are men, not women."

Sanday's cross-cultural analysis of more than one hundred societies demonstrates that warlikeness goes hand in hand with other characteristics of a culture. Typically, in cultures where men are culturally conditioned for war, they also dominate women, espouse religious beliefs focused on male gods, and are distant from their children because the gender spheres are separated. This cluster of traits has emerged from statistical study of tribal cultures, most of which have disappeared from the face of the earth; the records of their lives have been kept over the last one hundred years of anthropological research. Not all tribal cultures had social systems like the one above. Sanday found another pattern that looked like its polar opposite. In this cultural cluster, war was infrequent, the sexes were more or less equal, their work roles were relatively integrated, and the gods these people worshipped had both male and female forms. Studies like this have much to contribute to the discussion of gender change in America because they isolate some of the critical factors supporting sexual equality and inequality. Male proximity to children, for instance, turns out to be an important variable affecting all the rest. A sexual division of labor that removes men from taking a nurturant role promotes a masculine ethos focused upon domination and war.

One important implication of this work is to show that things do not have to be the way we see them in Western society. Men are not naturally warlike; the culture makes them so. Another is to point up the profound nature of the changes that are occurring in American life. If the cultural mechanisms of gender that operated in tribal societies are similar to those in ours—and there is no reason to think otherwise—then integrating the labor of men and women can be expected to ripple throughout the social order, making deep and lasting changes in national policy and religious belief. We already have indications that this may be occurring in the challenges women are making across a broad front in social life. But feminist activity may only be the most obvious manifestation of a more basic process that comes with merging the gender cultures. Many women in the battle for sexual equality believe that somehow their fight is associated with larger issues of war and peace. This analysis of equality and inequality among tribal cultures affirms that belief and suggests how it might work. Allowing men equal rights to parenthood, giving them a role (as fathers) that recognizes no cultural privilege for women in the sphere of human development, is a crucial part of the process.

Depending on whether a culture is focused on war or fatherhood, it will promote different dimensions of male personality. In tribal cultures, the masculine ideals (and attendant personality types) range from murderous to thoroughly humanized and peaceful. Among the

61

Lepcha people of the Himalayas, fathers often carried children on their backs on long journeys. Closely involved in their care, men fed children and trained them away from aggression. Inability to cooperate with others was considered highly undesirable. In general, the Lepcha emphasized similarities among people and diminished differences, which had the effect of discouraging competition between the young and the old, the men and the women, the rich and the poor. In the adult sphere of work, many activities were customarily done either by men or by women, but there was no reason why a man or woman couldn't switch work roles and they often did so, with no sense of shame or embarrassment to their sense of gender identity. Men were supposed to be better tree climbers than women, for example, but if a wife outstripped her husband in climbing a tree, he was likely to be proud of her, not ashamed of himself. The one thing prohibited to women was killing animals. In groups like this, the ideology of gender tends to be muted; sex cultures are weakly developed. In others, with a powerful division in labor and a warrior ethos, every activity of life can take on gender meaning, distinguishing men from women. Ultimately, adult personality conforms to the ideals. In cultures like these, gender personality may develop along opposing lines, emphasizing male aggression and female submissiveness.

Among the Iatmul people of New Guinea, a normal man was a killer; his occupation: headhunter. He was harsh, proud, and flamboyant, a person who bullied and swaggered his way through life, out of touch with authentic emotion. He could neither cry nor mourn. If a close relative died, he was likely to get into an argument over whose fault it was that the man died without passing on his mythological knowledge. Unable to weep, he ridiculed through imitation the dirges women sang to mourn the dead. Often obscene, frequently aggressive and histrionic, these men spent hours boasting to each other in the men's clubhouse. For them, life was a melodrama and they were on center stage, dressed in spectacular clothes, playing for the applause of the women they loved to ridicule.

The female personality could not have been more different. Cooperative, cheerful, submissive, and not at all involved with their egos, the Iatmul women did most of the work in the fields and all of the child rearing. Dressed in dun-colored work clothes, they ceded authority to men in public, although they did have some authority at home and they could be extremely courageous if the need arose. But, for the most part, their role toward men was to admire male activity, and they did so, encouraging the men to more and more dramatic behavior.

Sexual hostility between the genders was never very far from the surface. Men made fun of the female body and refused to watch the women's dances. Rarely did the women return the ill-will, but they would on occasion bar the men from their houses and stage all-female dances of stunning sensuality. Gregory Bateson, who developed this profile of Iatmul gender personality from field studies, obviously liked the women better than the men, whom he considered almost psychopathic. But he confessed to having some guilt about his attitude because it was obvious to him that the men had been conditioned to this behavior and they deserved understanding, even if they were unpleasant human beings. "As in other cultures, a boy is disciplined so that he may be able to wield authority, so [the Iatmul man] is subjected to irresponsible bullying and ignominy so that he becomes what we should describe as an over-compensated, harsh man—whom the natives describe as a 'hot' man."

Bateson's study shines a light on the possible source of a masculine ethos like this. First of all, he could find no real differences in the way the children were raised. Both genders were reared by their mothers exclusively—the men played no role—and it seemed to Bateson that mothers treated boys and girls more or less the same. But at puberty a significant event occurred. Juvenile boys were taken into the men's house and subjected to a brutalizing ceremony aimed at turning them into men. For several days, senior men humiliated and scarred the boys. Wrote Bateson:

> In the process of scarification, nobody cares how the little boys bear their pain. If they scream, some of the initiators hammer on gongs to drown the sound. The father of the little boy will perhaps stand by and watch the process, occasionally saying in a conventional way, "That's enough! That's enough!" but no attention is paid him . . . when pain is inflicted, it is done by men who enjoy doing it and who carry out their business in a cynical, practical-joking spirit. The drinking of filthy water is a great joke and the wretched novices are tricked into drinking plenty of it. On another occasion, a . . . bone is suddenly jabbed against the boy's gums, making them bleed. Then the process is repeated for the other jaw. In the ritual washing, the partly healed backs of the novices are scrubbed,

and they are splashed and splashed with icy water till they are whimpering with cold and misery. The emphasis is upon making them miserable rather than clean.

During these ceremonies, the novices were referred to as "wives" and shamed as women. The whole thing was aimed, Bateson thought, at driving out the emotional attitudes of the feminine ethos, and planting an aversion to female traits with an opposing masculine style.

Much has been written in psychoanalytic literature about the need for boys to break away from their mothers and, at the age of two or three, to develop a masculine identity. Everything associated with feminine is labeled unacceptable in the minds of little boys striving to emulate the male ethos, and this has been considered a universal process of male gender identity formation. But Bateson's study suggests a different dynamic. In cultures with a vested interest in high male aggression, the gender roles are separated. Boys are reared in a female world until adolescence, when they are literally wrenched out of it through a brutal experience linked to masculine identity. This is a time when the sex hormones run high, preparing the brain and body for adult sexuality. During this biologically vulnerable period, boys make the leap into a man's world which is so different from the one they knew before that it requires massive denial and rejection of everything associated with females. The cost to them, in terms of fidelity to the self and emotional balance, is enormous. But then, such cultures are not interested in developing a balanced male personality. They want killers, and that is accomplished at puberty through a dramatic encounter with senseless abuse, perpetrated by an institution of senior men. As for the women, subordinate as they are, they also have the freedom to be jolly, cooperative, and natural; they never learn to kill. A certain amount of submissiveness and a low profile may be the implicit bargain they make in exchange for a masculine type who is willing to commit homicide.

American society has no single masculine ethos, like the Lepcha or the Iatmul. It contains both types within its vast cultural complexity, and gender ideals for men are not homicidal. Nevertheless, the experience of these small tribal groups has some relevance for analyzing American gender roles. It is true that until recently in middle-class professional social levels, men and women have been trained for segregated work roles, and the masculine and feminine ethos, developed along opposing lines, reflects that difference. It is also true, until recently, that women have been given almost exclusive responsibility for rearing children and men have been trained for war in a process that depresses their humanity. The imprint of a warrior culture is upon us; at the same time the options for change toward equality run broad and deep. But the significant point here is to consider the sacrifices men are willing to make at the personal and human level in order to fulfill an economic or military function. From cross-cultural work, we can say these are uniquely male sacrifices.

Under certain conditions, men are willing to forfeit their humanity because they do not see themselves as central to the processes of life. They can support and protect life, but not create it. Their own personal lives can become secondary to performance in a way that few women understand who know that if they do nothing else, they can perpetuate the species, and that alone is valuable. Men can become peripheral; their humanity is not essential. This unique position of men, which makes them cannon fodder under some cultural conditions, also spills over into family life, where fathers, separated from active, nurturant parenthood, can more easily fall into the role of harsh disciplinarians. They become scapegoats for the world's meanness, giving it and receiving it back from their children in an educational process that makes them a focus of hatred and rebellion, while supposedly toughening their children. This gender dynamic is likely to happen in strongly role-divided families where men play little or no role in nurturing their children. They agree, in effect, to be the brutal ones, again at some personal cost to themselves. One woman I interviewed for this study, recalled hating her father and disrespecting her mother for his harsh domination and her soft conciliation. Years later, after therapy had given her some insight into her family legacy, she asked her father why he had been so harsh. He replied, "It was all right if you hated me, but you should not hate your mother." He was the scapegoat.

It stands to reason that organizations created by men trained to forfeit their own precious humanity would reflect an ethos lacking in human dimensions. By the rules of professional behavior in finance, expressed feelings are dangerous; personal life is expendable if it interferes with work. A mask of rationality is maintained at all costs. One emotional outburst—no matter what the provocation—can permanently halt a woman's (and presumably a man's) advance to the top. In this environment, communication among professionals follows a carefully marked narrow channel, not including the kinds of exchanges that vitalize the spirit or form personal bonds. A male executive succinctly expressed the deadening effects of controlling self-expression in a bank:

> You can't be yourself. My feeling is, you can't be. Otherwise, you're likely to put your foot in your mouth. At home, with my wife, we communicate. I tell her what I think of her, but there's a time and a place. If you don't pay attention to that, you wind up saying the wrong things at the wrong time.
>
> It takes a toll on you. You go home at night and you're dead. You don't want to do anything. You don't want to read a book. There is nothing you want to do. You can't taste dinner. I sit in front of the boob tube and fall asleep. I mean, nothing is very enjoyable.

In *The Anatomy of Power,* John Kenneth Galbraith attributes the extreme caution of a modern executive to the organization's demand for conformity. His thesis is that submissive managers and strong internal discipline strengthen an organization's power in dealing with the outside world, using a military model as an analogy. As Galbraith sees it, the suppression of self is nearly as severe in civilian as in military organizations. The executive makes an "extremely severe sacrifice of the right to personal thought and expression. And also of a wide range of personal enjoyments." He devotes himself to the organization "at the expense of family, friends, sex, recreation and sometimes health and effective control of alcoholic intake." Says Galbraith, nobody ever listens to the speech of a modern executive because it is so dull—he cannot speak for himself—and none of these men, with few exceptions, will ever make a contribution in music, literature, the arts, or serious learning. The executive is well paid for this sacrifice, but "it is worth something to give up so much . . . of one's own certain life."

Other theories have been advanced to explain the dehumanizing effects of corporate culture. The growth of rational bureaucracy is one. But neither theory explains why men have been willing to put up with roles like this and how they maintain their vitality over the long years. These questions take us back to gender culture and the unique position of men in sex-divided societies.

Cultures reward men for their sacrifices in military and economic roles by making them heroes. Without that reward, the loss of humanity would stand out in all its starkness, which happened during the Vietnam War when society reneged on its promise and disowned the war after putting its men in the field. The agony of the Vietnam War veteran could not be assuaged with money or retirement benefits; only heroism gives enough emotional and spiritual compensation for the brutality men endure in war. Through heroism, their culture gives them back a measure of the humanity it took away.

And through heroism, men gain increased value with women. Their personal lives, although distorted by the function they serve, can be renewed by women and children, who form an essential bridge to hope, optimism, and the benevolence of life, which would otherwise be destroyed by the warrior ethos.

Similar rewards compensate the corporate executive who sacrifices himself to the organization. Forfeiting the human dimension is tolerable because other people provide the emotional life and social enrichment the individual cannot supply himself—and these are absolutely vital springs. One can live without them, but not well. The personal erosions are too severe. This in turn raises serious questions about the well-being of executive women, who, like the Amazons of Dahomean culture, are frequently living out singular lives.

Women entering professions run up against the masculine ethos. Either they work as hard, or harder, than men do, making the same sacrifices of self, or they do not succeed—that is the message. But the cost to women is considerably more severe than it is to men. Women cannot start families at the age of forty, or even thirty-five, unless they have already spent years building a solid marriage. Their life cycles differ from men's in that the reproductive capacity runs out at midlife, so the tactics of postponing personal life for achievement carry far greater risks of permanent loss for women then for men.

Finding husbands who can provide the emotional nurturing a professional woman needs is sometimes difficult, but not impossible. Several women in this study had done so, and presumably the hunt for "a good man" will get easier as the sex cultures merge. Even so, professional women who want children will not be in the same position that professional men have been in for the last few generations. If women are lucky, they find domestic equality with a man. That is not a repetition of the old warrior culture in reverse form, but a new pattern of shared parenthood. Under the best of circumstances, professional women will be providing more parenting than men have done in traditional masculine culture.

But as a product of that culture, the corporate world is not inclined to relinquish its excessive demands on professional labor. In a recent survey of major American corporations, 40 percent expressed the belief that a woman with children could not hold senior positions in management. Almost as many, 37 percent, felt that men who were active parents couldn't reach the top either. It's encouraging that more than half of the companies felt otherwise, but few of them were doing anything to make changes in a system that discriminates against parents and exploits the labor of its best people, demanding a level of devotion that differs very little from the military. Not surprisingly, at the present time in executive roles most women are not married and most do not have children. The figures are stunning. Out of three hundred women executives polled by the UCLA Graduate School of Management and Korn/Ferry International, an executive research firm, 52 percent were unmarried (never married, divorced, or widowed) and 61 percent had no children. Their sacrifices were far greater than among male executives, of whom only 5 percent were unmarried and only 3 percent had no children.

The dilemma women face is real and external to them; it is not a product of their own internal conflict, although that exists too. Men and women have lived by different rules in this society. Masculine rules would strip women of their sexuality, in much the same way that the Amazons were stripped.

Over time, corporate culture takes its toll on the personality. Gradually, the professional identity—manipulative, image conscious, functional, independent, rational, emotionally inauthentic, and totally focused upon achieving an effect—erodes personal spontaneity and health, unless there are other sources of rejuvenation in a person's life. For the man or woman who identifies too closely with the professional role, the result can be a state of mind one woman called "tough fragile." That meant she believes she must act strong, independent, and rational all the time. As a single woman, she has few sources of emotional support, and she aches with needs unmet. But she cannot allow herself to express those needs; somehow, expressing them has become unacceptable. There should be no "chinks in the armor." Even the metaphor is militaristic. But who told her she must be unfailingly strong, independent, and rational? Who told any of us? Everyone and no one. It's in the air. It comes from entering roles defined by men whose lives are, at the bottom line, expendable.

Merging the two cultures successfully takes years, as a woman sorts out which parts of the feminine identity she wants to preserve and which parts are maladaptive in the new role. Both her personal and her private lives undergo the stress of change and growth. She may delay marriage and children for years as she works to master the professional environment. Family life is put off. In other cases, the changes result in divorce, as women stop taking care of men they once thought it was their duty to mother. The cycle of change follows a pattern that for some women has enabled them to have it all. Other women lost more than they bargained for, because they could not anticipate the forces they were coping with.

4

Gender Transformations

The first step in becoming a financial professional is to learn the rules of the prevailing culture, which are essentially masculine in nature. The behavior, style, dress, mentality, and value systems of professional groups developed from the needs and inclinations of Western men, so that women entering these fields are inevitably shaped by the type-casting of the other sex. In academic life, women learn to suppress what they know intuitively, in favor of an overly logical approach to knowledge. In medicine, they are caught by a value system focused on technology rather than touch. In business, they learn that many human dimensions of the personality must be kept out of sight during working hours. Learning to act like men, or at least, not to stand out as different from men, is an important first step in developing a successful professional identity. A woman may struggle against these models or refuse to learn them, but at her peril. The unreconstructed woman does not do well in a professional setting.

Many women in my sample described a process of change that came quite suddenly in their early working lives. Adapting to professional life meant giving up some part of their feminine identity. (Depending on the age of the woman and her background, this process began in business school or on the job. In several cases, when women were trained by their fathers, it began much earlier than that.) They cut their hair short, or changed the way they dressed. They became more serious and less playful. They stopped expressing emotions at work and kept personal details of their lives to themselves. They revealed less. They put off having relationships, often because there wasn't time to work and also play. At this point, gender differences do not show. People of both sexes devote themselves to the achievement ethic with singleminded energy. The opportunity to *be* somebody lies waiting for the individual who has energy, talent, and persistence. The world seems open and exciting. Money, high status, control, and influence—these are the rewards of the professional life, and they seem marvelous. The woman, like the man, goes for it.

Pauline is a banker, from the top of her neatly groomed blond head to the tips of her toes encased in medium-heeled pumps. She is twenty-nine and single. Almost nothing in her life compares in importance with work: "If tradeoffs have to be made, work would win. I make time to do other things, but they are easily dispensable. No one other thing commands nearly the attention that the job does." Her goal of moving into a managerial position at the bank where she works in San Francisco is the only goal she's sure of.

> My domestic aims are much less clearly etched in my mind than are my professional aims. That's why there isn't any conflict; they take a back seat. I do have outside interests which I pursue fairly actively, but I date infrequently.
>
> I think my preference is to be married at some point. But right now, I'm very ambivalent on the subject. I don't view it as being a situation I need to accomplish soon. It's more like a longer-range goal.

Pauline is also ambivalent about whether she wants to be a mother. She has not decided against it; she's just postponing the issue. It all depends on whether she finds a man she wants to marry, and she is not looking for him now. In spite of her very clear priorities, or maybe because of them, Pauline feels some loss in the home arena. She thinks she has surrendered slightly her desires for a home life in favor of work. That feeling comes from having postponed all these things.

This kind of singleminded, serious attention to the job is not new for Pauline. She has known since junior high school that she wanted to be a banker. All of her part-time and summer work were in the industry. She has never worked anywhere except in a bank. When she was ten, her father would take her to New York on business trips and she would lunch with bankers, a heady experience for someone that age. Her brother, more artistic than Pauline, would go along too, but he didn't like it nearly as well. Pauline loved it. She loved the supportive attention of her father, a corporate executive. She thrived under his serious, respectful treatment of her. Because she was a child didn't mean Pauline got bossed around. Both parents treated her with equality, but it was her father's professional grooming of her that made her set her sights as high as she did.

During the interview, Pauline sat very quietly, the image of a decorous banker, answering all the questions with a steady, intellectual rationality. Nothing broke the calm surface of her professional demeanor. She gazed at me unwaveringly, with hardly a blink. It was obvious from the answers she gave me on marriage, children, and femininity that the female side of her life has been put on a shelf, at least temporarily. She identifies very thoroughly with her role in the bank. She believes it is not possible for a woman to be feminine and also exercise power and authority. A feminine woman simply does not have powerful traits. The word conjures up ideas like dainty and demure or doll-like. Pauline thinks of a feminine person as being passive, bubbly, vivacious, and superficial. It is a negative concept—and outdated. The concept of woman, on the other hand, stands for strength of purpose and competence, used usually in a professional context. In Pauline's mind, there is no concept that stands for the adult sexual roles of women as wives and mothers, at least no concept that she identifies with positively.

Pauline works ten hours a day, which she doesn't view as working too hard. She is extremely serious about achieving recognition through competence and intelligence alone, rather than through female charm. The idea that she might gain something, even inadvertently, through her sexual attractiveness is anathema to her, so she carefully maintains personal distance from men at the bank and avoids even a hint of interest. If a single man there should ask her out to dinner, Pauline would accept the invitation, but "by not flirting and by making my conduct pretty obvious, it would be clear that if the intent were other than just friendship, and a professional exchange of ideas, there was not going to be a receptive person on my side."

Many young women in finance have the same serious intention that Pauline shows. Postponing decisions about family life in order to achieve professional ambitions is typical in the early years of a career. In fact, for these women, establishing a professional base first was instrumental in allowing them to have families later in life. But if Pauline's attitudes were common for her age and stage of career development, her background was not typical. She came into finance already carrying a professional identity; other women had to learn it.

Many of the women I interviewed made a radical break with the past when they moved into the financial world. Half could remember specific times when they deliberately altered their behavior to gain more respect from peers and to fit into the prevailing professional style. They told me of learning to be less warm, hiding real feelings, reacting less emotionally, concealing impulses of playfulness, sexuality, and nurturance, trying to lower their voices, being less supportive. Major aspects of their personalities were set aside in favor of a serious, rational, nononsense devotion to work. Sexuality and spontaneity were only some of the things that got swept away in the decision to become aspiring professionals. Humor, play, emotional contact, and idiosyncrasies of all sorts were kept out of sight for long hours of the day, while the young professional worked and waited for advancement. All of these changes, aimed at gaining increased power and responsibility, create the image of a reliable, sexually neutral, businesslike personality. It is a screen which allows the woman to function protectively in an environment dominated by the other sex. But it is also the beginning of a change in gender identity. The change is permanent, not ephemeral. Although most women eventually recapture their sexuality and sense of self, they do not become the women they once were. They move on to a new feminine identity.

Like many women who talked about these changes, Maria remembers a specific point when she radically altered her behavior to fit the professional stereotype. When she entered the office, she liked having fun, going out to lunch, having drinks, doing things "on a dime." Colleagues dubbed her the "bouncy blonde," while the upper echelon ignored her. Ambitious and politically astute, Maria realized before too long why she was being kept in a corner. She also knew that to change her image, she would have to change jobs. In the space of a few months, she made herself over.

> I dressed differently. I took on a more conservative demeanor. I got a new wardrobe. I couldn't afford suits, but I got outfits. I made a point of associating with other, more professional women. I made a point of going to security analysts' and financial women's club lunches. I began rejecting lunches and drinks.

Maria joined a number of professional associations and began appearing in public as the serious financial person she was. Her new image, calculated to win her the attention of the right people, worked. She rose in the hierarchy and by her mid-twenties was a senior investment officer in banking. By the age of thirty, she was a new mother.

Looking back on it, Maria remembers that the transition into a professional personality was awkward. She changed internally as well as externally. Before, she had run around with a fun group of young bankers—picnicking, roller skating, and playing volleyball. When she became serious, she stopped all that and began socializing with just her husband or maybe a couple. At work she set a game plan that included the careful selection of male associates. She chose men who had wives who worked and liberal views because she felt they would be more willing to help her. During the process, a shift in identity began to occur between home and work. She would be one person at work and then another person at home. At first, that bothered her.

> You feel insecure. You go home and say, "My God! But I was one person there and now I'm another person." Umm . . . but then it becomes natural. I can't tell you how long the transition took, maybe three years. It's like learning to make your bed in the morning. You do it twenty mornings in a row and you've established the habit. It [the new identity] becomes part of you. It is yourself, but it's the exterior. It's what you let people see.

For Shirley, the change was more painful. Promoted out of secretarial status, she had to prove herself publicly in the new role, which went against everything she had ever learned about being an emotional, loving, giving woman, helping and subordinate to men. The change required a wholesale suppression of the old personality, symbolized by cutting her hair shorter and shorter until it was an inch long all over her head. She lost her sense of humor and her feelings and her interest in sex. She became intense, with a driven energy that was only released through physical exercise. She withdrew from men at both personal and professional levels. She stopped revealing her emotions at work and watched people for clues as to how to behave.

> I had to unlearn things. I went through a very angry period. . . . I became real calculating. I watched people and found out I didn't have to

be so sweet and nice. I could say what I meant. There were a couple of women I respected and I watched how they did things. One of them broke down one day and cried. A lot of people saw that and reacted very negatively. She just had had it. She took all her files, walked into the hallway, and threw them up in the air. I looked at that and I thought, "I'm not going to be emotional. I'm going to cover that up. I'm not going to show my feelings anymore." To me, crying represented a weakness. I know now that it's not, but at the time, it was all the things I had been raised with that I had to fight. I was determined not to be that person.

Shirley's alienation lasted about a year in its most rigid aspects, but she was never the same again. Eventually, her feelings returned and she ripened into a strong and warm human being.

Changes like these repeated themselves several times in the stories of these forty-four women. Not everyone went through them. Some women came into professional life already geared for the new identity by their personal or educational backgrounds. A few refused to change. But many experienced a definite period in which they put away a significant part of themselves and learned a new identity. The end result for these women was to develop multiple identities. They became more complex and multifaceted personalities. Their private and their public lives became separated.

Marilyn swung into her office in the early morning hours, shuffled some papers around on the desk, and decided to carry out the interview in a conference room where there would be more privacy. She looked like a young version of Katharine Hepburn. Toasty, warm brown eyes gleamed out of a triangular face; her hair was piled on top of her head and she wore a string of jade beads on a tan dress that swirled around her midcalf. The dress had a jacket, Marilyn said, but she had taken it off and couldn't remember where she put it. At thirty-seven, Marilyn has the ego strength of a general and the authority to match it. She is known on Wall Street for having a thick skin. She described herself as "gritty"; others say she is "together." It took years to get there. Over the next two hours, Marilyn told a story of culture change that began for her in the South, where she learned that nice, well-bred Southern women should be warm, loving, and gentle, not aggressive or contradictory to the men in their lives.

My litany was that. All of the women I knew [while growing up] were very traditional women—mothers and homemakers—and supportive of their mates at all costs. They were terribly supportive of husbands and children, and that's what I thought women should do. The roles I saw did not prepare me for anything I had to develop. They gave me zero in terms of knowing how to behave at work.

Marilyn entered the brokerage business in her twenties and was immediately thrown into conflict. Could she be soft, wonderful, warm, and feminine? Could she be capable professionally? Could she be both at the same time? The conflicting messages of the two identifies stayed with her throughout her twenties. She could not figure out how to deal with men. She wanted them to like her, to think she was wonderful; yet being warm and wonderful was totally unproductive on the job, as Marilyn quickly learned. People did not take her seriously. The opposite alternative—to be overbearing and aggressive—went against the grain of her feminine training, so Marilyn was caught in a quandary: How to relate as a friendly human being but not as a woman, in the terms that Marilyn understood that word. One of the first women in her field on Wall Street, she had few rules to guide her development as a professional woman. That would come later. So she was on her own, testing out different solutions, evolving slowly.

> I don't know exactly when it happened, but I learned that you had to be slightly less warm, slightly less good-natured, slightly less laughing, carefree, and happy. You have to put on a more serious demeanor, to establish credibility more quickly. I don't advocate trying to be nasty, but just stop trying to be warm, wonderful, and nice. It works better.

One of the first things Marilyn learned was that her instincts to be accommodating and popular were completely inappropriate in the new environment. People didn't understand her behavior, didn't seem to know how to respond to it. So she drew a small circle around herself, including only those few people with whom she could be natural. With them, she was funny and coy and they understood. The rest she handled from a distance, with the no-nonsense, businesslike manner that professional women in this field routinely employ to keep personal exchange off-limits.

The second thing she learned was that somehow she would have to create new territory where sexuality was not an issue, a place where she and the men she worked with could meet as people. Marilyn found the solutions by trial and error. If a compliment about dress or appearance came her way, she returned it with enthusiasm, taking the remark at face value, pretending it was directed at her as a person rather than as a woman. If a man tried to make a pass at her, she looked him squarely in the eye and said, "I don't know what you are talking about." Time and again she wrenched a relationship back to an even keel, forcing a new sphere of contact that was stripped of sexual innuendo.

I'm not saying you should try to eliminate sexual attractiveness and femininity at work, but you need to learn how to use it. It really is counterproductive to use femininity for sexual attraction. If you want to be taken seriously, you just can't use it. You are female. There's no disguising that. Yet you have to not let that be the overriding element of your personality.

You have to deal with people as people; otherwise, you come on as a woman and the whole thing changes. I feel very strongly about that.

At home with her husband of thirteen years and her new baby, Marilyn reverses her priorities and drops the professional identity, creating the split between public and private lives that Maria and many other women talked about.

I switch gears when the day is over. That's one reason I don't socialize after work. On weekends, I'm another person. I'm a lot less serious, a lot more feminine, a lot more flirty, a lot more sexy and I do that on purpose. From nine to five, I'm one person. On Friday night, I change and the change has to do with clothes, personality, and vocabulary.

In spite of the fact that she splits her worlds and speaks of being two people, Marilyn has one integrated gender identity. Her experience with becoming a professional woman has altered her concept of what it means to be feminine, indicating that the change in identity has touched her deeply. Being a woman and being feminine mean the same things to her.

Traditionally, feminine means a person who is a little more kind, charming, and accommodating. Feminine is anything a woman is now. I think it's terribly feminine to be professional, successful, aggressive, and hardworking. I don't think those things are contradictory now. I'm coming to the belief that you are all of those things at some point in your week, but not necessarily at the same time.

That's what's so nice about this whole revolution. It makes people—

women, certainly—more complex persons, able to be lots and lots of things in the course of a week, month, or year. Men are quite excited about this. There are very few men who are not really excited to hear, "I'm a woman. This is what I do for a living. I really love it. I make lots of money, I'm very powerful, I think about my work a lot." Men just love that. Only men with low self-esteem are threatened by that.

The most dramatic, and in some ways troublesome, identity split was expressed by a thirty-one-year-old senior financial consultant in San Francisco. Sharing a house with a man she loves, planning marriage and motherhood with considerable ambivalence, this young woman was splitting between an aggressive, masculine identity at work and a subordinate, feminine identity at home. The split recreated the pattern of her parents' roles in a strongly father-dominated family, and the way this woman was coming to terms with her life was to act out an aggressive male role at work, but forfeit power at home to her spouse equivalent. This is the way she talked about the division.

> I have to admit, I feel like I'm caught in the culture change. I think I am one of those people in the middle where women were beginning to assume responsibility at work; yet they had a different persona.
>
> At work I don't think of myself as a woman. I am a person doing a job. It really doesn't dawn on me that I'm a woman until somebody brings it to my attention. I'm very aggressive. I'm simply doing what every other man is doing there, in a position of power—being aggressive. The guys you hear at work say, "Well, you're a women's libber. You must be terribly difficult," and it isn't true. I tell them that it's possible to lead a normal life at home, that I'm simply just like them at work, and I believe that.
>
> When I come home, I like being treated like a lady. I mean, there isn't even an issue of being equal . . . well, we are equal, but I like being dominated, having decisions made for me because I feel I've made them all day long. If we're going to do something, he takes care of all the arrangements. And I just get to go and have all the fun. I get back rubs every night. He goes out and buys me jewelry. I'm just spoiled. I'm terribly spoiled. It's almost like he has the final say. In buying the house, for instance, he made the last decision, and in buying the car, it was initially my idea, but he made the final decision on it.
>
> I almost have two lives, and the women friends I spend time with are very much like me. They have what you call a split personality and have

been able to handle it quite well. I'm very, very happy. I guess I feel fortunate that I've got two worlds.

Barbara had much more to say about the two identities. Dressed in silk, sitting in an elegant living room with a view of the San Francisco skyline, slim and very attractive, she talked at length about what it was like to live out two different lives, with states of mind that are opposed along the lines of power and aggression. She and her fiancé don't fight at home, but occasionally what they call Barbara's "aggressiveness" creeps in and she cuts loose. He says, "Well, you're beginning to act like you're at work," so she sits down and relaxes. The troublesome part of this story was the degree to which Barbara forfeited power at home. It seemed like a delicate balance that could be upset by the introduction of children. In truth, although the couple wanted children, each was delaying the decision for different reasons. I also wondered about the aggressiveness of her professional identity, so I asked Barbara if the workplace might suffer if women left their human qualities at home. She said:

> I don't know why it would get any worse. I'm simply doing what every other man is doing there. I mean, there are some human qualities I take into the office, but the bank is hiring me to get the job done and it's not different from the behavior the men have.

In a small exploratory study, it wasn't possible to answer all the questions that might arise with multiple identities. The women with children made different distinctions between home and work than Barbara did. Equality with their mates was essential. But what was true of the majority of women who maintained family ties or sought to establish them was a clear and definite separation of the public and private spheres.

What is this thing called feminine identity? How does it change? What does it stand for in the woman's psyche? The short answer to those questions is that feminine identity emerged from the interviews as a significant marker of what women were doing in regard to family roles. It was closely associated with attitudes toward motherhood, which should come as no surprise. Childbearing is the most basic gender trait of the female sex. But, although it seems obvious when you think about it, the link was not anticipated.

When I began the study, questions about femininity were included like any others for the purpose of exploring culture change. I had no reason to believe femininity would be important in the lives of these professional women. The concept could have become outdated and irrelevant. In my own life, I had struggled against the limitations of feminine culture, feeling the same anger that many women experience when they think they must act dumb, silly, or subordinate to men in order to be accepted as feminine. So, I had no predisposition to defend femininity, and it came as a revelation to discover that the majority of these women found the concept still very salient, very important in their lives, as a negative or positive force. Few thought the concept outdated. Even those who ferociously disliked the idea believed that it was relevant to them. Several discovered while they talked that they were disturbed by their negative attitudes and wanted to explore them further.

The conclusion was inescapable that among these women, a positive association with femininity as powerful marked a woman's movement toward motherhood. Connotations of weakness, on the other hand, were associated with rejecting or postponing that role. External appearance had nothing to do with feminine identity. How a woman appeared to me, how delicate or tough she looked, had no relationship to her sense of femininity. She might look like an angel and feel masculine or resemble a tiger and feel feminine. Those oppositions occurred, in fact. The woman called Marlene in Chapter 2 was by appearance the sweetest and most delicate-looking woman in the study. Internally, she felt like a man. By contrast, a woman I met later in the interviews looked very powerful. Stockily built, with short, cropped hair and broad shoulders, she stared at me for a good long moment with unmasked aggression. Finally, satisfied that I would not get nervous under her scrutiny, she sat back and began talking. She said she knows she intimidates many men and that's fine with her. When she was single and dating, her personal power served as a litmus test for choosing prospective mates. If they couldn't handle her power, she didn't want them. She has been married twice, widowed once, and never divorced. She is now enjoying being a stepmother and has a positive association with femininity.

Feminine identity proved to be internal. All the clothes and cosmetic ads in the world did not affect it. But a woman's attitudes toward men and children played a large role and those attitudes in turn were strongly affected by what she thought she needed to do to be a wife and mother. Most theories on gender identity do not cover this kind of cultural learning. Feminine identity has customarily been viewed in a psychoanalytic framework, as a product of early, unconscious forces. It has a hidden quality, like genetic predisposition. You either have it or you don't have it, and there is nothing much you can do about that, short of a seven-year analysis. Moreover, if you don't have it, according to analytic theory, there is probably something wrong with you. Women who reject feminine roles to follow a male lifestyle have been said to have a "masculine syndrome." These Freudian-based theories of classical psychoanalysis suffer seriously from ethnocentrism. They do not take into account the effects of culture or culture change; moreover, they have frequently functioned as cultural instruments enforcing traditional sex roles. I don't discount the power and validity of analytic thought in making these statements. The wonder of it is that much depth psychology remains useful in spite of its traditional cultural myopia. The anthropological concept of identity, however, differs in significant ways from the psychoanalytic one.

It is, first of all, conscious and learned, rather than the product of unconscious processes. Secondly, it carries no clinical implications for mental health or illness. Psychoanalysts believe that women who react against feminine roles suffer negative psychological consequences. By contrast, anthropologists make no claims about the health of individuals. They look for patterns of change that are common to many women and interpret the individual's state within a cultural framework, not a clinical one. The in-depth material these women gave me on family background, feminine conditioning, sexual behavior, and personal feelings is powerful material, very revealing of the individual. There may be issues affecting the mental health of some of the people I interviewed, but those are personal, private concerns. The stories of these women were used to illuminate cultural processes affecting many of us, and the interviews were given in that spirit.

Feminine and professional identities, as they are used here, refer to belief systems. They are sets of ideas the woman carries around in her head, telling her what she should do in life and what she should be like. These mental programs spell out the duties, privileges, responsibilities, and limitations of the feminine and professional roles. "A wife should not work," for instance, once acted as a powerful injunction keeping married women out of the labor force. Originally, the rule was enforced by institutional practice. A woman was fired or laid off if she got married. More recently, the rule has been maintained by the force of identity alone. Women *thought* they shouldn't work when they got married, or their husbands thought that. Whether verbalized or not, these mental tapes dramatically affect the choices we make in life. "A mother should stay home to raise her children." "A wife should make her husband feel powerful." "A professional woman should live for herself." The rules go on, setting up guidelines for making choices from a welter of possibilities. Created by the individual from a variety of sources, these identities are like computer software. They may represent stereotypes held in common by thousands of people, or they may be more individual versions, arrived at through personal experience. Whatever the source of the belief system—whether it be parents, movies, novels, history books, friends, the opposite sex, environmental stress, or a combination of all these factors—each person has her own set of ideas, and they are changing all the time. It doesn't matter so much where she learned her ideas, but how they affect her life.

This formulation of gender identity does *not* refer to sexual preference or biological membership in the female sex. A woman does not become sexually masculinized when she adopts the masculine ethos, but she does take on a man's social and cultural identity. The changes are deep enough that for a while some women may feel disassociated from their former selves. They may act in ways that feel unnatural or counterintuitive. They may think through everything they do. Nothing is spontaneous; everything is watched for effect. As a side effect of repressing the old feminine identity, a woman can lose touch with her sexuality or feel alienated from men. If the feminine ethos a woman learned in the past is sufficiently different from the professional identity she is learning in the present, she may be temporarily forced into rejecting large dimensions of her past life, which is to say, her past identity.

Everything associated with the feminine is brought into question. Motherhood and marriage may be postponed or rejected. A woman may stop flirting or lose romantic impulses. Externally, she changes her appearance dramatically, so that it is absolutely clear she is to be treated as a professional, not a woman. All of these changes represent a cutting loose of the old feminine identity, and—for a while at least—they can put a woman out of touch with her feelings. It is easy to be intellectual and distanced from people, especially when the culture rewards that behavior; hard to be emotional and close, especially when you no longer know how you feel about this business of being feminine.

Changes like these are characteristic of culture change. Anthropologists studying identity change among people in developing nations confronted by westernization have observed a similar process. Such similarities between change for these women and change for native peoples adapting to Western culture help confirm the contention that what we see in the masculine and feminine worlds are, indeed, two different cultures.

The first step in identity change, as described by University of Pennsylvania anthropologist Ward H. Goodenough, is the "act of eradication." People make a commitment to change by destroying their old symbols. They may become suddenly rude or they make a radical change in dress or manners, which is dramatic enough to make it impossible for other people to go on viewing and treating them as they were before. Destroying old symbols ranges from the mundane (cutting long hair short) to the profound (destroying religious icons); but in either case the person is taking the plunge, making a decision to change. He or she may not know what comes next. If there is not an alternative standing by, destruction of the old symbols can take on an antisocial appearance. When women of the 1960s burned their bras, the act seemed antisocial, but its cultural meaning was the same as when women of the 1970s stopped wearing dresses and appeared in man-tailored suits at work. In both cases, women were discarding symbols of the old feminine identity. Only in the second case, however, was there a new identity ready and waiting. In the intervening decade, the society had geared up for a massive change in female roles. No longer were individual women plunging into a new world without guidance. Legal and social changes encouraged masses of women to enter the professions, and an entire industry of books, magazines, clothes manufacturers, and change agents of various kinds sprang up to guide women into the new identity, to teach them how to be New Women.

The second stage of culture change is to learn the symbols of the new identity and conform to them. People watch others to learn what is expected of them. They shop around for models, suppressing their own intuition and individuality in favor of following the crowd. As the decade of the seventies turned into the eighties, a mass culture change of this sort occurred for women in finance. Within the short space of one or two seasons, women underwent a radical change in dress and manners. Following books coaching them how to dress and act for success, they rejected en masse the clothes associated with feminine identity and appeared in business uniforms designed to minimize their sexuality and maximize their sense of authority.

One woman, watching this process from her office in a bank overlooking a subway entrance in San Francisco, remembered her impression:

> It just hit me one day. The BART system empties out right here. People are purged every morning. I was going to a meeting about a quarter to eight on the surface, and as I crossed the street, a couple of trains happened to arrive simultaneously. Out of the bowels of BART came all these women, many who have worked so hard for identity—you know, to establish this identity, and what do they do with it? I stopped right in my tracks and thought, "Honest to God! They all look the same." The very thing they've been working so hard for, they've thrown away. I was very struck by that. All these women in their business suits and no makeup. Straight hair. If that's what they've decided, that's fine. But I can't believe they all decided the same thing at the same time.

However wrong it may seem in light of the American ethic of individuality, conforming is an important stage of identity change. People want to play by the rules; they want to be recognized as having a new identity. If other people don't recognize the identity, they don't have it, and that is a crucial element of cultural change. "Recognition and acceptance is vital," says Goodenough. "It is impossible to play the roles of a new social identity in a vacuum." In formerly colonial nations, Western officials often refused to acknowledge the changes being made by native people who made efforts to dress and act Western. By continuing to treat the natives as second-class citizens, westerners frustrated their movement toward identity change. The same lack of recognition can frustrate a woman's attempt to change. A few women in the study were having trouble being accepted at work, and because they were professionally stymied, they were also hampered in moving on to achieve other things they wanted in life, such as marriage and children. Some of them may have contributed to their lack of acceptance by holding onto old feminine behaviors and refusing to conform in certain ways to professional culture. Their motives were valiant, but the price was high.

Fortunately, the stage of conformity is limited. Once having dressed and acted the part, once having been recognized and accepted in the new role, people sooner or later regain their individuality. At that point, many reach back and rescue from the past the things that still serve the present. It was then that many women in this study reconnected with their feminine identity and they were aware of that change in no uncertain terms. It became crystal clear to them that the professional identity is only a hat they wear. It is not the Self. Moreover, the Self has several hats and several identities, which draw on and express different talents, desires, and strengths. A key thing to know about this theory of identity is that the I, the central decision maker and motivator of life, stands above and encompasses both feminine and professional identities. Although people may be caught in their roles from time to time and allow themselves to be defined by their jobs (whether in finance or motherhood), that state is experienced as a negative one. People struggle to master their roles. They want to control their lives rather than be imprisoned by a script in the social order. Ultimately, if they are to continue growing as adults, they achieve some control. With age and experience, the I takes over and begins directing traffic among the parts of life, which leads to setting priorities, determining limits, and making new choices.

Men in finance appear to maintain more integration between their professional and private lives, leading some observers to wonder if women are wrong to maintain a clear separation. But the overwhelming testimony of women who have clearly adapted to both roles suggests that multiple identities are healthy, if not necessary. Men whose masculine identity is more closely entwined with professional life may not need to make the same splits as women, whose feminine identity may stand a world away. But that could be to the disadvantage of men. If there is anything we know from the lives of men, it is the danger of becoming lost in professional roles. The creep of professionalism constitutes a clear and present danger to intimate relationships.

Between the ages of thirty and forty, many of these professional women came to a point in their lives when they realized that achievement lacked major satisfactions at the personal level and they reached out for solutions beyond work and public recognition. Men often reach that stage at retirement, but it comes twenty or thirty years earlier for women whose gender life cycle is different. Men may have new families until they are over seventy; women approach a reproductive limit in their late thirties. Unfortunately, professional income and status offer less help to women than to men at that point, and so the woman may face a crisis: What went wrong? Why doesn't my life work? Why did I sacrifice so much for this? Then, if not before, several women began to recover aspects of feminine identity. Turning around to recover feminine identity in more positive forms did not necessarily mean that the woman married and had children, although she usually did one or the other. But she did come to grips with the limitations of the professional identity and consequently decide to broaden her life.

One of the most outstanding women in this group—a leader of professional women and a rising star at work—arrived at that point in her mid-thirties. What makes her story so revealing is that she began life in finance with all the advantages of money, breeding, background, and ability. Renee fit into the world of achievement as though she were born to it. Which she was. Her father, an accomplished and powerful man, trained all of his children to excel. Renee grew up with high goals and high ideals, never experiencing discrimination because she was female, never feeling that because she was a woman, she had anything to prove. Discreet, politically sensitive, and full of self-confidence, Renee rose quickly at the bank in New York. She knew how to take care of herself and she was not defensive.

> I learned instinctively that people who work for you, let them get credit, let them do their own thing. To be nervous because I'm a woman or have to state my place, I just haven't felt that. I don't think I've ever felt that. I learned that if you treat somebody well, they trust you and they treat you well.

Renee treated the janitor and the senior vice president with the same egalitarian touch. She was comfortable with them both. They were human beings to her, not figures in a hierarchy of differential power. So she swung into New York public life without a visible flaw. She knew how to stand up in front of a room and tell jokes. She never thought about her appearance or her behavior. She was instinctively appropriate; it had never been any different.

Renee spent the first decade of her life in a professional whirlwind of hard work, public appearances, and social activities geared around professional contacts. Along the way, she met a man she wanted to marry. He was in his own social galaxy and together they spun a glittering trail of restaurants, parties, and public affairs. In the world of finance, Renee was a superstar. People clamored to see her. She seemed to have everything. She liked her financé's family and they liked her. She wanted children—the time was right.

Then her world began to collapse. The collapse came with warning signs because something had been eating away at Renee for some time.

> I felt extremely unhappy at times with all these things going on, and the reason I did. . . . There were many people who wanted to see me. All the social climbing that goes on, with the aggressive public image and superstar achiever.
>
> We would go incredible places night after night, and I came away with probably the best lesson I've had in life, which was that it really didn't add up to much.

Renee sought time to be alone with her financé, but they were always surrounded, until one night when the party couldn't make it. The two of them went out to dinner, sat across the table from each other, and discovered they had nothing to say. They had a dynamic public life together without an intimate base. "And that scared the hell out of me. I don't think that's the way to live."

Renee broke her engagement, resigned from all the boards she was on, and made time for introspection, seeking ways to develop the private, intimate side of her life with people who meant something to her. It was painful and frightening. The thing that depressed her the most was the lack of family.

> I truly liked his family. I was welcomed. I would have liked to have children. It was all there, but it couldn't have worked. You're so close and all of a sudden, it blows up in your face. For it not to work was shattering. It teaches you that there's one ingredient and all the other stuff doesn't matter. Why did it go wrong? I said to myself, "I'm going to sit here and figure this out."

One of the first things that happened to Renee was that she became vulnerable. In her search for understanding and new relationships, she opened herself up to people and they let her have it: "Well, you're so smart, tough, independent, etc. Do men really like you?" It was a crummy question and Renee didn't have the answer. She discovered that some people were not her friends and men couldn't seem to handle her accomplishments. None of those things would have been visible had Renee been happy. But she was in transition, wondering for the first time in her life if she, as a woman, could have a dynamic professional career and a family life as well. Theoretically, you could have both, but the strong, independent, rational qualities which Renee had in abundance were not the things that created emotional bonds. Maybe she should be more needy. She noticed that women who showed their needs for men got involved very quickly. But such feelings were not appropriate in a bank, nor were they very familiar to her.

Step by step, Renee changed her priorities from work to relationships and playtime. She stopped working on weekends. She fought to develop the emotional life and inner self that would give her access to intimacy. Slowly, a new life emerged, with friends who cared and relationships that lasted. At the age of thirty-seven, Renee does not know whether she will marry, and children may not be in her future; but she's happier, because in her former life, for all that was going on, she was at bottom isolated. Now that is no longer true. One sign of the change came recently when she discovered for the first time that she finds some men at the bank sexually attractive.

Renee resists the notion that her story reflects on a women's issue. "It's a person issue. It's a problem that people in this life have." To a large extent, she is right. Professional men have the same problems, but it is easier for them to find women who have the relationship skills they lack. Professional women often must humanize themselves, which brings them back to the traits that cluster around feminine identity: nurturance, emotional rapport, vulnerability, and the body in its full sensuality. These qualities are identified as feminine in American culture mainly because men, to achieve, have often had to sacrifice them.

B ut if women must adopt a masculine ethos to prosper in their careers, what about their private lives? What impact does professionalism have on their willingness or ability to marry and have children? Most of the formal restrictions—and there were plenty—that prevented women in careers from having families have been overturned, leaving a cultural fabric of unwritten customs that continues to perform the same function. Why, in an era of permissive integration, are so many financial women still alone? Do they choose this lifestyle, or do they arrive there by mistake, unaware of the forces they are coping with?

In the next three sections, these women tell the stories of their personal lives and family backgrounds. They tell us how they feel about being mothers and how their lives have been affected by the example set by their own parents. I've separated the forty-four women into three groups—women who reject motherhood, women who are mothers, and women in the middle who are interested in being mothers but have no children yet. These are not just arbitrary divisions; the statistical analysis revealed that a decision about motherhood reflects many other things in the life of a financial woman, particularly her own family background and the balance of power she saw enacted in her childhood home.

In the first group, we hear from women who have rejected motherhood consciously and emphatically. The sex roles they experienced in their families of origin are ones they do not want to repeat. Most of these women saw their mothers subordinated and they have difficulty perceiving any strength in feminine roles. The gap between the New Woman and the Old Woman is one of power, and it stands as a formidable barrier to reproduction.

II

Women
Who Reject
Motherhood

5

The
Daughters of
Patriarchy

Thirteen women in the group of forty-four said they were not interested in being mothers. There was no ambivalence in the way they
made that statement. Children were not in their images of the future.
They had made a definite decision against reproduction and were struc-
turing their lives around their careers. The remarkable thing about these
answers was the lack of any desire to be a mother. With the exception
of four in the group, these women seemed to feel no sorrow or linger-
ing regret, which I found surprising. Reproduction is a fundamental
need among all living things. It is not an instinct in the sense that every
woman should feel driven to bear children, but it meets a range of
physiological and emotional needs and helps to satisfy the great existential question: What am I doing here? When other things in life turn
bitter, human beings look to their children and say, "At least I did that."
So it was interesting to find a group of women who were very clear
about their decision against maternity. Sometimes, but not always, the
decision was made at an early age.

The four women who expressed some regret (two in each city) had
surrendered their desires for a home life to a greater or lesser degree,
for the sake of career. Two had surrendered only slightly. Said one:

> . . . that maternal instinct, that nurturing feeling, maybe, that I've decided
> I couldn't do. That has to be basic. No matter how I intellectualize it,
> there's still an emotional feeling of raising and giving birth and bringing
> another person in. Because of where I'm going now, I don't see that.

But the other two felt a great deal of loss. One became very angry when she talked about the choices women have to make. She raged at the thought of men who would say things like: "But don't you want any children? Don't you want a baby to say, 'I love you, Mommy'?"

"I want to kill them. What do they think I'm made of, ice cubes? Of course, that's got to be charming and wonderful. I mean, I wanted to kill him. And this was a man whose wife gave up a job, who stays home twenty-four hours and he's never home because of his job and she's nuts from it. And when I repeated it to her, she said, 'What does he know? What does he know about sacrifice?' " Beneath the anger lay a great deal of sadness, which this woman was insightful enough to admit. Still she feels she cannot have children because she is not giving enough. She is not good enough, not suited to be a mother.

The other woman had arrived at her childless state without ever making a decision against motherhood. She's sorry she doesn't have children, but not sorry enough to do it at the age of thirty-nine. Except for these few, the rest of the group seemed comfortable with their choices. They really did not have any great desire to be mothers. At least, that is what they said.

Most of them were still capable of reproduction. Only one of these women had had her tubes tied and only one was past the age of forty (age range: 31 to 42), so this was not a decision they had to make for biological reasons. In fact, the question sidestepped biology by asking, "Are you interested in being a mother?" Only women who clearly answered "No" were counted among the thirteen. A woman who was older than any in this group (forty-five), and who could not bear children for medical reasons, answered "Yes" to the question. "I'm always interested." She was counted among the women who might have children, even though her chances of biological reproduction are nil.

Eight of the group were married and a ninth was living in a monogamous union which she expected to become legal, so lack of fathers was not a problem for these women. Several seemed content with their marriages; they could have had children, if that is what they wanted. There were no more divorces or troubled marriages among this group of women than in the other two groups, the women who might have children and the women who already had them.

As you might expect, the thirteen women as a group were very positive about their work and dedicated to their careers. Several put in long hours—ten to twelve hours a day and then took work home—in the drive to achieve high professional rewards. Several of them were clearly excelling at work, either in terms of responsibility, money, or status, including a financial director for a development firm, a senior executive in a major corporation, a financial analyst who reports to top management in a large bank, and a senior manager in investment banking. Two of them had also been president of their own professional women's organizations, so these were women used to leadership. That does not mean that only women who refused motherhood were doing well at work. Many working mothers were also excelling professionally, but the ethic of work was so pronounced among these thirteen women that it was not unusual for them to put work ahead of all other considerations, including relationships. They liked to work; there wasn't enough time to do everything. So they made a choice.

> I hardly have time to do anything, much less go home at night and see a child. I don't like to cook and shop. It's not that I wouldn't want children, but they would get in the way. Once I thought I would have ten children, but I totally changed my mind. I like my life the way it is.

Another woman is just now coming to the conclusion that she doesn't really want to produce her own family. Professionally, she is moving very fast and it occupies most of her time and energy. The work is exhilarating but isolating, since there are virtually no other women in this particular financial field. She has no trouble finding men friends, but simply cannot nourish a significant relationship at this point in her life. She thinks that eventually she will marry someone who already has his own family, rather than becoming a mother herself.

> I can't say I've ever had any strong leanings in that area. I really don't like the idea of teaching and taking care of somebody's little needs. I think I'm past the stage of my life where I'd really . . . I just don't think I'd benefit from it.
>
> I've always felt obligated when I was dating a man, to have his children if he wanted them. But I've been putting it off and putting it off. Now I see creating a lot of things for myself. I see a partnership [with a man], creating a nice life for one another and maybe somebody else's family. I've never been that interested in a home life and I'm too young to do any of this stuff right now. I know I'm thirty-four, but I'm still too damn young. I'm a late bloomer.

The great majority of women who decided to forgo reproduction came from patriarchal families in which their fathers held high power and their mothers did not. Eight of the thirteen women came from such homes, where in the daughters' eyes their mothers lacked power and authority in the family. By contrast, every single woman who gave birth in the two samples from both cities came from homes of high maternal power. When the two groups were compared statistically—women from homes of high maternal power and women from homes of low maternal power—the difference was obvious and significant at the .001 level. The daughters of patriarchal families were not interested in being mothers themselves. They clustered overwhelmingly among the women who rejected reproduction.

It may seem obvious why the daughters of patriarchal families reject motherhood: They can't see themselves playing a role which in their deepest childhood memories had been a powerless one. But this kind of relationship has not been documented before, nor is it necessarily automatic. Patriarchal cultures that restrict women to domestic spheres often have a very high birth rate. Women follow in their mothers' footsteps whether they have power or not. But these are situations in which women have little option but to follow out a prescribed life course, which is no longer the case among American middle-class women. In the early seventies, only a little more than a decade ago, abortion was legalized. Combined with the spread of easy contraception, it gave women virtually complete control over their reproductive functions. During the same period of time, women gained a broad mandate to develop careers outside the home and become economically independent. One can hypothesize that in this environment, patriarchal families become maladaptive in a fundamental biological sense. In evolutionary theory, adaptation refers to differential rates of reproduction among competing species, and, in this study, patriarchal families were not producing any offspring.

Not a single woman who was the daughter of a low-powered mother had any children. Twelve women came from homes like that where, in the daughters' eyes, fathers had high power and mothers did not. Only four of these women had any interest in being mothers, and only one appeared to be in the process of doing it. At the time of the interview, she was engaged to be married. She and her future husband had decided to have children and there seemed to be no obstacles in the way. Incidentally, this woman had grown up as the only female in a household of men. Her mother died when she was eleven, and she and her brothers were reared by a strong-willed father who counseled his daughter against marriage and motherhood. He wanted her to be a professional woman.

Sandy has followed those precepts, and now, at the age of thirty, working in a brokerage house on Wall Street, she feels successful enough to challenge her father's psychological authority over her world. She told him recently that she will marry soon and he should prepare himself for that. Sandy doesn't know why he has always objected. She suspects that he didn't want her to live out the life his wives and other women he knew well had done, and he believed that if she had a husband and children, they would ruin her professionally. He always had high expectations for her academically and professionally, but having a social life was not important.

> He wanted me to look nice. I didn't go around in a hair shirt. But psychologically, I think he did inhibit me. I've always had more trouble accepting the femaleness of me than I've had accepting the independent, competent part, which might be thought of as the difference between the professional woman and your other life as a woman.

Sandy appeared for the interview wearing a dress. With her soft voice and gracious bearing, she looked every inch a lady. But she thinks that word is an anachronism and doesn't fit her at all. Sandy's conditioning for feminine roles was cut short abruptly by her mother's death. She remembers baking cookies with her mother in the kitchen and holding tea parties with her dolls. Then came a year's struggle with cancer which killed her mother, and following that, a lot of responsibility at a young age. Alone with her brothers and father, she tried to fit into a male role. Her father was very controlling.

> I think I was afraid of him. Although he presented a party line of rationality, and everything should be logically discussed, ultimately, if he didn't want something done, it was "This is my castle and you'll do it my way." So there was a kind of authoritarian stance, and you tried to avoid getting to that point, because if you did, he was the father and you were the

child. It was a no-win situation. I wasn't physically afraid of him, but his anger was enough. It was very emotionally upsetting to the whole family, so unpleasant that it [anger and yelling] became a strong deterrent.

Nevertheless, Sandy and her father had a fairly close relationship. About ten years ago, she became aware that she was not comfortable with the notion of being feminine. She had always thought of herself as female—that was no problem—but the idea of feminine carried negative connotations of being pink, frilly, not powerful, and not competent. It was not a good thing to be, yet the idea would not go away. Nor could she connect it with her self-concept as a female; so, like many women, she was left to struggle with it. About four years ago, something happened to change her perspective. It wasn't a spectacular event; she simply reached a level of professional success where she felt comfortable expanding her options and exploring neglected parts of herself.

> I figured out that I didn't have a very balanced view, that pink, frilly, and not powerful was not the sum total definition of feminine. I think as I became more comfortable as an adult and as I gained authority at work, it fell into place. It lost its weakness.
>
> I think I would equate femininity with acceptance of self. That's what it became for me. I've decided that if women have a better sense of their own femininity and are more comfortable with it, they are better at exercising power.

Sandy wants to be a mother, but her plans are slightly ambivalent because she doesn't know how she will react to childbirth. She wants to continue working, and from what she has seen among her peers, there is no way to anticipate her behavior once she becomes a mother. This is a path Sandy will have to forge for herself because in her memories of a warm and low-powered mother, there was no model for the New Woman.

Sandy is closer to integrating the professional and feminine parts of herself than are many other daughters of patriarchal families who have been strongly influenced by a powerful father. The first point to raise here is: What kind of power are we talking about?

Power can mean many things, from personal influence to tyranny. Some parents are powerful because they love their children and show it; other parents are powerful because they gain control of the house and make everyone else conform to their demands. The power may be beneficient or punitive, rational or emotional. In this study, definitions of power came from the women themselves in describing their parents. I did not tell them beforehand what power meant, except to say that the idea excluded power outside the home. People may be high-powered at work and low-powered at home, or vice versa. I wanted a measure of family authority, a picture of masculine and feminine power in their archetypal states, buried in the mother-father images. It called for a gut sense of power, a child's eye view of which parent swung the clout in the family; and that is what emerged from the answers. I posed the question this way:

> I am exploring family background along two dimensions. Personal power and authority in the family is one dimension, and emotional warmth is the second. So I'd like you to think about each of your parents and tell me how you would rate them on these two dimensions. This does not include power in the outside world, but only power within the family, in regard to each other and you. Taking your father first and then your mother, how would you rate him—as having high power or low power, and high warmth or low warmth?

Most of the women answered without vacillating. They had no trouble deciding which parent held the balance of power. Only a handful stumbled over the question, saying they couldn't relate to it. In exploring their memories, these women described an egalitarian style where conflicts were settled by discussion and children had a voice, or they were families where for some other reason the daughter never experienced conflict between her parents. There were not many families like that. The majority of women saw a power differential and they saw it without thinking very long.

By and large, this is a group of women from a tradition of high maternal power. Most of them are the daughters of powerful women. Active, energetic, verbally dominant, sometimes domineering and authoritarian, these mothers of the past generation wielded power in spite of their economic dependency on their husbands. Most were not professional women themselves. Although they had worked from time to time, rearing children was their main occupation. Thirteen women said their mothers were professional women; the rest identified them primarily as housewives.

In the total group of forty-four women, thirty-two said their mothers had held high power within the family, matched in nineteen cases with a low-powered father. Contrary to other sociological studies of businesswomen, these are not the offspring of primarily dominant fathers. Distant or absent, quiet, sometimes warm and supportive, the fathers of these women often lacked authority in the eyes of their daughters. For eleven women, both parents held authority. Two women had never known their fathers. Nineteen said the balance of power and authority was held by their mothers. Twelve said the power was held by their fathers.

The description these twelve women gave of their parents resemble the traditional European-American patriarchal family, in which the father's will prevails and the mother is clearly subordinate, sometimes willingly, sometimes not. Sara's story tells of her distress at seeing her mother dominated:

> My father would yell the loudest. If they were to have a fight in front of me, my father would have to win, just by being bossier. In a way, she had more power over me because she could get me to do things because I wanted to, or because she gave me a good reason. Later, after I started to study child psychology, I discovered that my mother was a genius. But I have to say that he had more power than she did, and I realized later that was because he had the economic power. He dominated her although he wasn't as strong emotionally. He didn't want to give her any credit for any intelligence or for doing any work or for contributing, and I didn't like it.

Sara's mother had a great sense of humor and seemed to be happy, but Sara didn't believe she was. She remembers her mother asking one day how they, the children, would feel, if she left their father. Sara said, "Great! Do it." But it didn't happen.

> And I wanted that very much, for her to be independent, to get away, to quit the whole thing, to get out, because I felt she was getting a raw deal and she had more to contribute to the world than this low status.

Sara grew up on a farm in the Midwest and doesn't remember being pushed into feminine roles. In fact, her mother seemed to be subverting that.

I remember saying about dusting the house, "I don't like this. It's dumb. It's boring," and she said, "Well, if you think it's boring, then don't get married. Or marry someone with a lot of money, so you have a maid, because that's what it is."

I got the idea. I thought it wasn't fair that women had to go through all the risk of having kids and also spend all the time with them, and that was your whole thing. But people didn't think too much of it. I got the impression that people didn't think too much of your being just a housewife. And I wasn't too pleased with that. Guess I was a bit of a rebel.

Sara dreamed of being a cavalry leader, in spite of the fact that she was female and very attractive. That was beside the point.

I was always a leader. In those days, I didn't know about any females who were leaders, with the exception of Queen Elizabeth the First. I loved history and I identified with the strong leaders in military history.

She decided a long time ago that she wasn't going to have any children; she didn't plan to get married, either. She was going to buy a house and live in it alone with a series of long affairs. But she did marry late (she's now thirty-three), and only recently, when her friends started having daughters, has she thought it might be nice—

if I thought *for sure* I could have a daughter. But basically, I don't really feel I'm missing a lot, and I did make a firm decision when I was younger.

I thought you had to be one or the other, and I wanted to go on with the independent career. I just didn't see myself as a mother. I wasn't really sure I was ever going to grow up enough to be a mother. You don't have to be that mature to make a lot of money, but if you have some little character you're forming, then you have to have your act together.

Several of the fathers in this group were like Sara's, domineering and aggressive. A woman in New York described power in her family this way:

He [her father] was a very hung up, unhappy man. Drank to excess; had terrible temper tantrums and he was a very cold individual. It wasn't until about two years before he died that he could even say anything nice to me. . . . But behind my back, I was the apple of his eye. I was his favorite child, the best of the bunch, but he could never say that to my face. When I was really getting my career off the ground, he came by, put his hand on my shoulder, and said, "You know, I wish I had a son like you." I said, "Thanks a lot, Dad. Thank you, Dad."

There was only one way, his way, and if he didn't get it, you'd pay hell, so you'd give in. Whatever he wanted, she did. Being married to an individual like that, you subjugate your personality. I thought she was incompetent because she put up with his idiocies. I asked her, "How can you let somebody put you down all the time?" I never wanted to be financially dependent like her.

And the woman who spoke these words has no desire to be a mother:

I like to visit my sister's children, but they get tiring to me. If I had one, I'd want to take care of it for the first five years, but then you'd have to put me in a padded cell. I need the outside activity. I'm very awed by women who are good mothers, but I don't think it would do for me. I might not be a good mother.

For these two women, the feminine images they grew up with at the most intimate level are ones of being dominated and even degraded. Their defense against falling into the same state is to walk a wide circle around maternity. Motherhood represents a loss of power. Financial independence represents the solution. These women really believe they cannot do both; and psychologically, they can't. The issues of power and status stand in the way. If they were to have children, they would have to work through and reject the internal messages telling them that motherhood imposes a state of inferiority, or else fall victim to the same subordinated status.

The fear of deteriorating into a state of feminine powerlessness, if they pursue love and marriage to its ultimate conclusion, forms a solid barrier for these women, who are in many cases out of touch with feminine identity. That is a strong statement to make, and it demands explanation. No criticism is intended when I say that many of these women are out of touch with feminine identity. They told me so and indicated in numerous ways that they were confused and sometimes angry about the issue. Typically, the women who did not want children and who came from patriarchal backgrounds were reacting against femininity as soft, giving, and weak:

I dislike the word "feminine." It conjures up all those little things I was trained to be . . . the connotation that men are powerful and women follow.

I don't feel feminine. It's not relevant. I hope I'm feminine, you know, in someone else's view. I suppose I am. I'm probably feminine. It isn't a harmful thing. I think a feminine woman can exercise power. I could also, if that's what I was.

I don't like the word "feminine." It connotes pink. I don't like the stereotype of women as nurturing and supportive. My husband is an infinitely more nurturing person than I am.

I don't think of myself as being particularly feminine. To me, it means—Oh, words like "gracious," "socially adept," "charming," "soft spoken," "genteel," "pink," and "ruffles." It conjures for me the manipulative, coy aspects of femaleness.

These responses from four daughters of low-powered mothers represent the dominant attitude among the group of eight and coincide with the rejection of maternity. One of the women quoted above raged at the thought that society discourages women from having both careers and families.

I think society has set up choices that are totally unfair. No one has ever said to a man, "You can't have a family and also a successful job," because you had a lackey at home, a slave maintaining the other side. That is a totally unfair situation.

This woman remembers, with the same anger, being conditioned for feminine roles:

I was conditioned to be such a pretty little girl that you would vomit. I didn't partake in sports, I didn't ride a bicycle and do not to this day ride a bicycle. I never got dirty. I was clearly restrained [to have] good and wonderful behavior.

But while these women didn't like the idea of feminine, neither did they feel masculine. "Is there a third way to be?" asked one woman with a sense of anguish. There is in fact a third way, but it calls for women to complete the cycle of identity change, extending the sense of authority they now experience at work back into the home, transforming the notion of what it means to be feminine.

In the testimony of several other women, I learned that that was what they had done. They had succeeded in working through the issue of powerlessness and low status, emerging with a stronger concept of femininity and a better sense of themselves as human beings.

6
Not Like
Mother

S hirley is a warmly radiant individual, who seems to have her life in order now at the age of thirty-seven. She has a man she loves and a good job. Eventually, she will probably marry this man, if they both can get over their phobias about commitment. By now, they know the masculine-feminine roles they learned were not the best. Shirley's father walked all over her mother.

> Get my laundry. Do this. Do that. He made her seem dumb. He berated her like she was a child. Everything was dictated by him and he was untouchable. I was afraid of him as a child, but I found out as an adult that he's a marshmallow.
>
> He was the titular head of the family. Mother is the classic submissive, passive . . . it makes me so angry! Powerless. Just totally. I even think she didn't have much power over the household. She used to pay the bills, but everything was dictated from my father. She defers to him constantly. I don't know if she even made the menus. She put up a wall around him, separated him [from the family], and covered for him all the time.
>
> He was very critical. I wanted his blessing, his response that I had done a good job. I wanted to please him. But I was closest to her. She has a wonderful sense of humor and feel for life. She adored the children and sheltered us totally.

Until she was fully adult and entering professional status, Shirley expected to follow in her mother's footsteps. In fantasy, she played at being a mother. In reality, she became a secretary, accepting as a matter of course her subordinated status in relation to men.

I knew females were supposed to be passive. You should let the man win at all costs. You always built up *their* egos. You always listened to what *they* have to say and make *them* interesting. You don't talk about yourself. You take care of them; give to them. And I looked for someone I could take care of. That's what my mother did.

In her private as well as in her professional life, Shirley played out a subordinate role until, at the age of thirty, she began training for a professional position. The opportunity had been won through legal action on the part of a group of women, and Shirley, as one of the beneficiaries, had to perform. People were watching. Either she learned to take responsibility for authority or she would fail publicly. She drew into herself, cut her waist-long hair until it was an inch all over her head, and dressed in blue and gray suits.

In place of the expressed emotionality of the old feminine ways, Shirley became calculating and rational. She began to observe how other people behaved. Consciously she selected new behavior patterns for herself. It felt very unnatural, very painful, and yet it was necessary, because out of this process of emotional distancing, a new identity would arise, an identity capable of handling power.

During that period, I was very professional and businesslike. I had absolutely no sense of humor about myself or about life. The only thing I did was tap dance—six hours a week. That was my way of letting things out. I was so intense and I think I was removed from people.

At one point I lost feeling. I think I became asexual. It lasted for about a year. I stopped dating. I thought all men were real jerks and I didn't need to be with jerks anymore. I was very hostile during that period. Some guy would say, "Good night, girls," and I would say (sarcastically) "Good night, boy." A lot of men didn't want to be around me.

Meanwhile, new patterns were being laid down. In therapy, Shirley learned that it was all right for her to be smart. At work, she pushed past the knots in her stomach and put herself out in front, until she was comfortable being at the center of things. And then, when all that was done, her private life began to change. Alienated from men for a long time, she allowed one nice man back into her life and then another. They were different from men she had dated before, more tolerant and more giving. Finally, she met the man who has become her lasting companion: "And we became friends. I began to realize I didn't have to be angry anymore. I was ready to start over again and be vulnerable, if that's what it meant."

Shirley doesn't want children now, although she has always been told she would be a good mother. She enjoys children, smiles at them, buys baby clothes for her friends who are pregnant, and goes on her way, relishing her free time. She thinks that if she had children, she would be like her mother—overprotective and totally consuming, living her life through the child—and she doesn't want to do that. It takes too long to grow up.

> It's taken me a long time to know who I am and what I want out of life. I just couldn't give that [time and energy] to a child. I'm still finding out about myself. I don't think I want to stay home with a child for five years.

As Shirley became revitalized as a New Woman, her opinion of what it means to be feminine underwent a dramatic transformation from negative to positive. Now, instead of being powerless, the concept carries humanistic connotations for her: "soft, gentle, and caring, emotional at times, *strong,* aware, sensitive, and compassionate." Shirley surprised herself when the word "strong" popped out, along with all the sensitive adjectives. "I don't know why that's there," she said. "It didn't use to be."

Life is sweet. Shirley likes her job as an investment officer in a bank trust department. She likes her free lifestyle. And she loves the man she lives with. Recently, he moved to take a job in another city, and Shirley requested a transfer to be near him. But she doesn't want people to know why she is relocating. A professional woman is not supposed to put love ahead of work.

N ot all the fathers in patriarchal families were aggressive in imposing their will. In some cases, it seemed that mothers actively promoted their husbands as the power in the family. The men took over responsibility for shaping their daughters' lives toward career values that devalued feminine roles. The father's influence was simply overwhelming. It was his home, his standards, his values. Often, it seemed as if the daughters in these families were more identified with their fathers than with their mothers. They saw themselves as being not like their mothers.

Sally, a serious professional woman in New York, calm and rational, is struggling to find herself as a person after five. She has no problems at work during the day. She works well; she uses her head; adapting to the work environment was not very hard for her. "I wore suits as a kid working in offices during the summer. I never really thought about being unusual. My dad wore suits to work. What frame of reference did I have? Maybe that was it."

But feminine roles are giving her real problems. When she dates men, she has this idea that she should go soft and weak and it makes her so angry she can't do it, so she goes on the competitive edge instead. It is a vicious circle that cuts her off from genuine warmth. Fortunately, Sally knows where her issues lie and is talking with a female therapist to develop what she calls her "warm side." She also wants to become more comfortable with power, and the idea of using it. The words "warmth" and "power" came out in the same breath, which is not surprising. In Sally's images of the nurturant, warm mother there was no power, and in her images of the authoritative father there was no warmth. At the psychological level, power is not mitigated by warmth and warmth is not strengthened by power.

> My father is very Germanic, into precision. There's right and there's wrong, but you have to work hard at recognizing a demonstration of warmth. It's there. I hesitate to say he was punitive because I only remember being spanked once. But it was his disapproval, if disapproval counts. There were rules and regulations.

When she was young, Sally wouldn't see her father for days on end because of his work and she remembers being very disappointed about that. She respected him—with a feeling verging on fear—but she had no sense of affection for him until she got out of college. "That was a maturing process for me. Plus, he changed. As he got older, he let down his Germanic guard a little."

Sally's mother, on the other hand, complemented him in the classic patriarchal fashion, with high warmth and low power.

> She was never the stupid, fluffheaded wife. She was a college graduate . . . but she deferred to him in terms of money, household, buying a car—all of those things.

> She was the classic caretaker, homemaker, wonderful homemaker, chauffeur, dinners, the whole business. You know. My father didn't know where the kitchen was. She was a wonderful mother in those caretaking things . . . but . . .

Recently, Sally's mother turned up unexpectedly at the door of her Manhattan apartment and told her that she was breaking away from her husband's control. Sally was stunned. She didn't know what to say and she spoke of the event in a deprecating tone of voice. It was as if they were very different sorts of people.

> My mother decided to bust out from my father's control when she was seventy. She decided it was time to get liberated and she showed up here on my doorstep. She had decided she'd had it with being a good little housewife and I'm sitting here thinking, "Oh, my God! How do I respond to this?" And I responded very poorly is the answer. I mean, I was totally ineffective. I just sat and listened.

Sally's closeness to her mother began to wane and shift to her father when she got out of school. She thinks that happened because she went into business and finally, after all these years, he has decided that maybe she *does* like to work.

Sally doesn't want to be a mother, even if she could hire a full-time housekeeper. Some of that is fear and some is natural disposition. Sally never liked dolls in particular and never fantasized about being a mother. She thinks she would not be a good mother—the common remark of daughters from patriarchal backgrounds. But what comes through strongly is the conviction that if she ever had a child, she would develop negative buoyancy and sink. Sally has a college friend who got married and had children; she continued growing while her husband did not. Now the two are separated. Sally has watched this drama of marriage and motherhood and it validates all her fears. "Seeing the conflict in her [the friend] is a terrifying thing for me. I don't want to be put in that position. She personally came out very short. She's a smart capable lady and if she can't do it, I guess I can't." Not very long ago, Sally ended a relationship with a man who got joint custody of his children.

"See, it's all backwards," she burst out suddenly. My brother is like I should be, stereotypically, and I'm doing the things that he as a man should be doing in this society."

109

Associations of weakness for the word "feminine" were evident throughout the interview, as was Sally's sincere desire to recapture a sense of femininity for herself—that something which is in her and probably also in her mother. She doesn't want women to act like men. She thinks women bring special strengths to the world, including greater perceptive ability, particularly at recognizing voices and body language. She thinks men should be actively involved in child rearing. Yet in that mental recess where the idea of male-female relations are formed, a feminine person has no power.

The last question asked of each woman was: "Do you think a woman can exercise power and authority and retain her femininity at the same time?" Sally's answer was logical and honest:

> I guess I have to say no. And I'm sorry I have to say no. But any of the truly powerful and successful women I know do not fit my definition of feminine. I'm not saying they're unfeminine. . . ? I *am* saying they're unfeminine. How do I explain that? [There was silence as she thought] Well, there's conflict there. They're ladies. They are ladies. But they're not—my stereotypical feminine. I'm sorry to say that. But I just . . . *Femininity does not wield direct power.*

The idea seems written in stone, it is so resistant to change. Here is a woman who wants to be more feminine, yet by its very definition, the feminine identity is unacceptable to her as a professional person. There is a deadend sense of self-defeat in that proposition. "I want it; I can't have it." "I need it; it will diminish me." If a woman becomes powerful, she loses her femininity. If she gains her femininity, she loses her power. The women who carry on this tradition of femininity, which was born in European cultures and nurtured by American wealth, are finding themselves blocked at domestic levels. The feminine roles they learned are not reproducible.

Pregnancy and childbirth are a time of intense reidentification with one's own mother—a time when many of the conflicts between mother and daughter resurface, to be played out again and hopefully resolved. A female sociologist, hearing of this study, recalled the identity crisis she passed through when she became pregnant. The daughter of a patriarchal family, she had been told by her mother, "Don't follow me. I've done it wrong. Do something else." For years she obeyed, following a professional path to academic success. She saw herself as strong;

her mother as weak. Then came the pregnancy, and the conflict erupted in a brief but terrifying internal struggle. "It was something I had to get through, literally a passage." For a while, she was overwhelmed by the threat of being like her mother, when she had taken such pains to differentiate herself. Then came the resolution. One day she looked at her fingers and realized they were free of arthritis. (Her mother had had arthritic fingers.) "I am not my mother, I am me," she said, and the crisis passed.

Most of the women from patriarchal families in this study were choosing not to go through such a process. And there are major benefits to a decision of that sort. Many of the women who rejected motherhood conveyed a strong sense of independence and invulnerability. They are free of conflicting domestic desires, for one thing, and can pursue their professional aims with an undivided consciousness.

Susan is the financial director of a development firm in which she has the potential for making far more than the $50,000 she made last year. She is so turned on about her job—"The sky's the limit"—that everything else pales beside the challenge of going all the way creatively and financially. She doesn't have much time outside of work. She puts in ten to twelve hours a day, ending at the health club. Often she will spend weekends doing the same thing—half work, half exercise. Incredibly, she manages to carry on two significant relationships with different men, and date other people as well.

A very pretty and dynamic individual, Susan exudes health and confidence. You have the impression that she will always get what she wants and that she has exactly what she wants right now. She doesn't want children, and while men are important to her, relationships are not a priority at the moment. The one with a man she nearly married is on the decline. He pulled back from marriage because he was afraid that she would

> wake up one day, chew him up, and spit him out. He felt that I'd never really needed men, ever, and that I always had a lot of attention from them, which is true. I *have* been very independent and I've enjoyed a lot of people. He just didn't want to be a casualty.

Susan's apartment in San Francisco looks one cut above college days, which is appropriate because she is living out an extended youth and has neither the time nor the interest to maintain a home life. At thirty-four, she thinks she is still too young to get married, although she would have married if her friend had not rebelled. He told her she needed him as a base for her flight; that he was supposed to provide the house, the comfortable social life, the unchanging foundation, while she soared into new and higher spheres. He was the rock, she was the bird; but he wanted a better deal. After he said that, Susan started to think.

> He was right, one hundred percent right. I had to give him credit for everything he said. And he was looking at it with an awful lot of concern for both of us. I said something very childish. I said, "Why is it in my life that some men have been able to accept me exactly as I am and not try to change me?" So he asked me, "Well, where are they now?"

Susan laughed, a pure and clear sound. He was right again. But it didn't really matter, not at the moment, not when she had so much ahead of her. "I think I'm still too young. I don't see any point in rushing into a mistake," she said,

Susan has consciously and deliberately selected against the kind of supportive, nurturant traits she learned from her mother and other women in her family. She discovered that those qualities (nurturing and supportive) were not effective in the working environment, so she dropped them.

> The only quality I found is not effective in the working environment is that particular quality—nurturing. You can get all wrapped up in some little secretary's problems and it's not necessarily beneficial to the professional relationship. It goes against my nature—and you don't do it openly— but you just learn to tend to your own onions.

And the same change occurred recently in her private life. She had been acting out the role of the perfect hostess—running around, making sure she had the right dress, thinking ahead for other people, trying to be thoughtful and have everything there at the right time. Then . . .

> When I started this new job, all that went out the window. I had a behavior mode with [her boyfriend] that I didn't have time for when I took this job and I kind of cast it aside. I had been more concerned about his interests before. Then, all of a sudden I was not. I slipped last year into a different behavior pattern. Some concern was still there, but often I'd be found forgetting or not paying attention or something like that.

She paused. "This is starting to make me think. I was using my supportive . . . I was being a female in that relationship. And you see, that was my only avenue for that sort of behavior."

Susan comes from a family in which her father exercised total authority. When asked to characterize him as having high power or low power, she said:

> Is there something above high power? Omnipotent? He was the authority figure, and cold. Underneath there was a lot of warmth, but he was gruff and very stern. You brought back a B on your report card and there was a lecture as to why that wasn't an A.

He raised her on an equal par with boys. When she wanted an erector set, she got one; she and her sisters were both tomboys. They played all the games that boys play and they knew they should learn to take care of themselves, because their father stressed this. "It was very important to him to raise children who would be independent." Susan's father, not her mother, was the disciplinarian, but gruff and stern as he was, he didn't scare Susan. In fact, she thought he secretly enjoyed her misbehavior.

> I was very naughty, but I always knew that actually he thought I was kind of funny for pulling stunts. He was amused by it. He wouldn't let me know, but I knew. He was gruff and would say, "Now, put your keys on my dresser and your license," which really restricted me. I never did anything really wrong except to be out of the house when I was supposed to be in it. I would tell Daddy I was listening to the radio in the garage. He never really bought that.

In spite of the strict standards, Susan felt adored and encouraged. "I was given a lot of faith in my ability. Anything I wanted, I could have. I was absolutely the most wonderful thing . . . we were just the greatest."

Her mother was the model of a nurturing, supportive female, very polished and without authority.

> She has no power that I recognize. Isn't that interesting? When we came home from school and were upset about something, Mother was very soft and gentle with us. She was gentle when we were alone, but she did kowtow to Daddy's performance requirements. She would say, "Your father

is the head of this family and what he says, goes. But I'm going to try to soften the blow." That is the way she handled things. She didn't openly confront him on anything. She did in private discussions—and maybe that's what you're supposed to do—but I wouldn't do it that way. I want to be at least equal.

And her mother willingly conceded men's dominance in affairs of the world:

> She always had this blind faith in the supremacy of the male. I can tell you, it was just unbelievable. Whatever they said, you know, blind faith in the government: "Well, dear, they wouldn't be President if they didn't know . . ." That kind of bullshit. Totally subservient to authority. Never made any effort to understand the mysteries of the world. I think I'm running away from this image of femaleness as being frail and unable to take care of herself.

Often, women from these patriarchal families had negative associations with the word "feminine"—negative as in weak, overly emotional and frail. Susan's connotations were mixed, and so were her attitudes toward the concept. She said she doesn't think of herself as being feminine or not; the concept is not relevant to her. But then she added, in a low, soft voice: "My mother always told me that being feminine doesn't mean being frilly. It means being soft, gentle, and thoughtful of others, kind and considerate. . . . I am feminine, I think. It's nice to be those things."

Some of the women who rejected maternity had mothers with high power. Obviously, maternal subordination is not the only thing that turns women away from reproduction. Five people in the group of thirteen were daughters of powerful women, yet for various reasons they choose not to become mothers themselves. One thinks parenting is not rewarding. A second just doesn't like children:

> I'm definitely not interested. I just don't like children. If they're six and can take care of themselves, OK, but I'm not the kind to want to take care of other people. I can't understand friends who are close to forty and have a four-year-old brat running around. I never really wanted to have kids, and I do think women can do both.

A third woman, Sharon, thinks she is like her own mother—too perfectionistic and compulsive to make a good mother.

These three described mothers who were quite powerful and authoritative, but low on nurturance and warmth. As daughters, they did not confide in their mothers, and if they found solace with either parent, it was usually with their fathers. Nevertheless, the women seemed to be identified with the maternal figure. No one said she had followed her father's role model, but they would say, "I'm like her," sometimes followed by an expressed or implicit sense of "I wish I weren't." None of the three was close to her mother. Sharon believes that her driving professional ambition was an attempt to equal the power of her mother, a power she had experienced as a critical force when she was a young girl. In effect, Sharon is doing what her mother said she could not do— be successful. The two have had clashes over authority for years.

The fourth woman lost her mother when she was ten years old. She never rejected motherhood; she just ran out the biological clock, with a great deal of ambivalence and some sorrow at having missed childbirth. In the fifth case, the daughter, a product of two powerful parents, sees herself as substituting for the son her father never had. She is the oldest of several girls and remembers choosing to identify with boys in grade school. She would sit in the back of the bus with the boys when all the rest of the girls sat in the front. She refused the dolls her mother offered and chose a cowgirl suit instead. Her mother, a woman of some wealth, tried to inculcate traditional upper-class feminine attitudes ("You'll want to marry a man who is better than you are"), but without success. Her daughter didn't believe her, and thought it was absurd not to beat a boy in competition, if you could do it.

In spite of her youthful alignment with boys, this woman, Sheila, is happily married and has no apparent conflicts over femininity. She said she could "take motherhood or leave it" and has decided to leave it. But her husband has had a vasectomy, which is potentially reversible, in case they both change their minds in the next five years. Sheila is now thirty-one. She thinks—like the daughters of patriarchal families— that the roles of mother and career woman are complete opposites. Contradictions. Her sisters have become mothers, she has become the career woman, and neither can imagine living the life of the other. It was her mother who told her she would have to stay home if she had children.

7
Revitalization

Many of the women interviewed who don't want children appear to be suppressing the nurturant parts of themselves. It's not that these feelings are lost to them; but they just are not useful at work. Since most of their time is spent either working or in a social environment involving work, there is no opportunity to express the behaviors linked with maternity, including nurturance, bonding, and the willingness to invest time and energy in human relationships. The bundle of maternal behaviors is there to return to, when and if the need arises, but while these women are so preoccupied with achievement, it hardly shows a glimmer of life. All the emphasis is on professional rewards.

They also seem to have made a full transference of psychic energy from family involvement to work involvement. They spoke of liking to work hard, of not missing a home life. One of the thirteen is a model of professional behavior for other women in her New York firm. From the words she used to describe professionalism, one could hear that very deep feelings were wrapped up in that idea. I asked her what it meant to be a professional and she replied:

> I know it when I see it. It's . . . it's like aesthetics, an intuitive thing. I can tell it when I see it in somebody. My boss was a total professional. He thought about his job; he thought about the individual; he thought about people, and he was one hundred percent attuned to the company, and to doing a very good job, not just for him, but for the company.

Those words show a sense of altruism and commitment of the sort that people make to parents, children, siblings, spouses, and very close friends.

Another woman who maintained a more cynical view of the workplace was nevertheless thoroughly devoted to the drive for success. She was going to get it, with the same intensity that a woman of a generation might have spoken about marriage. "I just want to su⌐⌐⌐⌐. That's all. The horror is wanting it and not getting it."

The single women in this group were all delaying marriage or ending relationships because they might interfere with work. Only one of the five single women said she would like to be married, but she is reconciled now to the idea that she will be alone. Another single woman said she views marriage as a form of retirement to happen in her mid-fifties.

The married women in San Francisco were an unusual group in that several described marriages to men they might not see for days at a time, because both partners were pursuing different activities.

> My husband can work until midnight or 1 a.m. We don't see each other every day. We do different things. He'll call and ask for a date. But our home life is just fine. We can go for a month and hardly cross paths, which is terrific. We'd get bored if we were together all the time.

Another woman had been married for twenty years but likes the idea of living alone. She feels she doesn't need a man and would not marry again if she were ever to become single. Descriptions like that were given only by women in San Francisco who had ruled out motherhood. No one in New York said—as they did in San Francisco—"I don't really need a man." On the whole, the women who rejected motherhood, particularly the daughters of patriarchal families, were an unusually independent group, more willing than others to be alone.

The idea that patriarchal families might be maladaptive in a modern American context was suggested thirty years ago by psychoanalyst Dr. Philip Slater. Slater found that in families with strongly complementary roles in the area of authority and nurturance (a demanding, disciplinary father with an expressive, supportive, and lenient mother), children had trouble identifying with the parent of the same sex. As a result, they failed to internalize the values of the parents.

The more denying and strict the father, the more lenient and supportive the mother, the more the son identified with the mother. He might learn to fear his father and obey him in his presence, but when

117

the father was out of sight, the son felt no motivation to follow his rules. Because he lacked warmth and support, the father did not attract his son to make a shift in identity from mother to father. Slater argued that in families like this, cross-sex identification may be of benefit because the child identifies with the parent who is least rigidly committed to a role.* Children internalize a parent's values when discipline and support come from the same source, said Slater, a point widely accepted in psychological theory. Other authorities, including H. Wecksler, found that the children of families with this pronounced division in mother-father roles were more likely than other children to have conflicts in self-image.

These family studies of thirty years ago are dramatically supported by the finding that career women from patriarchal backgrounds don't want to be mothers. They seem not to have internalized maternal values. The emphasis these women place on work as opposed to relationships supports that interpretation. Their values appear to be drawn from the male world. Lifestyles reflect the belief that motherhood and careers cannot be mixed. You can be one or the other, but not both, following the traditional idea that a mother's proper place is in the home.

From this perspective, development as a New Woman puts you beyond the pale of motherhood. Maternity can occur only in one context, the one on the other side of the world, the one requiring extreme devotion and service, where a "true woman" altruistically denies herself for the sake of her children. It is probably significant that the daughters of low-powered women, who have rejected motherhood themselves, kept saying they are not good enough to be mothers. The ideal of motherhood was simultaneously raised so high it was unattainable, and so low it was undesirable—the classic portrait of feminine behavior in nineteenth-century Western patriarchal society. If the same process is occurring widely among career women in other professions, it could lead to the rapid disappearance of familial patriarchal traditions in the middle class through lack of reproduction.

But what of the women themselves? Do they suffer? It's no sin to reject motherhood; in fact, it contributes to outstanding professional success, perhaps because the women are able to focus all their creative energies toward one goal. The time is past when people generally as-

*Cross-sex identification had no pathological consequences in this group.

sumed that to be a *real* woman, you had to have kids. The task of integrating motherhood with careers is difficult enough that many women may give up reproduction because giving up the career is worse and they can't get things together fast enough to do both. All that is true, and yet there is a risk, a risk that women with these values will experience a severe lack of personal fulfillment. The costs did not appear until these women entered midlife, when they became aware of a whole set of needs unrelated to work and they began to change. It was the testimony of the women aged thirty-five to forty that convinced me something very important is happening when women show no interest in being mothers. If it were simply the inconvenience of combining careers and children that led these women to reject motherhood, the issues of feminine identity would not exist. But there was a pattern, a pattern suggesting a breakdown of identification with mothers in the context of a general devaluation of femininity.

The good news is that the issues appear to lie in the arena of cultural values rather than in any core sense of female identity. All of these women were obviously feminine in dress, manner, style, and sexual preference. In spite of their often negative attitudes toward femininity, they clearly thought of themselves as female, without ambivalence. No one wanted to be a man and no one professed a homosexual preference. Most of them were married. Nevertheless, the daughters of patriarchal families were more strongly identified with their fathers than with their mothers, on the whole. There was much variation on this issue. Some women seemed to differ from their mothers from the time they were little and followed their fathers instead. Others said they did not take either parent as a role model. But only one of the twelve daughters of patriarchal backgrounds identified her mother as a role model.

The fact that so many women who reject motherhood came from father-dominated families indicates that a major reason for turning against feminine identity lies in the cultural subordination of women. Unable fully to identify with the mother who lacked authority, the daughter differentiates from her and from the value systems underlying maternity. Sometimes, it looked as though the parents collaborated in turning the daughter away from maternity. Neither wanted her to follow the old patterns of female dependency, and they sent her out into the world to do it differently.

At some point, women achieve enough success to begin questioning the singleminded pursuit of careers. The feminine grows up, so to speak. It becomes an adult and takes on connotations that are a mixture of gentleness, sensitivity, toughness, and strength. Besides Shirley, two other women in this group were starting to place more time and energy into relationships. There was a sense in them of opening, exploring, expanding, and humanizing their ambitions. All three had recently found new partners (two marriages and one cohabitation). They were the only women in the group with new primary relationships, and their bonds highlighted and reflected the internal changes these women were going through as they reintegrated feminine identity in a more powerful form.

Sara

Sara, a gutsy, expressive woman of thirty-three, rebelled against the low status of female labor when she was a girl. All of her girlhood heroes were male, except for one, a liberated English teacher who was married with four sons. "She was a big, tall, beautiful, happy woman and I liked her whole act. Nothing vindictive. Nothing petty." Other teachers, however, pushed sex roles, which incensed Sara as early as the third grade. The adults in her family, when they talked about Sara's future, would ask her, "Do you want to be a teacher or a nurse?" There were only two choices. Her father thought she ought to marry a senator. But Sara had other things in mind, namely, escaping from the confinement of feminine roles. She decided not to get married . . . well, at least not until she was forty.

Sara went to work on Wall Street and rose to professional levels through hard work and a serious attitude. Most of her friends were men; there weren't many women at professional levels in finance during the late 1960s. Anyway, Sara needed to learn the rules of this new world. And the learning was rough. "I wasn't ready to fight for my life. . . . I thought logic and reason counted in this world and I sure had to get over that thought!"

The insecurities of a very aggressive and competitive business gradually dawned on Sara.

If a new person takes over, the people the other one brought in get kicked out. That bothered me. That was a conflict [with her own values]. I like to feel I can be loyal to a firm, that I will work just for that firm, do my best, and somehow they will notice it and reward me. Well, A, it didn't always work out that way, although it does occasionally. B, it doesn't matter how loyal you are, you can get kicked out for a number of reasons. There's a merger or something else.

A good friend, a male mentor, told Sara she had better learn to lay her cards on the table and fight like a man. So she did that. She learned to swear and fight back aggressively, but without losing her cool.

You don't try to manipulate or whine or wheedle. You stand up to people and sometimes you say things that are really insulting, if that's what you have to say. But you try not to get excited.

Another thing you learn is that if you're going to confront someone, you don't do it in front of other men. You get them off into another room and say something very calm, like, "Well, I think we have a problem in this situation."

Sara stayed with the business through her twenties and early thirties, learning to produce tangible results with clients, learning to trade and sell under severe pressure. She wanted to be the best broker on Wall Street, not an unusual ambition in her business.

So many people tell you, "I am the best. I mean, I am telling you, *I am the best!*" And, of course, a lot of us are just kidding ourselves. [She laughed] But I was not kidding myself. I knew I was going to be the best, and I knew I wasn't going to do it forever.

Meanwhile, Sara lived in apartments and carried on love affairs without getting married. The only domestic ambition she had was to own a house; she didn't want children. She was also very sensitive about the notion of being feminine. She was outraged when a man she was dating said he didn't want to see a woman not be feminine. "I thought, 'That's bullshit. As long as I can do the job, why should I care about whether I'm feminine or not?'"

Somewhere along the line, Sara found her own internal power. Maybe it happened the day she confronted a man at work and scared him, not intentionally and not verbally, just by the look on her face.

> I must have looked deadly because I really scared the guy. I never thought I could do that to anyone, but obviously I did scare him. He turned red and backed off. People didn't pull much on me after a while, after I had a little more status.

Seven years before her deadline at the age of forty, Sara married a man who has grown children and wants a different kind of marriage than he had the first time around. That suits her very well; she wants a partnership marriage and they have a lot in common. They like to do things together. At the same time, she is changing careers from finance to psychology because she wants to give expression to the generative parts of her personality, and she never intended to stay in the money business forever.

> I personally don't think it's graceful for a woman to be doing this kind of work when she's heavy into middle age. It even looks funny for men if they're a certain age. It's more a young person's business. You go in whether you are sick or not. You hassle them to get two weeks vacation in a row. It's so totally profit-oriented. I wanted to be more of an Erik Erikson or something, at that age [midlife], doing more to give to other people, as opposed to this accruing kind of work.

Sara's description of what it means to be feminine follows the course of change, revealing a shift in values along with a stronger sense of herself. Her testimony started out, as usual in this group of women, with "feminine" and "woman" representing opposite sets of traits. But the words shift in mid-passage:

> Feminine has connotations of weakness. Yet I honestly believe that women are emotionally stronger and will survive better than men do. I think I'm a woman enough, but I'm not sure about being feminine enough. My friends have always said they thought I was feminine and men I went out with said that too, but I don't see myself that way. Maybe, I'm fighting it because I know I always react negatively when someone says, "Well, women need to be feminine."

Then the shift began.

I would rather be feminine than unfeminine. However, I think I don't want to be the old-fashioned, stereotypical feminine, which involves too much flightiness and dependence and those kinds of negative things. "Oh, if you leave, I'll just die." That kind of thing. Feminine should involve stronger kinds of personality traits, stronger, as in more positive, as in being able to relate to people, being able to console and comfort. Actually, I think I see that as a big part of feminine, the more supportive, but supportive in a positive sense—helping people.

Sara is reclaiming the nurturant parts of herself. She thinks women make fine bosses. She's seen them exercise power and retain their femininity, so it isn't a weakness anymore, like a disease that keeps you in bed three days a week. Sara's new definition of what it means to be feminine is based on what she is herself—sweet and tough—and it reflects her recent decision to find meaning in helping other people. Sara has become a humanist.

Sharon

Sharon has been a striver since college. She graduated the outstanding woman in her class and hasn't stopped since. At the age of thirty-seven now, in glowing good health and married for the second time, she stands close to the top of her profession, in senior management of a major corporation. One more step up the ladder would put her among the elite who populate boards of directors. And she's beginning to question it all. As I walked in the door of her San Francisco office and sat down, she said: "I'm in an existential crisis. . . . How much more do I need in terms of achievement and recognition and so forth? It gets a little absurd."

Sharon is not depressed about this situation. She has many options; the difficulty is choosing among them. Money is not a factor. She and her husband have more than they need for even the best standard of living. Nor does she have any doubt that if she wants it, she can have the next promotion. The problem is this: All her life, she has striven for recognition, to be somebody, to have power and status in the public realm. Now that ambition is being challenged by a new need, the need to find a stronger sense of personal identity and self-expression. She faces a crisis of meaning and purpose in life. Until now her sense of self has been drawn so strongly from the professional role that she wonders who she is beneath the mask.

Corporate life, for all it can deliver in terms of money and recognition, has major drawbacks in the human realm, which are compounded for women. The role playing is extremely rigorous; everything must be processed through a well-developed political sense. Said Sharon:

> It takes me a couple of hours sometimes to relax [after work] and be more like myself. I have to watch what I say, have to watch the way I dress, I am constantly on guard. My lunches are either with bankers, investment bankers, or in the executive dining room, so again, I have to be up on sports, able to kid around, able to be the buddy-buddy, without being too strong, so no one is offended. My lunches are always—tension is too big a word—but I'm always on guard. I have dinners too and receptions. I'm in a corporate mode most of the time. [She paused] Which I've enjoyed. Which I've enjoyed, but then all of a sudden, I hit this situation. . . .

Sharon is angry now because the political climate in the office has become dramatically worse lately. A new manager has fired a number of people arbitrarily, just because he didn't like them. They were very good people, in Sharon's estimation, some of them her friends. There is no appeal from this autocratic behavior, and the close encounter with it brings home the facts of corporate life: "You are at the whims of the organization."

Moreover, being female in a male-dominated organization is like trying to eat with your hand tied to your waist. In Sharon's experience,

> You have to be strong and assertive without offending people. So you push a little and then back off, push a little and back off. You're always testing the waters to see how far you can go, trying not to get angry, trying not to be confrontative, trying to think of other ways to say, "You're not right," without attacking the person. It's getting more and more difficult the higher I go. . . . If you just look at it as a game, then you can survive all this. When it starts becoming so much of you, then you're into neurotic.

Sharon decided four years ago that she would not have children. That was a firm decision. She thinks she is too perfectionistic and compulsive to handle a child. In her opinion, women who are able to cope with both career and children must be very laid back, the kind who can entertain coming in with the groceries while people arrive on the doorstep. "I'm very much a financial person. Everything has to be in place, and I thought, 'Oh, what a terrible environment for a child!' "

She thinks she learned some of these traits from her mother, who was very high-powered and not very high in warmth. Often opinionated and inflexible, her mother could be downright intimidating at times. You could never challenge her on a subject. She was always right and she made the rules. Sharon's father, by contrast, was a soft, warm, and friendly person, a pacifist by nature, with an outstanding intellect. Occasionally, when her mother was being too strong, he would look at her in a certain way and Sharon knew that things would change. But that didn't happen very often. Usually her mother took all the power, and Sharon clashed with her many times over authority.

This experience with her mother has been a central factor in Sharon's driving ambition. One of the things that scares this very bright and insightful woman is that as she gets older, she sees more and more of her mother in herself.

> That's one frightening part of staying in the corporate world. I don't want that setting in. It's not worth it to me to be at the state she's in now. She had practically a perfect life until forty-five and it's just gone downhill. She's completely alone, very critical of people and not many friends. So, I say, "Oh, what's the use? Get off this treadmill."

Her new husband, a very nurturing man, is teaching Sharon to get in touch with her feelings and to let down a little. She had been a nontouching person with her first husband: "Just to say 'I love you' to someone. God! I'd rather stand up in front of a board of directors than have to say that. I used to say it and choke. So there was some barrier I put up."

Now that the nurturant part of herself is being given expression, Sharon feels exhilarated—and a little rusty. Her husband has to take the lead in this area. He moves in, when Sharon gets angry or depressed, to make her whole again. She can't do that for him, not yet. But she is seeking to change, using the techniques of gestalt therapy, imagery, and meditation to achieve more awareness and find her center. Ultimately, she will decide on a new course in life. Other financial women, at this point, have the opportunity of giving birth and rearing a child. That

125

option is permanently closed for Sharon, but there are choices she can make. She can change careers, become self-employed, change companies, take a year's vacation, or stay where she is with a different sense of herself. "When I think about it, having all these options is exciting. I just want to make a good choice."

Sharon's concept of being feminine, by the way, has no connotations of weakness. It never has had.

> I've always resisted the idea that women are supersensitive, soft and emotional. I don't see these as feminine traits.
>
> Feminine means an air of confidence without being loud, a warmth, but ambitious, a person who takes some time with appearance, without being too obvious. She probably sets her own standards.

Her description reflects the caution of a powerful woman in a power structure dominated by men. A woman's authority is very carefully displayed.

After fifteen years or so of devotion to the quest for money and other rewards, professional men and women who have slighted their private lives need to find new reasons for being alive. Learning to make intimate connections is the way they can do so. The women described in the next chapters deal with this point by having children for the first time. The women described here have refused that option, but the need to do something is still there. For them, the route to revitalization is to retrace a path into the feminine self, wherein lie the things that bring intimacy—love, trust, vulnerability, spontaneity, and wonder. It doesn't have to be done by having children at the age of thirty-seven and finding out that the mother-child bond is marvelous. It can be done—as these women recommend—through self-exploration and finding new directions. Having children is the easy way.

In Section III, we hear from the working mothers—who they are, what they come from, and how they cope. They are women from traditions of maternal power. Their ability to make transitions swiftly enough to get in under the wire of the reproductive countdown was helped along by a strong feminine ego. By and large, they did not have to cope with the issue of feminine subordination in their own personal histories.

126

III
Women Who Have Children

8
The Daughters of Matriarchy

Of all the issues raised by sexual equality, the most important is whether women can take major responsibility in the public sphere and still rear children. Both roles are demanding; both require large stores of attention and energy; both give deep-seated ego satisfaction. And they are, in many ways, completely at odds.

The professional role was shaped in the image of ambitious, middle-class men who were able to support their wives at home and focus their attention completely on professional achievement. Not all professional men followed this pattern, but most did, and the standards of the professional workplace reflect a competitive emphasis on work at the expense of personal life. The mother's role, by contrast, was shaped in the image of women who had no other important work to do but rear children. The amount of female time, energy, and ego involvement that have gone into the production of American middle-class children has been excessive compared to the standards of other cultures and other times. Women cannot meet these standards of child care and become professionals at the same time.

So, the conflict is set up by cultural tradition to be absolute. Mothers can work—that's all right—so long as the job remains a secondary occupation, which doesn't compete in time or energy with child care. But if mothers aim for professional careers, they challenge patterns of feminine behavior that have been maintained for generations. The more demanding and competitive the career, the tighter the tension between home and work. Women who think they must do everything right, meeting the standards set out by career experts on the one hand and by child care experts on the other, will almost surely be caught up in a dilemma that will deprive them of one of the two major satisfactions in life—work or children.

In 1984, two decades after Betty Freidan's prophetic vision reawoke the women's movement, many people of both sexes still believe women cannot be good mothers and good career people at the same time. Their opinions reflect a world in which the sex roles are still firmly dichotomized into jobs that make all-or-nothing demands. Anyone who tries to cross over these boundaries runs up against careerism on one hand and the mother cult on the other. "I'm struck by the number of women who still find the problem insoluble," commented Tufts University psychiatrist and former president of the American Psychiatric Association, Dr. Carol Nadelson, who has been counseling female students and other women on these conflicts over the past two decades. In this study, as well, several women said they think it's too difficult to be a working woman and a mother at the same time: "I'd have to stay home for five years"; or, as another woman put it, "The lifestyles are complete opposites." Interestingly, most of these opinions came from women who do not want to be mothers; the women who already were mothers never made statements like that. In fact, some complained that society discourages women from having it all by creating the image of Superwoman, as though an ordinary woman could never combine the two roles.

Who, then, are the working mothers in finance? And how are they coping? Have they been overwhelmed? Are they Superwomen, as the popular image suggests? Or are they ordinary women with uncommon knowledge?

The first thing to note about them is that mothers constitute a minority among financial women in both cities. A child care questionnaire sent out to the three hundred members of the Financial Women's Association (FWA) of New York in 1979 brought back forty-five replies from women with small children. The FWA has no figures on the total number of mothers in the organization; nevertheless, a 15 percent return on an issue that generated keen interest among these women is small indeed. The majority had no children, and that remains true in 1984. In San Francisco, working mothers were even harder to find. Sev-

130

eral financial women I interviewed didn't know of even one. Maria, who tells her story in this chapter, searched her memory for women like herself who are married, with small children, and still working. She came up with the names of four, out of a total of 150 women she knows in two financial organizations. Maria thinks that most of her peers have decided not to have children at all. "It's a demanding business," she said.

The second point to note about these women is that they were not overly torn, stressed, or on the verge of a breakdown from too much work. On the contrary, they seemed especially free of debilitating internal conflict, in spite of very full schedules. Usually, they didn't have time for themselves. Their hours were filled from morning to night, but no one talked of being swamped. They talked about careful management of time and about being more efficient at work.

One exception among the fifteen mothers was a young woman with two small children, no full-time help, and a high-pressure job as head trader of a bank. Close to being overwhelmed, she said that if her work had been this demanding when she decided to have children, she would have put it off. "I just would have said, 'Later, later, later,' and it would have been too late." But the other fourteen did not appear to be unduly burdened. For one thing, they had learned to control the excessive demands of the professional role. As for motherhood, they were stepping out on a frontier, violating the dictums of the child care experts by going back to work when their babies were one to two months old.

Nearly all of these women expressed positive attitudes about femininity, about their lives in general, and the mothering experience. Bright spirits, in spite of the fact that they followed highly structured routines, these women did not tell grim stories of anger and resentment. No one spoke of marital conflict in terms of having to satisfy a husband while developing their own careers, and the word "guilt" came up rarely in terms of having enough time to spend with children. In short, this was a select group of women. One can assume that mothers who wanted to stay home with new children, or who felt overwhelmed by the two roles, had dropped out of the work force and would not appear in this sample. By the same token, women married to traditionally minded men who think mothers should stay home would not turn up here.

The distillate left is a group of women with some special knack for mastering their jobs early enough to reproduce and for choosing husbands who were willing to share the child rearing. To a man, these husbands helped with the children; a few had less high-powered jobs than their wives and one was temporarily unemployed. The women ranged in age from twenty-nine to fifty-seven, with children from one to twenty-two years old. Two of the women were pregnant with a second child at the time of the interview.

As the family background and cultural data of the different groups were compared, a profile of these mothers gradually emerged. In sharp contrast with the women in the previous chapter, who were not interested in being mothers, each of these women was reared by a woman with power. Three of them had parents who were equally powerful, but twelve of the fifteen described a matriarchal pattern, in which their mothers held the balance of power and authority in the family. It was a reverse image of the patriarchal pattern of the last chapter, with one important difference. In their daughters' eyes, the fathers in these families were not subordinated as were the mothers in the patriarchal families.

People often wonder whether matriarchal authority will take the same form as patriarchal authority if women are given access to power. The answer has to be that it depends. In this case, they were not the same. The patriarchal personality described by daughters in the last chapter was consistently cold, authoritarian, and sometimes harsh. Wives deferred to male authority; husbands showed little warmth or sensitivity. Mothers were experienced as warm and powerless; fathers as having excessive control. These men ruled, in other words, by virtue of their position and gender rather than through emotional bonding. Seven of the eight fathers from patriarchal families in the last chapter came across to their daughters as powerful, but with low warmth. By comparison, nearly all the mothers in these patriarchal families had high warmth, as well as high power. Authoritarianism was rare. So, the kind of power wielded by the matriarch and the patriarch were different—in this case. But not always. These results hold only for the two groups at opposite ends of the spectrum: women who are mothers, and women who aren't interested. Women in the middle who might have children because they expressed an interest in so doing showed different patterns, especially for patriarchal families. There were four women from backgrounds of predominately male authority in this group. Three of them had fathers of both high power and high warmth.

In addition to high-powered mothers, the feminine tradition of power for these fifteen mothers often included grandmothers as well. Several spontaneously mentioned a strong or independent grandmother who played a role in their lives. Finally, these women had, more often than not, escaped restrictive feminine conditioning. A minority of the mothers (six out of fifteen) said that they were affected by traditional feminine training, compared to the great majority of women without children (twenty-two out of twenty-nine). Often they had learned that they could do whatever they wanted in life. And since they did not observe it in their immediate families, female subordination to male authority was not part of their childhood gestalt. All of these elements add up to create an image of women who learned power and authority in a feminine form from the time they were children. As a result, they were spared some of the internal conflicts that work to keep many women from integrating the historically divided sex roles. Femininity—the sense of comfort and satisfaction with feminine roles—was not at war with professionalism.

This greater internal integration reflected itself in the connotations these women gave for the concept of "being feminine." Most had positive connotations. A sampling of the responses of six mothers shows the integration of "feminine" with "woman":

It means being comfortable with myself as a woman. It's a level of security with yourself, being comfortable that your body is different. Sensitive.

Feminine means strong more than weak. It means being a woman. More positive than negative.

Guess it means being comfortable with the fact that I am a woman. Working and femininity are not contradictions. I know people who are very feminine and very take charge kind of people. What's the difference between men and women? Well, the difference is obvious. I am not an androgynous person.

A person who is feminine is a little more kind, charming, and accommodating. Femininity is anything a woman is now. It's terribly feminine to be professional, successful, aggressive, and hardworking.

It shows quality in a person. Goes with taste. I like to think of myself as being feminine and I admire it in other women. I don't connect it with being a housewife versus professional.

133

Feminine means being a sensitive and sensual individual, being able to feel, to have emotions, to relate to people, particularly those who are closest to you, to be able to let your guard down and love.

I asked the last woman if she had ever heard of the identification of feminine with "silly" and "stupid." She said, "Yes. The dumb blonde. But I don't identify with it. I've witnessed it, but personally, I've never experienced it." Usually, these mothers were not ignorant of feminine stereotypes, but they had not identified with the characteristics of the stereotype. One young woman, however, gave a surprising response. Asked if she had ever heard that females were supposed to be warm, soft, and non-contradictory to men, she said, "Oh, never! I'm sure I was never told that by anybody. Even when you say it now, it sounds so foreign!"

Comparing her comments with those of other women only a few buildings away, who were suffering from a sense of deep disgust at the image of a weak and dominated female, one can only conclude that American life contains a vast range of cultural experiences. What some women take for granted, others have never even heard of.

Who were these mothers of mothers and what kind of power did they wield? Seven women with children recalled their own maternal figures:

She had the authority; she raised the children.

"I'm your mother; therefore, I'm right."

Very energetic woman. Very smart and high-powered.

The backbone of the family; always pushing me.

An easygoing lady. Very laid back and warm.

Intense organizer; she did everything.

High-powered, warm, and domineering.

Usually, these women did not use the words "supportive" or "nurturing," nor did they talk about the "classic homemaker" when they spoke about their mothers. Instead, they mentioned discipline, emotional involvement, vividness, and high energy levels.

Some, but not most, of the older generation were professionals:

She had high power and warmth. She was always available, but she had other things to do. She was a professional woman. She gave positive reinforcement for achievement. I felt close to her.

Most were homemakers with personal authority:

She was a very energetic woman, very smart and high-powered. She would have been a successful professional thirty years later, but in her era, she was child-oriented. She was the opposite of my father, who had unpredictable business dealings. She would have sat down, figured it all out, and made [the business] work. My mother was very adventuresome and felt that people should get out in the world and find out what's going on. She said, "Ah, go do something." I have the feeling that was the genesis of things for me.

Some were better educated than their husbands:

She has more education than my father. She was the dominant figure in the family, the one you could go talk to. She was the one who managed the money. She was ambitious. She knew and could foresee things—a good person. I think she was ahead of her times. But she's so outspoken, sometimes people are offended by what she has to say. She's really the pillar behind the family, now more than ever. She's always wanted to write, but she never got that opportunity.

Usually, these women handled the discipline in the family:

She was an intense organizer. She did everything. She can't sit still. Discipline was done by her. She's very emotional and warm. I used to be more like her. Now we're close friends.

Occasionally, the discipline was dictatorial:

My mother was a very impressive person. She had a tremendous amount of influence over decisions that were made in general, specifically about what I was doing. "Where are you going? What are you doing? Who are you going out with? I approve. I don't approve." She got right in there. "I'm your mother; therefore, I'm right." I can tell you I heard that more than once in my life. There was not much room for disagreement. Discipline was not an uncommon event in my house, and Mother handled more of it. I can remember getting whacked with a belt more than once by my mother. Child abuse—I grew up with it.

The fathers of these women usually pulled marks for low power. In spite of that, most of the daughters felt good about them. Having a low-powered father was not a negative thing for them. They liked and respected their fathers (with some exceptions), and their experience with maternal power did not mean they saw their fathers as dominated. Only two of the fifteen women felt that their mothers had dominated their fathers ("She wore the pants," "She was bossy to him"), and they didn't like it. But that was not the common experience. As a rule, these men were easygoing and laid back or more quiet. A few were distanced. Often, low paternal power resulted from a choice the fathers made to let their wives have their way. These descriptions of their fathers were given (in order) by the five women quoted above on their mothers:

A few fathers seemed ineffective to their daughters:

> I always felt he was less in touch. My father definitely had less on the ball at dealing with problems. You could never disturb him on a Saturday morning or a Sunday, or if he was in a bad mood. He had a kind of impotent anger. It was just unpleasant at the time, something to avoid. He would yell and scream, then it would be done, and I knew it was just noise.

But more often, they gained influence through warmth:

> When I was a child, my father was a strong figure and very powerful in the family. I give him low power now, because as an adult, I realize he was not the powerful figure he seemed. He was enormously successful and enormously unsuccessful my whole life. In retrospect, I look back and realize his business dealings were unpredictable. I have more communication with my mother, but I feel very sympatico with my father.

Some were easygoing men from the working class:

> He was a brushmaker, in industrial brushes. He is a very easygoing figure, scared to hurt anyone. He never raised his voice. He has a tremendous sense of humor, very warm and loving. I don't think my father finished high school.

Several conceded domestic authority to their wives:

He was a very easygoing person; he let her have her way and she idolized him. He was a physician with a private practice and he had evening hours, so he was gone a lot. But even if he had been around more, I don't think he would have been any different. Even once in a while, if we ran into problems—when Dad laid down the law, he scared you. And then you knew, you didn't cross the line. I always admired my father, because he could control his emotions. I admired what he did. I was proud of him.

The few who exercised authority used it positively:

He had high, high power. I was very attached to him. He was really a terrific person and very close to his family. Home at six every night, involved with us, individually and collectively. His expression of love was overt. He was comfortable with hugging. Very open. Communicative. But we grew up in an authoritarian household. "I'm your father and you do what I tell you." Otherwise, wham, bam. Both of them. High power. Not always as well wielded as I would like.

Mary, the woman who spoke those last words, has a three-year-old son and holds down a responsible job with an investment bank in New York. She is highly placed enough to set her own policy; nevertheless, she still works about ten hours a day, gets home to spend an hour with her son before his bedtime, and only then, late at night, has time to be alone with her husband. Time for herself is taken walking from her house to the subway in the morning.

Popular writers have described this kind of scheduling as requiring superhuman strength, but Mary denies that.

People act as if you are Superwoman to be able to do all this. That, I think, is a form of discouragement [to other women who might want children]. A lot of people see me in that category and I keep wanting to say, "Now, listen, I'm really a perfectly normal human being. I know there is nothing extraordinary about me. I have faced a particular set of circumstances that I have dealt with over the course of my life, but I haven't done anything brilliant. In the end, if you want to do it, you do it. You fit it in."

Mary is unusual in the risks she has taken. She once tried to start her own business, working seven days a week. She broke her own sexual taboo against dating anyone in the office and, in the process, found a new husband. And she ended a nine-year marriage on the fifth month of her first pregnancy, told no one about it, and came back to work a single mother. Asked how she could have so much control over her emotions, she said:

> Because I strongly believe it would have affected people's image of me. It just cripples their brains. They say to me, "How could you have coped with that?" Also, it put up a wall around some of those feelings so that I could get through the day.

The oldest of six children, Mary doesn't remember much about growing up with feminine training. She came into this world as a bright light in her grandmother's eye.

> I understood that I was a girl and that was wonderful. My grandmother had three sons. I was the first grandchild, and I was a girl. To this day, we are very close. She is eighty-six now and in a nursing home, but she still tells me I am her girl. I am terrific. I am wonderful.

In the sixth grade, Mary was hit by the realization that being female could restrict her options. A softball coach wouldn't let her play on the team because she wasn't good enough. "It was the first time I recognized that along the way I had been deprived of a few things that my brothers were good at." Mary sat on the sidelines and complained until she finally was put on the team as catcher, where she got hit in the face with a baseball bat. "I still hate that man," Mary recalled. The policy of winning at all costs was contrary to the teachings of her father, who thought the personal development of the children was more important, and Mary still hasn't forgiven the coach for his inhumane values.

In order to be promoted at work, Mary had to learn not to be more aggressive but to be more charming. She had been in the habit of expressing her honest feelings about people in business ("He's dumb!"), and the word got back to her that many people hated her. With characteristic adaptability, Mary took a course to develop professional charm and learned to be as dissembling as the next person. It made her more effective and more promotable, a factor which becomes important in the lives of professional women who want to be mothers. The sooner they gain control of their careers, the more likely they are to get in under the wire of the biological clock that ticks away the reproductive years.

Now, at the age of thirty-three, Mary is in control of a team setting bank policy and developing new markets. It is highly challenging and she's out in front. It's like having her own bank. Yet she says her son is her greatest achievement.

> I see motherhood as having a whole much, much larger dimension than I ever thought. I knew I would have a family. I didn't know, and there was no way anyone could tell me, of this incredible thing. Just no way. It has made me believe, Don't write anything off, because there is more there than you realize. As I've become more comfortable and confident, I have been able to cultivate and let those sides expand. Like listening to music. I think it's maturity, a sense of myself.

Asked if she has any conflicts between herself as a woman and as a professional, she said no. "The only time I start having problems is when being a woman keeps me out of things. That makes me very angry. The conflict is certainly not within me, it's a conflict the world has."

Throughout her life, Mary has set her own course, demanded her rights, taken risks, violated norms when she had to, and learned to adapt when there was no other way to get where she wanted. That is the kind of woman who, in this sample, has children. To do so, they must violate one of the most widely held and cherished standards of the American middle class—that a woman should spend the first few years in full-time care of her own child.

Mary spent four weeks at home, then went back to work, leaving her baby son in the care of a full-time housekeeper. She turns into a full-time mother on weekends, but from Monday morning to Friday afternoon there is not much family time. "I do my best. I get down on the floor, but it's hard. Sometimes I'm tired and not enthusiastic."

The mothers in this sample know they are setting a course for which there is little precedent. They don't know how things will turn out.

> Surely, there are times I'm not sure Jerry will get all the attention he needs. Then again, Gloria [the housekeeper] is probably a better mother in these days and times than I am. She is a much better mother all day long. It's "our child." She's good. She takes him to the park and sits there

for five hours. I can't sit in the park for five hours. So, it's a difficult question.

Although all of these women shared a tradition of maternal power, they differed in other ways. Some had grown children, some had infants. Some were relatively young when they gave birth; others were hitting the upper range of the reproductive cycle. These factors made a difference in how they handled the tension between home and work. The older women, being usually better established in their careers, could make work conform somewhat to their needs. The younger women were more likely to take a hiatus in career achievement—although continuing to work in the same job—until their children were older. Older women with older children often had offspring before they became full-time professionals, so child care and professional development came at different times in their lives. The mothers separated easily into three categories: women over thirty with young children; women under thirty with young children; and women over thirty with children over thirteen.

Seven of the fifteen mothers had children when they were in their thirties, after a decade or so of career development. As a result, these mothers, in New York particularly, had reached a level where they felt they could set their own standards without being trampled upon. These women had learned to say no to work when it threatened to interfere too much with their private lives. They could mentally switch gears at the end of the day and leave their work at the office. They also knew by experience that they could negotiate with employers over travel schedules, extra work, and all the other intrusive demands of a career environment shaped by a male lifestyle with no parental responsibilities. Women without children were more likely to allow work to dominate their lives than were the working mothers, often because they just did not realize they had some latitude to say no. (Employers may also be more willing to shift schedules around for women who have children than they would be for single women.) Whatever the case, the mothers in their thirties with small children had a command over their workplace that was impressive.

Myra walked into the interview laughing and joking, supremely sure of herself. Married for sixteen years to the same man, Myra waited ten years to get pregnant, so she could build a career first and gain some control over her working life. With a clarity of vision and intent that was uncommon fifteen years ago, she looked around, saw the pitfalls for women, and set her path accordingly:

I had two eyes. I could see that opportunities were denied women with children and I realized I had to get to a certain point in a career where I could say, "This is what I want to do," rather than have somebody tell me. . . . I got married very young, when I was twenty-one, so I had lots of time. I waited and figured out what I wanted to do. Things have worked out pretty much as I planned.

Now in her late thirties with a six-year-old child, she is a director of financial analysis for a major corporation in New York and she wears authority naturally.

There are many things you think you have to do to be successful in this business that you don't really have to do. You don't have to go on a trip when they say you do. Things can be rescheduled. Sometimes, you have to work long hours. But most of the time you don't. You can take work home. These rules change.

Myra says no to her boss frequently. Usually she reschedules professional demands to accommodate her life as a parent, but sometimes she will say no, period, and he accepts that answer.

I know a lot of people who believe, men and women both, that if you give that answer, you'll get fired, be demoted, not get your raise. But it doesn't matter. I have to tell you, *it doesn't matter*. . . . I've made the decision that certain things in my family life come first. I've also made it clear that I won't travel when my husband travels. If I didn't have the ability to say no at work, I'd be a lot less happy.

At the same time, Myra is warm and friendly. Occasionally she will hug an officer of the company whom she likes, which is not the rule for professional behavior in her business. One time, a senior officer whose work she reviewed kissed her on the cheek before a meeting with the chairman, who joked, "Do you always kiss your lead reviewer?" Such easy male-female relations in the office are not common among this group of professional people. Men return Myra's warmth without sexual overtones. She has never been sexually harassed. How did she arrive at such a firm sense of her own power?

Myra attributes it to an independent upbringing in a world of women. The daughter of a single mother, who was divorced early and worked all her life, the granddaughter of a woman who ran a millinery store and a farm, Myra sees herself as the third generation of independent working women. In high school, she wanted to be a doctor, and although her ambition changed, she never had the thought: "Only until I get married." She expected to work all her life. Reared in New York, she attended an elite all-women's college on the East Coast, where authority and aggression were matters of personality, not gender. She thinks that as a result, she was spared the stereotyping of masculine and feminine behavior along lines of power and aggression. She was also spared the consequences of too-close parental control. Asked if her mother had high power or low power, Myra gave a response that was unique among these women. "The children had the most authority," she said.

> My mother was a very easygoing lady, very laid back, not at all punitive or controlling. When I hear about my friends' mothers, I wonder where these ladies come from! They are controlling even now. My mother was very warm. I took her as a model and I like her very much. I use the same terms of endearment. I love and pat just the way my mother did, exactly the same. I don't think I dominated her; I always felt we were equals.

Myra's six-year-old daughter expects the same equality. Self-sufficient and independent, she says things like: "This is reasonable, this is only fair," and her parents concede. "I'm a believer in equality. That's where she got it. My brother said he would love to have equality with his children, but he hasn't quite achieved it yet. I feel lucky. No question about it."

Myra laughed frequently while answering every question with a quick, sure response. She had no conflicts of the sort I had been picking up from other women, no feminine conditioning (that she remembered), no confusions over professional and feminine identity. She was her own woman, not a Superwoman, just a clear woman. I played with the fantasy that women of the future would have that kind of clarity. The second and third generations of professional women will not even remember there once was a role conflict that set women against themselves.

Myra's daughter is being reared during the day by a housekeeper. She and her husband took a month off after the birth and then went back to work. Asked if she were aware of the advice by experts that a mother should spend more time with her child during the infant years, she said:

> Yes—but they're wrong. I was raised by a mother who worked and I turned out OK. My daughter is being raised by a mother who works and she's OK. It doesn't make sense to me. I know nasty people who were raised by women who stayed home and nasty people raised by women who worked.
>
> I read the books [on child rearing] and I came to the conclusion that it didn't matter. Nobody had good evidence. If they had shown me a sample of one thousand kids, with a control group, showing really significant differences in the contentment of the child, the way they viewed themselves, their IQ, the way they dealt with the world, I would have thought twice. But they didn't. . . . It's clear to me now that my daughter comes to me more than anybody as an authority and comfort.

Like her daughter, Myra doesn't let anyone tell her what to do. She looks around and makes her own decisions. Without that ability, she might have been discouraged from trying to mix a career and motherhood.

> The world around you tells you how difficult it is. It's not difficult per se, but very time-consuming. There are two points of view in the women's movement. You can have it all or you can't have it all. I believe you can have most of it.

But, as Myra would say, you must learn to say no to the powers that be.

> People have power over me who can persuade me that their point of view is correct. They have power over me in a corporation, a hierarchical thing, but they don't have ultimate power over me, only over a segment of my life. The worst they can do is fire me.

Not all of these fifteen women remembered their mothers with the kind of easy, unconflicted love that Myra had. A few thought their mothers had been manipulative, or controlling or undercutting or not warm (three of the women gave their mothers marks for low warmth), so

143

there was a negative as well as a positive side to the maternal power. One of the women in San Francisco remembered her mother trying to force her into a feminine mold that she hated. In rebellion always, she played with guns instead of dolls from the age of five. Her mother turned her over to her father finally because she could not handle the girl. Another woman, in New York, went to work initially to develop a realm of her own where her mother—vivid, appealing, smart, high-powered, and neurotic—would have no impact. All the women in her family were independent and forceful compared to the men, and although this woman longed to escape from her mother, the image of maternal power stayed with her. "I grew up with the idea that power was natural to women."

9
The
Maternal
Force

F our of the mothers in this study had children who were either already grown up or in their teenage years. Because these women, aged thirty-eight to fifty-seven, gave birth many years ago, they reflect the distance women have traveled in the past two decades, from feminine roles or low-level occupations to professional rank. There were few similarities among the lives of these women, except for the curious fact that they were the only mothers in the sample who were not currently married. All of them were single, including three divorced women and one widow.

They show the battle scars of an intense struggle for upward mobility, and their stories tell of the epic changes women have come through in only a few years. Unlike Myra in the last chapter, these women were not following a well-laid plan of career development and motherhood. They could not foresee what lay ahead. Blinded by fast-moving historic events, they were forced to act and then cope with the consequences.

Margaret is a passionate woman from a Southern dirt farm family. Ambitious, aggressive at times, as beautiful as a Scarlett O'Hara at the age of thirty-eight, she is the mother of two nearly grown children. I interviewed her while she was having her nails manicured in a private salon in San Francisco. Wealthy now, she was destitute as a young mother eighteen years ago. Under the same circumstances, other women might have chosen the safe course and stayed home. Not Margaret.

Her first son was born when she was seventeen and ignorant of any other purpose in life for women but to marry and have babies. Her daughter came a few years later. Three years into the marriage, working to support the family, she decided she didn't need her husband. She didn't need to come home from work and have her husband yell at her to get the kids out of his hair, while he read the newspaper and she cooked dinner. She might as well be doing it herself, without some man exercising his authority, telling her what she could and could not do. So she left him, when she was only twenty, living in San Francisco where the family had moved for his college education. Only twenty, with two small children and no skills. "I was starving. I couldn't even feed my kids. I would run out of money before the next paycheck came. That's how poor I was. And he never came around."

Margaret worked and took care of her kids. That was all. Nobody wanted to date her, even if she had had the time, which she didn't. Waitressing on weekends, coming home to children she was beginning to hate, afraid she was ruining their lives, Margaret felt headed for a crack-up. Then her husband started coming around to torment her. He accused her of ruining his life. He would take the family for a ride and threaten to drive off the cliff or kidnap the kids. He wrote her letters full of diatribe and hatred. She began having nightmares that the children were being stolen through the bedroom window. She told herself: "If I can ever get through this, I can do anything."

One day at work, another waitress told Margaret she was going to Europe for $100 on a special charter and asked Margaret to come with her. "I couldn't even imagine going to Los Angeles, much less Europe." But all of a sudden, there it was—the great escape. Margaret picked up her kids, took them to her husband, who was by now remarried, and told him, "Here, you're going to have them. I have no life. I have no time. There isn't enough money. I can't do it." And then she disappeared, leaving behind her unpaid bills.

> It was the most remote, ridiculous thing that a person in my position could ever come up with. I went to stay a month and I stayed nine months. I hit London and it was a foreign language to me. I had no idea what to do. Bumping from one experience to another—it changed my whole life. I stayed in Majorca for five months and thought of every way I could possibly imagine to get away from my kids, to abandon them and never come back. Every possible creative thing, I mulled over—sending a letter

that "Your mother has been killed." Everything I could imagine. And then one day, I just said to myself, "They're my kids." And I knew there was nobody in the world to take care of those kids but me, and there was nothing in the world for me to do but to come back and take them. Because I wanted to do that.

Margaret came back a changed woman. Her goal in life—to raise her children—was no longer a question. It was only a matter of how. She made her plans with hard-headed logic, and the very first step was obvious: She had to get a man. Before, when Margaret had dated men, she played the coy "I'm not trying to nail you" game. When she came back, she was thoroughly honest:

I had blinders on about anything else. I knew what I had to do. So I recruited a man. Instantly. Before six months was up, I was living with him. I said, "Listen, do you want to live with me or don't you?" I cut the bullshit and I never stopped cutting through the crap from that point on.

Margaret lived with her helpmate, a poor, struggling artist, for several years. He helped her with the children and with her own emotional problems. She gave him aggression and drive. Meanwhile, Margaret became a broker and began an ambitious climb to a peak of financial success from which she has never wavered. Last year she made $100,000. But it took years to get there.

It was a private men's club when I started in the business. They'd say, "Oh, you want to get registered?" and throw the books in your lap and watch you die, laughing about how these women wanted to be in the brokerage business. I was a secretary to thirty brokers [at one point] and they loved me, but when it came time for me—the little boys went to training class and got coddled and lectured and all this stuff, but for me, the New York Stock Exchange rules were thrown in my lap. I didn't go to any lectures because I was too busy typing letters. But that was the beginning of my education and I got it.

Five years and several jobs later, Margaret was registered as a broker. The more professional she became, the more she diverged from her artist-companion, who hated the business world and the stockbroker part of Margaret. The relationship did not last.

He was loving and I had a wonderful time with him. But he was there for a purpose, not to spend my life with. I was there for him for a purpose. Once we took care of those purposes, we did not need to get married. He was not my kind of guy.

Margaret is like her mother in many ways. Both were princesses in their otherwise mundane families; both saw themselves as better than other people. Both had a fantasy of escaping the rural South for some more glorious place. That place was San Francisco. Margaret's mother fled when her daughter was four years old, leaving the child in the care of the grandparents. Separated from her father, Margaret's mother was stigmatized in her home town and forced to choose between moving back in with her parents or leaving. She left. Forbidden to take her daughter with her, she left anyway, and Margaret was reared by her grandmother, right down to the breast-feeding. (She had an uncle a year younger than herself.) Like the two younger women, the grandmother was powerful, but unlike them, she exercised her power through traditional roles.

My grandmother ran everything. In her own little quiet, martyred way, her own poor, little weak "I don't know anything" way, she was like the fucking Rock of Gibraltar. Like, she gets her way and you don't even realize it. Made of iron. She's this "Oh, poor little me," and she has everyone scraping and bowing and doing everything she wants you to do.

I was not suppressed or controlled. I got to do anything I wanted, and I never got into trouble. I could always break the rules and not have anyone know. But everything in my life was centered around making my grandmother happy. I knew that was the most important thing—to make her happy.

Margaret visited her own mother in San Francisco once a year—an awkward event because the older woman didn't seem to know what to do with her, except to criticize her clothes and manners. They were never close, and it took years for Margaret to work out the resentment she felt toward her mother; nevertheless, she sees the older woman as powerful. "I think it took a lot of guts to do what she did, to leave. It took a lot of guts for her to survive on her own."

Now that her own children are almost grown and in college, Margaret has feelings of ecstasy about them. She is avoiding a relationship with a man who loves her because the most important thing in her life is spending the last couple of years with her children at home.

> I used to think people lied to me when they told me that having children was a very rewarding experience. I used to say, when my kids were young, "The sons of bitches; they lied about this. This is pain and suffering. Nothing but work. They take from you all the time. They don't give back anything. Having children is certainly not rewarding." But since they got over their obnoxious puberty years, it's been nothing but rewarding and I am so happy spending the time with them.
>
> I know my job with my kids is the most important thing that I have ever done or probably will ever do. When I think about that job, I don't care how much money I make.

And that statement is from a woman who says in the next breath that she aims to be the best broker on two coasts, and you don't doubt her intentions. But the job, ego-satisfying and financially rewarding as it is, is a game. Her children are a miracle—and that's a totally different realm of thought and feeling. She has this image in her mind of her grandmother, her mother, herself, and her daughter all sitting together, looking alike, being alike, maintaining the thread of continuity through time and past death.

> This image is so glaring. I see first of all the physical part of it, the heritage of having the same shape. Our personalities—stubborn, willful, unbending, having certain attitudes that are hard to get along with, sort of intolerant, being miserable little bitches. My grandmother especially, getting to know her as an adult, I realized I had always thought of her as this saintly person, and then to see her as the manipulative person she always was. And seeing things about my mother that are identical and seeing things about myself that I always denied and seeing the same things in my daughter. . . .
>
> There's nothing I can ever do that will outshine that one. I love my job, but the kids are perpetuating the species. I mean, what's it all about? You just make up the job to keep you occupied through the years. It's a game. But the kids—What are we doing? Where are we going? Where did we come from? That's what the kids are all about.
>
> This is probably my egomaniacal, mistaken sort of projection, but I think that if you have the secret genetic code, the strong pass it on and the weak don't. If you don't have it, it doesn't get passed on. I'm just proud that I could do it.

When Margaret finished with these words, the interview was over. In her egomaniacal eloquence, she had said it all—the primordial maternal value, based on the unique capacity of a woman's body to generate new life. Intellectuals of many persuasions call this the "feminine" principle, meaning the nurturing, life-giving impulse associated with fertility, earth, water, and other natural productive processes. Creating life is the central meaningful act.

But sublime as it may be, this procreative impulse has kept so many women in a culturally subordinate position that it comes to represent a kind of divinely inspired double-cross. The double-cross is that the ultimately meaningful act—the only hedge against death—is capable of crippling a woman's life if she is not prepared to be a parent. And preparing to be a parent for a career woman requires a careful passage through some very difficult social and mental transformations.

Margaret gave birth when she was too young to make a fully conscious choice. That is not the case with most of these mothers, who live with a new set of circumstances for women. In the past, many women reproduced who did not want to. Now women have fully sanctioned opportunities to choose careers and let the children go. Moreover, these women move in a professional milieu that more often than not discourages women from having children. The values they are confronted with every day, the lack of benefits for maternity and paternity leave, the almost total lack of community supports for child care—in this kind of world, those who decide to become mothers are doing more than follow out a blind impulse. They are expressing a value system based on the authority of a powerful internalized feminine model.

Women understand, through experience with their own mothers, whether mothering will be easy or difficult, happy or unhappy, confining or liberating, rewarding or not rewarding, and make their decision accordingly. For a career woman to undertake the months of pregnancy and dependency involved with childbirth, for her to put her body where her head is and assume the intimidating task of creating another human life, she must be motivated by something more than an impulse. She must *want* to be a mother, expecting that it will enrich her life and believing that it is the most significant thing she can do. Otherwise, it is too difficult to raise the children and too easy to delay the decision until the choice is gone.

Many women in this sample wanted to be mothers but hadn't done so yet. Some were unmarried, some were delaying their decision, some were vacillating, and others were in the process of planning the event. Potential mothers were a mixed group, some of whom will surely realize their ambitions for a family and some of whom will probably not. The number of women with unrealized domestic dreams was large. Difficult problems stood in their way—problems with work, and problems with finding the right man to marry. They were up against the clock and they knew it. They could see that time might run out before they figured out a way to correct whatever mistakes they were making. In many ways, these women are like the housewives of the 1950s that Friedan wrote about, but at the opposite end of the spectrum. They did what they thought was right, and now find themselves bound by a web of unseen cultural forces and circumstances which have no name, unable to experience their lives in the full richness that these mothers speak about. They have, so to speak, lost their birthright.

But, regardless of these real-life circumstances, the overwhelming majority of these women who were interested in being mothers were themselves the daughters of women with power and authority in the family. The desire for children was not automatic for these women; it was not an instinctive genetic reaction. Rather, it was culturally patterned and strongly influenced by a tradition of maternal authority.

Maternal power has a bad name in theories of psychoanalysis, for reasons that have now become apparent to women who know the field. Freud's theories of psychosexual development, as well as those of many other male thinkers in the field, were inevitably influenced by a masculine perspective and by a culture that relied on male dominance. They knew, as only men could understand, that maternal power could threaten a son's masculine identity. What they didn't see was that men, disappointed in their fathers, could project their anger onto their mothers, equating female authority with fears of castration. At midcentury so much was written about the domineering mother that to the educated public, all maternal power seemed to take a negative form. To be sure, some mothers were indeed the domineering, critical women their sons described (and psychiatrists wrote about), but many were not.

In the 1950s, a female Harvard psychiatrist and clinician at the Beth Israel Hospital in Boston, Dr. Grete Bibring, decided to take a good look at the matriarchal family that occurred so frequently in the stories of her male patients. The mothers in these families were pictured as domineering, strong, and active, often better educated and more competent than the fathers. They were also the targets of considerable fear and hostility on the part of the sons, who blamed their mothers for their own feelings of sexual inadequacy. Upon close analysis of the verbal reports, Bibring concluded that these matriarchs were not the negative figures their sons perceived. They were basically thoughtful women, but too close to their sons. The father's authority and connectedness had been missing, leaving the sons overly involved with their mothers and unable to shift their identity firmly into a masculine mode. They converted this difficulty into a fear of female power. Such neurotic reactions were a function of a common American problem—there was just too much of mother. Fathers had not assumed enough of a role in raising their sons.

Bibring also had reports on daughters who grew up in these matriarchal families, and they revealed a different picture. Apparently they were not damaged by their mothers, because they were less likely to reject feminine roles than were the daughters of patriarchal families. Unfortunately, Bibring never published her data on the daughters, and she died without putting the material into a usable form. But her evidence suggests that positive forms of maternal power have been swept indiscriminately under the carpet of abuse. The critical point, for these purposes, however, is the difference Bibring perceived between the daughters of matriarchal and patriarchal families. It is one of the few indications we have that American women are more accepting of feminine roles when they grow up in families that cut across the cultural grain, violating norms of male control. The point here is that the patriarchal family as we have known it—involving female subordination—is doomed in an era when women have choices.

I do not wish to defend matriarchy at the expense of male authority. It does not seem desirable to concentrate power and authority in either parent, even if it is true that daughters reproduce more often under one than they do under the other. The ideal situation is to combine . authority and nurturance in both parents equally. That was the point of Philip Slater's work on values and parental identification in the late 1950s. Children identify with and internalize the values of their parents when discipline (authority) and emotional support (warmth) are combined in the same individual.

Slater contradicted such traditionalists as Talcott Parsons, who assumed that the classic patriarchal family was the lynchpin of a healthy personality. The family defended by Parsons was one with strongly divided sex roles, split along lines of male authority (he deals with the world) and female expressiveness (she gives emotional support). When Slater looked at the effects of this kind of family on a group of Harvard students—all men—he found that the sons were rejecting identification with fathers who had been judgmental and lacking in emotional support. They might conform outwardly to paternal rules, but when alone, they followed their own devices. They had not internalized the older man's values.

Slater had no way of knowing whether women would react the same way men did to strongly role-divided patriarchal families, but this evidence suggests that they do. Women absorbed the family values of their mothers when authority was combined with warmth, but not when their mothers acted out a supportive role and conceded power to their husbands. As the sons failed to follow their fathers when they had no warmth, so the daughters turned away from their mothers when they had no authority.

In a more structured, traditional society, it may not matter what the children think of their parents, because they face an entrenched value system everywhere they look—in the community, the extended family, the church and school. But this kind of framework no longer exists for most of the American middle class. Opportunity now carries both sexes away from their backgrounds, and if the values don't go with them, those values and perhaps the people as well will be lost. New women long for an internal guidance system based on parental models they can love and respect. That is, by and large, what these mothers have been lucky enough to get.

In deciding to have children, the timing of the birth had important effects on the way these women handled the tension between home and work. Older mothers in the group typically had a firm grip on their jobs when they chose to switch gears and give birth. None of them expressed worry that children would limit their professional horizons. This greater maturity provided other advantages as well. The woman who made a mistake in choosing her first husband had time to get divorced and remarried before she had children to support. A few of these mothers went through that process—early marriage, divorce, some years of exploration in the single world, marriage again, and then family. Early marriage seemed to facilitate the task of combining careers and motherhood, because women had time to experiment and work out the bugs in their private lives. A good ten to fifteen years of professional development and personal growth with husbands produced the integration that finally allowed these women to have it all.

Four of the mothers, however, had children when they were still in their twenties, two of them making a deliberate decision to break away from prevailing patterns. One of the women, whose mother had been treated during pregnancy with diethylstilbestrol, was afraid she might not be able to give birth when she was older. So she went ahead when most of the other women in her professional circles were delaying the event or deciding not to have children at all. A second young woman, in New York, wanted to get child rearing out of the way early, before she had a lot of responsibility at work. She felt she could more easily shift her priorities home when the demands at work were not very high. Both have accepted a hiatus in career advancement. A third woman had children before she became professional and is close to being overwhelmed by her new status.

10
Obstacles and Tradeoffs

Never was the tradition of maternal power more clear than in the case of one of the young mothers in this study, a woman I call Maria. Thirty years old, blond-haired and blue-eyed, Maria is the daughter of a woman from aristocratic roots in Latin America. Her great-grandmother (who wore a diamond in her tooth) earned the first teaching credential given to a woman in the South American nation of her birth. The next generation of women lost the money, and Maria's own mother was reared poor in a Spanish-speaking enclave in San Francisco during the Depression. She was proud, very proud, strong-willed, distant, and conservative, determined never to be poor again. She controlled the purse strings; she made most of the family decisions, pretending all the while that her husband was in charge, because that's the way it was supposed to be in her Latin culture. Struck by polio when Maria was two years old, the mother had to be hospitalized for a year. Nevertheless, she worked throughout Maria's preschool years, going full time after Maria reached the age of five.

Maria's father could not have been more different. A warm and gentle Irishman who grew up in foster homes, he was the kind of man "who always voted for the underdog." In Maria's mind, he was a "good man, a gentle, gentle man."

> He wasn't a great thinker or anything like that. He was happy working with his hands and he believed in certain morals. Integrity and honesty were the two most important things in his life. He believed in fair play. He would not cross a picket line. We boycotted a local movie house for a year and a half because the janitors were on strike—that kind of thing.

Not a leader, but a supporter, and if you got his support, you could be sure you had it all the way—a very loyal man.

Tears rose to Maria's eyes as she talked about her father, who died ten years ago. The love between them was palpable.

He was a very warm person. I was the apple of his eye. He raised me like a son. We'd have debates over pancakes on Sunday morning and when we'd go out golfing, it would be just him and me. I'd be the caddy. When he'd go surf fishing with me, I'd sit on his shoulders while he'd run out and cast the pole in the surf. I'd get up at five in the morning to go cat fishing with him.

One of the reasons I wanted a daughter was that I had such a great relationship with my Dad and I wanted my husband to have that.

Although Maria always felt much closer emotionally to her father, she sees herself as being like her mother. "I'm afraid I am very much like her. She pretty much knew what she wanted."

As the love bond with her father stood out, so did the powerful example set by her mother. Maria has been called a "pushy broad" on several occasions by unliberated men who felt insecure and did not want to hear her opinions. She has a characteristic way of dealing with these insults. She stares back and says nothing. That happened with a former boss whom she questioned in a meeting. Rather than answer her challenge on its merits, he said, "If there's anything I can't stand, it's a pushy broad." The room went dead quiet as people sucked in their breath and Maria blushed. But she kept her eyes on him and her mouth shut. Eventually the meeting continued on a more serious note and no one ever mentioned the event. But he was embarrassed, and the next time around, Maria spoke up again.

As she told this story, Maria's body stiffened and her eyes took on a steady gaze, as though she were a matador about to pierce a bull between the eyes.

I said, watching her, "You have a lot of gall—that's not the right word—but to go back and do it again."

"In Spanish, we call it *cojones,*" she said. "That means balls. So you can quote that."

Both parents encouraged Maria, who lagged in school achievement when she was young. She spoke only Spanish until she went to kindergarten. But her parents nurtured her confidence, never putting her down or threatening her. A few times her mother tried to slap her ("I was a smartass, so I'm sure it wasn't without provocation"), but she would run away and because of the effects of polio, her mother couldn't catch her. Once the slap hit home and Maria was never within range again. (Another mother in this sample tells of putting a book in her pants when her mother spanked her, so these daughters did not always suffer punishment willingly.)

Although she was reared in a Spanish-speaking culture in which women took care of men and female children were not allowed to participate in sports, Maria escaped the deep imprint of feminine subordination that children learn in the immediate family.

> My mother was never a role model for being submissive. Submissiveness was not evident in my family. Everyone pretty much spoke their minds. I was never told to keep quiet. Also, my father, being raised in foster homes, had no traditional roles. He didn't know what it was like to see a woman cater to a man. He didn't know how to treat me as a daughter. He treated me as an individual.

Nevertheless, Maria experienced conflict for about three years when she entered the securities business at the age of twenty-two, acting like a flighty, bouncy female in short skirts and long hair. Business associates nicknamed her "Blondie," and her bosses kept her in a corner where she made up her mind that if she did nothing else, she was going to be taken seriously. Maria changed jobs, bought a conservative wardrobe, cut down on socializing in favor of work, and joined professional organizations, with the result that in a short period of time she gained new respect and new responsibilities. At the time of the interview she was a senior money manager, responsible for investing $100 million in stocks and bonds. She was also the only mother in the group who enjoyed a major benefit from her company. For as long as she needs it, as a new mother, Maria works twenty hours a week with full pension, vacation, and seniority benefits. When she is ready to return full time, she will resume the supervisory responsibilities she has temporarily given up. This uncommonly generous "prime time" program was offered by her employer, who first told her that her job could not be done on a part-time basis and then changed his mind.

He said, "You know, I was wrong. I was just perpetuating the male dominance in this industry." At first, I tried doing both jobs and decided I was going to burn myself out. I made it known here and my boss reinforced it. He feels I do 80 percent of my previous job in 50 percent of the hours. He is my best supporter.

Childbirth changed Maria's perspective dramatically for the second time in her short professional life. Before the baby, she had been the perfect professional, going to all the meetings, sitting on all the podiums, lunching with economists and other money managers, maintaining the visibility that goes with a public role. She didn't even know there was another side to life.

I was one of those people who was going to take six weeks off and be right back at my desk. I was in the recovery room after [a cesarean delivery] and I couldn't feel a thing from my chest down. I looked at the clock; it was eleven-thirty. I thought, "My God. I've got a luncheon appointment at twelve-fifteen with another money manager." That's where my head was.

It took a good week to get that out of my system. The pain! I couldn't move. I couldn't turn over for two days. I couldn't walk upright for two weeks. Finally, I just closed the door and said, "Forget it." Plus, everything was under control here.

At home with the child, Maria's identity deepened as she got in touch with the life beneath the blue suit.

It wasn't until I started being home with my daughter that I realized there was more to me than just my profession. A lot of people don't realize that. Women judge their value by their net worth, their salary and their professional responsibilities. I did that. I am Maria . . . I'm an investment officer, therefore, respect me. All of a sudden, you realize, hey, your personal life is much more important.

Now, her priorities have been reversed. Maria comes first, then her family, and only then her profession.

At work, Maria became more efficient:

It took me about six months to get it through my head that I had only so much stamina. Now, I'm very selective. People are amazed. I don't chitchat on the phone. I have better organization. I don't look at a piece of paper more than twice. I've definitely gotten quicker with decisions.

But the question of who would care for her child erupted into a series of crises. Many of the older women used housekeepers they had employed for years. Maria didn't have one. Nor was she prepared for the conflict she would experience over going back to work so soon after the birth of her new child. At home with her infant for four months, Maria wrestled with the issue of finding a substitute mother. She couldn't bring herself to make the phone calls or place the ads:

> I don't know if it was procrastination or what. It was almost a physical inability for me to even consider calling a referral agency. Later, I found that was very common in my mothers' group. I was not an isolated case. But it was a terrible time.

Maria finally found a college girl who was good with children; confident that her daughter would get the love she needed, she went back to work, psychologically adjusted now to the idea of being a working mother. The girl left to return to school. Maria found another woman, only to discover six weeks later that she was stealing things from the house. At that point, Maria decided to go for day care and recoiled from what she saw:

> There are so few competent child care facilities that it's frightening. Some places I walked into, I cringed. You'd see all the children in walkers or playpens with the soap operas going all the time, and you'd say, "Nooooo, thank you."

The first day care center Maria settled on lasted six weeks. She would come home from work and find her child on the floor with a runny nose and nothing on her feet.

> I asked the woman to put on my kid's shoes and socks. She thought I was being too difficult a mother and without notice, she said, "Don't bring your child back." That was it. Goodbye. I said, "How about until the end of the week?" She said, "No."
>
> There is no greater crisis than being a working mother and having no place to put your child when you're at work. You utilize all the contacts you have.

Finally, on the fourth go-round, Maria found what she wanted, an excellent home with a professional woman who had given up her own managerial job to care for her second child. She hadn't been able to find good day care, either. There are five children in the home and Maria is full of praise for the experience her daughter is having as the youngest of the lot. She thinks her child is better socialized in this center with other children than she would have been at her own home with a housekeeper:

> I used to think that having someone come to your home was the best of all worlds. You don't have to get the child up when she's sleeping. You don't have to change their clothes and take them out into the cold when it's raining. Sure, there are advantages, but they're short-sighted advantages. I'm looking at the total socialization of my child. I think a housekeeper is more of a convenience for the woman than it is a benefit to the child.

The belief that their children are better socialized growing up with other kids is a common one among mothers whose children attend day care. Maria's description is not unusual:

> My child, at twenty-two months, has a vocabulary that is just amazing. She understands 99 percent of what you tell her. She can communicate with adults. She's not learning this from adults; she's learning it from the three- and four-year-olds. My daughter is now 80 percent toilet-trained and I never had a thing to do with it. Neither did the day care lady. She looked at the older kids who were so proud of themselves when they went to the bathroom and she's just mimicking them. It's a big deal. I would not trade that. My daughter helps with the housework. She picks up her toys.
> And she's not a pushover. She can stand up to other kids, and I think that's important, particularly for little girls. When I was growing up, little girls were taught to play by themselves. They dressed in dresses, they didn't rough-house, they were taught to draw and paint and play tea. My daughter plays on the slides and the monkey bars. She's active. It's so important that they not be inhibited but are able to explore.

Maria's enthusiasm contends with beliefs at the opposite extreme that day care is harmful to the child, and that the mother who does not stay at home with her infant in the early years risks creating emotional and intellectual damage. Much of the force behind this argument comes from John Bowlby's work over the last thirty years on mother-child attachment and the effects of maternal deprivation during World War II. Bowlby maintained that an infant requires a close, nurturant relationship with one caretaker, preferably the mother, in order to grow into a healthy, stable personality. To conclude, however, that a mother must be home all the time to preserve that bond requires a leap of faith, and until recently, there wasn't good information bearing on the subject. Now that information is becoming available, with stunning effects. It is found that there are few, if any, differences between infants in good day care and infants reared at home. But the day care *must* be good.

One of the most comprehensive and controlled studies was done by a Harvard team headed by Dr. Jerome Kagan, who followed sixty Boston infants over the first two and a half years of life. Half the infants were reared during working hours in an experimentally designed center, with a loving staff and a stimulating environment. The other half were reared exclusively at home by parents, from the early age of three to five months to almost three years. Throughout the period, the children were tested for social, emotional, and intellectual development.

The conclusion was that "A day care center staffed by conscientious and nurturant adults during the first two and a half years of life does not seem to produce a psychological profile very much different from the one created by rearing totally in the home." There were just as many shy children in the day care center as there were at home. Anxiety levels and reactions to uncertainty were the same. Intellectual progress did not differ. And, finally, all of the children, no matter where they spent their days, preferred their mothers over day care people by an overwhelming margin. Emotional bonding was not affected by the experience. Children still ran to their mothers in times of distress, and they developed profiles typical of their family backgrounds. In short, the family remained the salient force in socializing these children, in spite of the mother's absence during the day. The family is such a powerful emotional force that it overrides other effects, concluded Kagan. Day care adults cannot compete with parents.

Slightly different conclusions were offered by Dr. Michael Rutter of the London Institute of Psychiatry in a comprehensive review of day care research. Rutter noted that infants reared in day care may have some tendency to be more active, more aggressive, with better peer relationships but a lower tolerance for frustration compared to infants

161

raised at home. These conclusions were tentative, however, and in need of further study. In no case were the differences indicative of psychological disorder; they were simply differences in social behavior. On the crucial issue of bonding, both authorities agreed: Children in day care develop emotional bonds in much the same way as children reared at home, and the bonds are with their parents. Said Rutter: "Early claims that proper mothering was only possible if the mother did not go out to work . . . were not only premature but wrong."

Results like these give much-needed support to those mothers who are stepping out on a frontier when they return to work one or two months after delivery. Nevertheless, the uncertainties and difficulties they face in finding substitute care remain a major problem. For instance, the ratio of adults to children is crucial in the first three years of life. A caretaker should not be responsible for more than three infants, according to Kagan. Higher ratios may retard the child's intellectual and emotional growth, at least temporarily. For the same reasons, infants should not be kept in cribs or playpens, which is what Maria saw during her search.

Finally, there seems to be a critical period during the life of an infant when it is vulnerable to separation anxiety and fear of strangers, a period lasting from the age of seven or eight months to eighteen months. Mothers who want to use day care should probably do it before seven or after fifteen to eighteen months. But it's unwise to admit the infant during the first month of life, which is the period the infant needs to build up resistance to disease and time the mother needs to enjoy her new baby. Said Kagan: "Even the People's Republic of China, which encourages early group care of infants, allows the mother two months with her newborn infant at home."

Whether because of these problems with day care or an ingrained tendency to keep the children at home, most career mothers in business are choosing babysitters for their infants. A 1981 national survey of 815 two-career couples in corporations found that 58 percent of the children under one year of age were being cared for by babysitters. Only 14 percent went to a child care center.

The price Maria is paying for motherhood is a temporary hiatus in her career. She can't expect to be promoted while working part time; nor can she keep up with office politics on such an abbreviated schedule. But on the whole, she is lucky. She has it all and she's only thirty.

Men are thrilled when they hear about her work schedule, and want the same for themselves. The only person who reacted negatively, Maria remembers, was a young woman who has decided not to have children. She cannot understand why Maria gave up the fast track to have a baby and now, in group situations, finds it difficult to be around Maria.

"I don't know why. Maybe I threaten her."

Twenty-nine-year-old Megan was pregnant with her second child when I saw her, and, like Maria, she is accepting a temporary lull in professional advancement until her children are older. She works full time, but her job at a New York bank is boring, and rather than look for more challenging work now, she plans to sit it out for a year or two. She has vague worries about this:

> I'm willing to take the life stream of titles and earnings more slowly, although I know it's a competitive world. When people I started with get another promotion because they don't have kids and they have more time to work, it will hurt somewhat—if it happens that way.

Nevertheless, Megan thinks she is happier with this choice than waiting until she is older. She rebels at the Superwoman image conveyed by older women with high-powered jobs and new babies.

> I'm better off doing it this way than being one of these women who waits until they're thirty-five and a vice president with a lot of responsibility. Then they have a baby, hire a housekeeper, feel guilty because they're always out at business dinners and can't give up their other responsibilities. I just don't want to do things that way. When I'm really ready for more responsibility and travel, my kids will be older. I know people with preschool children who travel 70 percent of the time. What kind of a life is that?

Megan's perception of the older women may be colored by her own choices. But taken together, the young mothers demonstrate, as the older women do not, the very real problems professional women face in deciding to have children while working in an industry that makes few allowances for family responsibilities. In spite of the fact that both Maria and Megan have supportive husbands who share in the child care, neither feels willing or able to put in the extra time for travel, overtime work, or professional entertaining that go along with a career in finance. They also need time for themselves. Reflecting on a day spent by an energetic mother she knows in New York (not in this sample), Megan said:

> I was crushed. I couldn't have lived through it in a week! I can't be on the go like her every second. And she's got it all planned, you know, like a computer. It's amazing! You just look at her and ask, "How does she survive?" I have a high degree of need for doing nothing, for sitting on a sofa.

Maria is able to take the time she needs for herself during the afternoons when she doesn't work; but other mothers, particularly in San Francisco, were having a difficult time keeping up with the pace.

Mona is going full throttle in a high-pressure job on a trading desk. She looks wonderful, alive and vibrant, which is partly due to her recent success. She has become a winner and people are talking about her on the Street. Sometimes when she is risking money and winning, a flush covers her neck and face, which reflects a complex mixture of excitement and unfamiliarity. She is not used to being a winner.

Her two small children go to a day care center, and although she has some help with the house cleaning, it is only twice a month. Mona loves her family with an emotion that infuses her whole being; her husband is supportive. But she gets five hours of sleep a night. She sticks to a rigorous routine and often wakes up with a headache. She can feel her heart pounding much of the time. She is on a roll and does not want to stop. Her doctor has told her not to worry, there is nothing wrong with her; but she wonders what the pace will eventually do to her body. Mona likes her work so much, she cannot contemplate the idea of staying home. Unfortunately, it also runs over into her personal time. "I'm supposed to get off at three o'clock, but if I'm involved, I don't. There's always a rush. I don't know what the answer is. Because I can't have my cake and eat it too."

Mona differs from the older mothers in two ways. She's new at her job and she does not have full-time help at home. Several mothers in San Francisco, including Mona, reject the idea of a full-time housekeeper on principle. They believe their children should be growing up in the company of other kids. New York mothers had very different opinions, summed up by a mother on Wall Street: "You've got to have somebody full time. They don't have to live in, but you've got to have full-time child care. Period." In the 1979 survey of its membership by the Financial Women's Association, 72 percent of the mothers were employing full-time housekeepers. I had the impression that this difference in the choice of substitute care was having a profound effect on the lives of the mothers in the two cities. Whether it has an equally profound effect on the lives of their children, as Maria believes, remains to be seen.

Many of the problems working mothers face lie not with themselves, but with the ethics of the workplace that put such emphasis on competitive, early success. While work morality is changing with the influx of large numbers of professional women, decisions like the one taken by Maria's boss are in the very small minority. Many employers may agree with him, but few will act upon their knowledge—until women begin organizing to confront their employers with the issues of parenting and family. As long as women accept the grief of trying to integrate careers and families without protest, they will be suffering alone.

Throughout recent history, the vast majority of professional men have had families; the majority of professional women have not. Current attempts by an avant-garde group of women to have it all only indicates how far we still have to go in creating a world where women have access to a full life.

The next two chapters describe the lives of the largest group of women in the sample: the women who are interested in motherhood, but have no children. The reasons for their unfilled ambitions are complex: Identity conflicts, postponement of marriage, trouble at work, the Cinderella syndrome, unenthusiastic spouses, and a preference for leisure time all play a role. But one theme stood out as a potential source of trouble for women who want it all. Some of these people held on to a feminine identity in a situation where it was maladaptive. Refusing to learn the rules of masculine behavior left them vulnerable and open to attack, hampering their private as well as their working lives. In declining to go through the process of identity change, they lost the opportunity to master the issue of power.

IV
Women in the Middle

11
The
Price of
Careers

P otential mothers are women in the middle. They don't have children, nor have they rejected the idea. This was a diverse group of women, gathered together only because they expressed interest in being mothers but had no children. A few were only vaguely interested, "If the right man came along," but many felt strongly about their still unfulfilled ambitions for a family. Some of these women were on the verge of doing just that—preparing to marry or become pregnant. Some were postponing the decision, and several saw their hopes dimming, as they held onto the dream of having it all and watched the biological clock tick away. Most of these women came from families with maternal power; a few came from patriarchal backgrounds. There were sixteen women in the middle.

In reality, this group would be far larger than it was in my sample. I sought out working women with children, an equal number in each city, so the total group is skewed toward family women. The true number of professional women in finance without children is much larger than this. It is a majority. Who are these women?

Marlene, described in Chapter 2, is in the middle, rocking back and forth between the professional and feminine parts of her life, unable to see the path to integration. In addition to her own internal conflicts, and probably contributing to them, she hears from the important men in her life that she shouldn't have children because they will ruin her career. In her heart, she wants children; in her head, she thinks that

169

becoming a mother might destroy an important part of herself—her professional identity and ability to work. Her father and her fiancé confirm that belief, leading Marlene further into a pattern of thinking in which she is bound to surrender important life goals on one score or another.

Sandy, who was thirty when I met her and a year older than Marlene, is on the verge of telling her father that his perspective no longer controls her life. He always cautioned her against getting married and having a family, and she followed that advice for years, but lately she has come to the conclusion that professional life by itself is not enough for her. She and her fiancé have decided to have children when they marry.

A third woman, at twenty-nine, was also engaged to be married when I interviewed her and looked forward eagerly to the prospect of having children. Terry, who is a nearly perfect financial woman—clear and rational, organized and intelligent—has considerable insight into her feelings and she believes strongly that "you need to have something for both sides of you." For several years, work came first in her life. If she had a date and then discovered she had to work late, she would call up the guy and tell him she couldn't make it. Men did the same to her. It was taken for granted that work was more important than social life. But then Terry began to question the primacy of work.

> When I first started traveling, oh, my God, I was excited. Now it's like— all the hassles of it. Do I have enough shirts so that when I get home . . . or, you immediately run to the cleaners and pay your bills. Then, there are the places you have to go. Everyone wants to go to certain cities in Germany, but who wants to go to the East Berlin border, look at a plant that's a million years old, in a city that closes down at 9 p.m.?

Terry stopped putting work first all the time and began to make decisions like saying no to work demands at seven o'clock on a Friday night, because she wants to be with her fiancé. She makes up the work some other time, but she wants control of her hours. Terry estimates that it will take her three years to work herself into a position where she has enough control over her hours to risk having a child.

Terry's fiancé, however, does not share this philosophy. In an allied profession, he believes that sacrifices must be made:

I can't tell you how utterly resigned I am to my fate. I'm resigned that I have to go in at eight and stay until seven. Men are resigned to the fact that they're going to have to put up with the boss, that they're going to have to hustle, that 50 percent of the job is putting up with certain kinds of abuse.

I sense that Terry fights that. She fights the idea that if you're going to be committed to a career, you have to be singleminded and you have to make some choices.

All three of these women were on the verge of getting married when we met. All three wanted a family. But only one was having a clear shot at it in the sense that she and her prospective husband had agreed to work on the practical issues of combining the two roles. The beliefs of the other two men echo the classic perspective of a masculine ethos. The dedicated professional sacrifices personal life for work; careers and parenthood are not compatible. For men, that philosophy has never been so uncomfortable that they had to challenge it. As Terry's fiancé easily acknowledged, "The choices for men are easier."

Two of the women in the middle were married, with supportive husbands, and both had full opportunities to make a choice. One woman was trying to become pregnant; the other, at the age of thirty-seven, was indecisive. Her husband, who has three children of his own, keeps telling her it would be good for her to have a child, but she is not convinced. She likes her independence and is afraid that a baby would make her vulnerable and dependent. Even if she kept on working—which she certainly would want to do—a child would limit her options.

I wouldn't have the freedom to flit off and do the stuff I do now. I go to the opera one night a week, the ballet one night. I do things with my husband and without him. I go out to dinner and teach classes at night. I have all this freedom. I can take off on the spur of the moment and go to Vail for a week. I wouldn't be able to do that if I had a baby. It would be like having a hostage to fight, somebody more important to you than yourself, impinging on my personal selfishness, I suppose.

Two years ago, when she was single, the woman who spoke those words was thinking of having a child by herself. But married now, with a teenage stepdaughter whom she enjoys immensely, she feels her needs for intimacy have been resolved. That was not an uncommon theme among married women in San Francisco: Opportunities for the good life are so available in that city that many women opt against childbirth to preserve their leisure time, not their working time. It is a clear choice, without sacrifice.

Pauline and Renee in Chapter 4 are also women in the middle. Groomed for professional life by their fathers, these women grew up knowing instinctively how to behave as women in finance. Their ambition since they were children was to move in the world of public authority. Independent, rational, and discreet, with a clear sense of their own powers, they have had no trouble being accepted by the male hierarchy. Both are comfortable with senior management. Until recently, both were thoroughly immersed in the professional identity; but Renee, who at thirty-seven is eight years older than Pauline, went through a profound shift at midlife when she confronted needs for intimacy that would never be satisfied in professional circles. Crucially aware that for all her popularity she somehow lacked intimacy, afraid that her maturation as a career woman might put her permanently out of the family sphere, Renee radically changed her priorities. She wanted a family and she felt the loss deeply.

Drawing back from a score of professional activities that had been taking up her free time, Renee began to look inside herself for the feelings that establish bonds. "I don't want to be just a banker," she said. Pauline feels the loss too, but more remotely. Family connections lie ahead as a long-range goal. For now and the immediate future, work is her life, while she postpones the search for significant relationships.

Ten of the sixteen women were single, and it was in the lives of some of these women that the stresses of having careers were taking their toll. The married women and mothers seemed to be more buffered against stress, but the single women in the middle were people with gaps in their lives. Only two of them said they were happy living alone; several spoke of their need for close connections with feelings ranging from mild discomfort to outright crisis:

> I think women in their late thirties are in a period of total crisis, especially women who would like to have a family, but haven't gotten married and are now verging on being too old, or maybe it won't ever happen, or, if it does, it's too late.

Karen is thirty-six years old, a willowly, black-haired woman from Nebraska who works and lives in mid-Manhattan. From an upper-class background, she is a lady with a Woody Allen sense of humor. In a sing-song voice, she recited all the dutiful female behaviors she grew up with. "You will not cut corners. You will do things right. You will be polite to people. You will work very hard. You will make A's and everything will be OK."

If she had stayed home and married the town lawyer, that lesson plan might have served her well, but as a New York investment counselor, it didn't quite serve. "I wouldn't say it's been fabulous," said Karen about her preparation for adult work life, "but it's gotten me through." At first, the ethical feminine training was useful because she worked for a nice, well-educated group of people. Now she works for a man who prowls the halls making sure people stay in their offices working and who monitors the length of the lunch hour. He regularly blitzes Karen with memos detailing all the things she has done wrong. She takes it for a while and then closes her door and uncorks. A couple of men she's talked to there tell her, "You can't go on this way. You have to march straight into his office and tell him," but Karen is reluctant to do that. "That's not the kind of person I am. Anyway, I'd be in tears in his office and that's worse, because then he knows I'm really knuckling under."

Karen tries to keep this stress inside to maintain a cool professional image. Usually she succeeds, but she can't help venting behind closed doors. Nor can she release the anger and anxiety through her considerable humor.

> Everyone around here is too totally uptight to have someone cracking jokes or acting a little bit lamebrained. We're all supposed to act like we know *exactly* what's going to happen next and can predict it. *Total* professionalism. [She spat out the "t"] The desire to be thought of as professional is so paramount that you feel if you walk into the office and say something goofy, they'll say, "Uh . . . do we have a lightweight on our hands?" So I have always totally guarded against that.

Besides the frustration at work, Karen feels stressed by her efforts to maintain a social life and do volunteer work as well. Two years ago, she got so run down that her heart began to thunder in her chest. It wasn't a heart attack but an accelerated rhythm, as if someone had shot a load of adrenaline into her arm. She was rushed to the emergency room of a hospital, where doctors could find nothing wrong with her heart. But the symptom comes back, perhaps two or three times a week. Karen hyperventilates and feels lightheaded. The doctor suggested she see a psychiatrist. He told her, "You're a nervous wreck." She said, "Fine. At least you know it's nothing too severe."

As Karen told her story in her office one evening, the din of traffic on Madison Avenue rose through the city's canyons to the fortieth floor, filling the room with its cacophony: A siren wailed in the distance, mixing with the continuous blend of horns and engines accelerating from stop lights. Even in her gracious office, with its thick carpet and carved wooden desk, the background noise was barely muted.

Karen looked as if she were dressed for dinner. She wore a beautiful blue print dress, accented by pearls and white earrings, which is the way she typically dresses for work. She can't stand the man-tailored suits—those "ridiculous blazers with full skirts and little ascots at the neck. I don't feel very comfortable in those suits. I feel like I'm a . . . my whole attitude about myself is different when I have one on. Even a blazer. I feel very sporty, like maybe I shouldn't be in the office."

Of all forty-four women in the sample, Karen was the only one with negative connotations for the concept of "woman." The strength, competence, and power that other people talked about, Karen saw from a different perspective, the perspective of a fallible human being trying to meet those standards. She burst out in a comic monologue when I asked her what being a woman means:

> I think it means you've been battered around by all this. You're trying to figure out what you want to do versus what people think you're supposed to do, and how to get there. You're fighting against your own self-perception and the world's perception of a working woman in her thirties. Being a woman now means being able to do everything well. You are expected to be feminine, expected to be intelligent, expected to get married and raise children without missing a beat. You are expected to get all the marketing done, collect the laundry and do the cleaning, drive the car long distances, have nerves of steel, and never look like you're wearing or fraying.
>
> In New York, being a woman means always looking nice, competing in some very high-powered situations, finding yourself at a dinner party with a client, standing up at cocktail parties where somebody asks you what you think is going to happen in the next six months and wanting an answer. It's a total image thing.

It's very unchic these days, when somebody asks you what you do, to say, "Underwater basketweaving." They go, "Oh," and turn right around and don't want to talk to you anymore. New York men have gotten so geared up they think when they ask a woman what she does that she will say, "I'm the executive vice president of blah-bi-blah-bi, and I'm going to the Far East tomorrow, so I've got to rush home right now and pack my bags. Tootles!" This is what they've come to expect. There is no space for failure. That's another thing that being a woman means right now. In any area. It doesn't matter what it is.

Karen knows many women who feel the same way she does, and one of the things that presses on them is the knowledge that time is running out on their reproductive cycles and they are not in a position to have the family they always thought they would. The experience is something like going to the moon. You grow up thinking you will have a husband and children, and instead, find yourself fighting for your life in an executive suite during the day, and, in the evenings, meeting a parade of potential romantic partners, most of whom could not pass a mental health test. It is all totally unexpected.

Five years ago, when Karen thought about being a mother and a career woman, there was no question in her mind about how to do it: Get a live-in substitute and go back to work. Now she's coming to the conclusion that temperamentally she couldn't handle it. The whole thing seems too difficult. But what are her alternatives? Karen circles around and around the issues.

> Am I going along at as rapid a pace as I should be? Maybe I'd better change jobs. So that stirs up a whole new set of things to think about. Am I happy with this career? Maybe I should get into another field. Maybe I should go back for my MBA. Maybe. Maybe. And all of these things start playing on you, not to mention the fact that if you have a social life, you're trying to maintain it, or if you don't have one, you're trying to get it.

> When I say women are in crisis, this is what I mean. I am confident it will be worked through. I think. Unless one day, you just find me on the sidewalk somewhere, having died from all this.

It was tougher being single in New York than in San Francisco. Fifteen times larger than San Francisco, with a harsher climate and a more aggressive human environment, New York has stresses that people across the continent glimpse with a mixture of fear and admiration. Professional ethics demand overtime as a sign of commitment. People hide their personal idiosyncrasies out of a real need to protect themselves from aggressive, political machinations. "The corporate world is not friendly," said one male executive on Wall Street. "People like to find out stuff on you. They do stupid things to get ahead, childish, immature, destructive things. Everybody needs to protect themselves."

The tough, achieving cultural scene is played out in a physical environment where the struggle for survival is visible, imminent, and remorseless. New Yorkers know in visceral ways the consequences of not making enough money to escape the streets. They work overtime to earn enough money to take taxis rather than ride the subways. They see around them many homeless, pavement people, a constant reminder that the bottom is not far away. A few mistakes, a lack of incentive, the loss of a job—these things threaten life in a way that the residents of San Francisco cannot comprehend. People are driven to the top by the images at the bottom.

Quite apart from the human factor, it is possible to die in New York during a winter without money, while in San Francisco you can drift with barely a penny in your pocket and never really suffer. The temperature may dip below freezing during a winter night, but it won't kill you, and the sun comes up in the morning, warming the air to 60 or 70 degrees. One winter day, I saw that difference in an unforgettable contrast. While the drifters of San Francisco warmed themselves in bright, vivid sunlight, I saw on television the street people of New York huddled over burning trash cans, the only thing that stood between them and a brutal, cold death. The news commentator announced that five people had died that day in subzero temperatures. But from where I sat, the daily struggle for existence seemed remote and far away. A woman I planned to interview that afternoon had canceled the appointment to go sailing on the sparkling waters of San Francisco Bay.

Up and down the scale of human achievement, the benevolence of the physical environment in San Francisco surrounds and supports the population, muting aggression and cutting into the work ethic. A male bank executive who moved from New York to San Francisco likes to crystallize the difference with a story about bus drivers.

I used to ride the bus home and one night it stopped at a Kentucky Fried Chicken. The driver got off, walked inside, ordered a snack pack of Kentucky Fried Chicken and a Dr. Pepper, got back on the bus, and proceeded to drive off, eating his chicken. In New York, they'd have beaten the guy to death. In San Francisco, everybody said, "Hey, he got a Dr. Pepper. Boy, that's good."

Even at the top, corporate executives sense a difference. As another man in San Francisco said:

Managing people is far different here than in New York. Motivating them is tougher. You can manage professionals in New York and ask them to develop their own personal image and reputation. Here, that doesn't work. Here, they work to play . . . the competition is here, but it doesn't permeate the whole society. There is a group of people who are competing, but then, there is a larger group of people you wouldn't find in New York who are basically letting the world happen to them. The competition doesn't cascade down through all the strata.

People work for money to play in San Francisco; they work for promotions and higher status in New York. The distinctions were obvious in the lower stress levels reported by single women in San Francisco. Nevertheless, in spite of these very great differences between the physical and social environments of the two cities, the stories told by single women were similar. In both cities, they described the difficulty of maintaining a professional life without intimate supports at home. The professional culture was not that different whether you lived in San Francisco or New York.

On a warm day in January, I walked with Becky into a park near her San Francisco apartment to tape the interview. A flock of white swans glided by on the surface of a pond while we talked and the sun broke through the trees in a filigree pattern of light. In the midst of this serene beauty, personal reflections came easily. Becky had some important things to say about the impact of the professional identity on her private life.

She is single, a relatively young woman of thirty-four who came to San Francisco from the East Coast several years ago to take a job in financial planning. She came with her husband at the time and both were looking forward eagerly to bright new jobs in their respective fields: finance for Becky and the academic world for her husband. They were a modern, dual-career couple with high potential.

From the moment she started, Becky loved her job and she moved up quickly, putting in long hours as part of an ambitious professional team. Her husband was working hard too in a college, hoping to establish a strong record for tenure. But he was running into problems. The Western environment didn't seem to suit his personality. For a long time, Becky didn't notice the erosion in her husband's spirits. They weren't talking much, for one thing, and they weren't spending a lot of time together. So, without any great awareness on either side, the marriage began to crumble. Becky's husband, feeling painfully rejected at work, became frankly depressed, but he never asked for her help. As for Becky, she was riding so high she didn't see his troubles, and often, she didn't care.

> I was obviously enjoying my career and being very successful. I guess I wasn't in any mood to be real supportive. I was having a good time. I was on a winning trip and I just didn't have any time for this down trip. I really had no idea how hard it was.

One day her husband came home and told her that tenure was not forthcoming. The news hit Becky with a shock of awareness. It was the first time she understood how badly he felt. Still, she had a hard time empathizing. "Get up and fight," she told him. But he couldn't, and after a few months of his depression, she moved out of the house and eventually out of the marriage.

Becky regrets that she did not tune in earlier when perhaps she could have helped him with the crisis. If they had only talked, things might have turned out differently.

> One of the things that's really important when you have two people involved with fairly demanding careers—not only intellectually, but personally and psychologically—is that you've got to be more careful about talking to each other and to say what's on your mind. Just because you love each other doesn't mean you really understand what's going on in the other person's head.

Becky rested her chin in her hand and fell silent for a moment. "The home life does sacrifice itself," she went on. "When you both have stressful jobs, you don't have the time to spend on home and relationships."

In spite of her self-portrayal as an insensitive wife, Becky is a soft and somewhat shy woman. The professional identity covers a personal vulnerability, which more often than not produces a feeling of neediness. Work does not satisfy those needs because, although the environment is supportive and friendly and everyone has a good time producing a product, her friends there belong to a special category of people called "work friends." Conversations revolve around impersonal topics and no one lets their hair down.

> It's that old vulnerability deal. You don't want to let it show. I don't know why, but I know that it's true. I think people would get real uncomfortable if you started to talk about your personal life at work.

Moreover, the financial environment, oriented toward evaluation and criticism, rarely produces an emotional stroke such as "Thanks, that was a wonderful job." When things go wrong, you hear about them. When things go right, the silence is deafening. Becky has trouble keeping up her self-esteem when positive feedback comes once a year in the annual report and there is no one at home to fill the gap. Paradoxically, the gap in emotional reinforcement has widened as Becky moved up the professional ladder, away from concrete tasks into conceptual areas. Sometimes she loses a sense of having achieved anything at all. As a potential means for getting positive feedback, Becky is considering becoming a Big Sister or helping out battered women. The idea is appealing for its human elements.

Becky is not driven to have children. If she had a husband who really wanted a family she would consider it, but basically she doesn't see how a child would fit into her career in corporate work. She also likes her independence and freedom on weekends. But Becky still faces some large and unresolved issues. For one thing, she wonders whether she will need that family down the line, ten years from now, even though the impetus at present is not powerful.

> I don't know if I have come to terms with the issue of leaving a child to be my progeny on earth to go on and on. I don't think I've come to terms with that, but I also don't think I feel a strong need that way.

Besides the existential issues of meaning and continuity, Becky recognizes other needs she faces on a more immediate basis. She lacks that private sphere where trust, loyalty, and mutual interdependence build a sanctuary against the outside world. It's not just the emotional support that's missing, but a crucial human element, where people deal in feelings rather than impersonal rationality. Becky calls it "people feedback," by which she means exchanges that feed the soul because they deal in such ancient currency as giving, gratitude, and joy. Without a family, these emotional gifts are harder to find.

> I hadn't thought about this before, but you know, single women in jobs are often considered cold or hard or something, and it may be that we sort of build up this wall so that we won't even need it, because we aren't getting it. And then it makes it very hard to even get into relationships or to take praise, because we've built up this "I don't need it" syndrome.

Unfortunately, in her current relationship with a man from the company where Becky works, these needs are not being taken care of. For one thing, the professional identity continues to get in the way long after they've reached home. Particularly if they have worked together that day, getting out of the business mode takes hours. Conversations about work drag on until the tongue is dry as dust. Moreover, the professional personality, which is not supposed to show any "weaknesses," is hard to drop when your partner is from the same place. Becky feels she must be tough and self-sufficient all the time. A new woman is not supposed to say, "I need you. Give me some attention. Hold me."

> You think that men will only like you if you are strong and self-sufficient. If you're weak and dependent, they don't respect you. The trouble is, we confuse that with the need for attention, emotion, and love. And so, we can't ever say, "I want you to love me and pay attention to me," because you think that's a chink. And it shouldn't be. That's not a weakness. And men do it too. We become like them, which is the worst of all possibilities. I think we should be adding our humanity and emotion and softness to the world, rather than turning into men. That doesn't do us any good.

The issues Becky is facing are extremely complex and difficult. She may not have all the solutions yet, but one thing she knows: The corporation is not the place to go for the missing human element. Many single women who find themselves unexpectedly without families look to the work environment as a substitute, but the political nature of a power hierarchy makes that solution dangerous. Work relationships are kept at an impersonal level for good reasons—emotions interfere with the need to do business and they make people vulnerable.

> If you try as a woman to find that human element at work, you're not doing your work real good service, because that's not what the work environment is all about. Maybe it should be, but it's not . . . not now.

Becky is separated from her family of origin by a continent and does not have a family of her own, which means that many of the emotional and spiritual anchors in her life are lacking. Those people who would keep her connected to the past and future have left, and Becky is forced to seek out alternatives. She believes that friends can substitute.

> A family is not just bloodlines. You can have a family through other means than children. I have several good friends out here that I consider family. I'm not sure the only way you can have closeness and friendship is to have children or grandparents or whatever.

Perhaps. But establishing a niche with friends that equals the depth and permanence of the bloodline takes special people and possibly a special living environment as well. Many have tried and failed. It may be that the culture has not grown up yet to the task of replacing the biological family which is being stripped away by technological development. The alternatives are still evolving, and so is Becky's life. But it is she and women like her who will find the solutions, because they must. Somehow, the deep connections and the dependencies nurtured since the dawn of the human race in families must be transferred to special friendship networks capable of sustaining the individual in a difficult world.

Throughout this century, individual women have chosen to forgo feminine roles to follow their own stars. Motivated by talent or

181

special circumstances, often influenced by their fathers rather than their mothers, many of these women did not expect to marry and have children. From an early age, they saw an unbridgeable gulf between feminine roles and personal achievement, and they made a deliberate choice. But the ranks of these women have steadily been swelled by professional women who never made a choice like that. They expected to work for a few years and then get married. In another era, they would have been teachers or nurses, occupations specially designed for women who intend to make the family their real careers. In this era, they have become lawyers and stockbrokers.

These would-be mothers—the women in the middle—represent a cut right out of the feminine mainstream. Their crossed expectations, the fact that they are still single and hoping to have a family, indicate how complicated the issues are. Why haven't these women found men they wanted to marry? Why are so many of them still single? From my interviews, I could find no simple answer. There were many reasons, one of them being that the more money and status a woman achieves, the more she expects from a prospective mate. No matter how good she is, he must still be better. Shades of the old double standard, female variety.

Judy, thirty-two years old, was probably the most wholesome-looking woman in the sample. With an open, laughing face, blond hair, and a vivacious spirit, she looked like the original Golden Girl of California. She could have posed for an image on Wonderbread. From a large Catholic family, educated in a private girls' school, Judy grew up with the American dream: good parents, beautiful surroundings, and money. She had a close, warm family; her memories of it sound like a television script. Her mother, whom Judy loves and admires, would dress up for her father every afternoon and meet him at the door with a kiss. A happy woman, devoted to her children, in love with her husband and strong in her own right. Intending to follow in her mother's footsteps, Judy got engaged out of college. But the man wasn't right for her, so she broke the engagement and went to work, planning to work for two years and then get married. The longer she worked, the more independent she became.

About the age of twenty-six, Judy looked around and realized for the first time that she might never find Prince Charming. She made the decision then to put both feet into her career and really work, with the ambition of getting the things for herself she thought would come with a man. "That's when I thought I'd better get my ducks in line. I definitely got more aggressive. I registered as a stockbroker, worked my way into sales and changed firms."

Each year, Judy made more money. Each year, her expectations for a husband grew taller.

> It gets difficult when you've lived alone. You're independent and making good money. Your expectations are so much higher than they were at twenty-four. The older you get, and the more money you make . . . your expectations. I don't want to marry somebody who is making—you know—I guess I should say it: somebody who's making less money than I am.
>
> So, how much money did you make last year, Judy?
>
> Fifty-eight thousand dollars. . . . So, it gets difficult.

Judy is no clinging vine. With a strong and well-balanced personality, thoroughly at home in the Bay area where she grew up, supported by a network of childhood friends, and able to draw a high salary, Judy doesn't really need a wealthy man. Moreover, her attitudes toward her own gender have undergone a revolution in the last decade. A few years ago, she couldn't have imagined a woman as President; now she thinks a woman would probably be better than what the country has had. She's seen women growing into power, she's seen how good they are, and that makes her proud. At the same time, she's seen more and more insecurity on the part of men, and that turns her off. She thinks most of the "crap" women go through in careers can be traced to the existence of so many insecure men.

> You wouldn't have to worry about women's rights if you had men who were secure in themselves and could understand that you can be equal; yet, you can still be feminine and he can still be masculine.

But alongside this strong feminine ideology runs the expectation of finding a more powerful mate. He doesn't have to be more intelligent than she is, but the money is important because, as she jokingly explained, "then I can retire." Judy laughed and retracted the statement in her next breath. She couldn't stay home now, she'd get too bored; but she wants a few months off. The contradictions were piling up, leaving her laughing and sputtering.

> It seems so logical to me. . . . I meant what I said . . . but, ummmm, I
> do want somebody who makes more money than I do. . . . Maybe, I
> want him to think of me as an equal, but he doesn't have to be equal? I
> don't know. Now you've got me stumped.

Why do women like Judy search for an equal with one mind, and
with the other—mostly unconscious mind—hold out for a man who
can beat their own best hand? It's a way of returning to the nest, and it
doesn't work. The childhood images defining how male and female
roles are to be played out form an indelible matrix in the mind, pushing through all the new learning. In Judy's past, her father was the
"head of the household." Ergo, her husband should be "head of the
household." But that patriarchal model is completely at odds with Judy's development as a new woman. She cannot live out the American
domestic dream, yet she hungers after it. Like many of us, she wants to
recreate the family home she knew as a child (or the ideal of one), but
that family home is permanently out of reach, unless a woman is content to go home and be the mother her mother was. Unfortunately, the
great American dream family was always more fun for children than it
was for mothers. And so the single career women are left with a dream
they cannot recreate and an image of masculinity that will sink them—
if they succeed in finding a man who fits it.

Some of Judy's friends have given up good jobs to go home; now
they are bored, and they envy her life. Judy spends weekends in Palm
Springs. She flies to New York five times a year, and runs to Boston just
for a party. Her married friends with kids look on this lifestyle with
envy. They want what she has: independence and no responsibility for
anyone but themselves. One of them told Judy recently that she wants
to leave her husband and three children to pursue a career. Judy gave
her the keys to her apartment and told her to stay there all weekend
by herself.

> I told her to really stop and think about it. "The grass is not greener on
> the other side. Just because you're looking at what I'm doing, don't jump
> to any conclusions. There are a lot of lonely nights, a lot of times I would
> rather have your existence than mine. If you don't love your husband,
> that's one thing. But if it's this career, go out and get a career. Do it. You
> can do both." But she feels she must divorce herself from everybody to

do it. She cannot be this total woman and have a career, if she doesn't blow four people out of the water. There it is.

When Judy came home, she asked her friend what she had done for Saturday night dinner. The woman had ordered in a pizza and gotten sick. No glamour there.

So what are Judy's solutions? How will she fill the gaps in her life?

I keep thinking, I'll wait, make all my money, and if I'm not married by forty, I'll adopt. That's what I keep telling my parents. But I still think that some day I'll marry and have children. That's the Catholic in me. The old family. Keep it together. Keep it going.

I don't want to live the rest of my life alone.

The agonizing gaps faced by these three women—Karen, Becky, and Judy—are the reverse of those described by Betty Friedan's housewives of the last generation. These women have the jobs but not the families, the opportunity to be effective and powerful but not dependent, the chance to use their minds and lose their hearts. Exactly that kind of reversal was picked up in a study of patterns of love and work among contemporary women, called *Lifeprints*. The authors studied a random selection of three hundred women in a city near Boston, ranking them along two separate dimensions. In one measure, the women were rated on their level of mastery, referring to having a sense of control over their lives, high self-esteem, and low anxiety. On the other measure, they were ranked on the degree of pleasure they experience in life. The pleasure index was a cumulative score of items reflecting happiness, satisfaction, and optimism. As it turned out, these two measures functioned quite separately in the lives of these women. One tied in with work achievement; the other reflected personal satisfaction in relationships.

The profile of the married homemakers was a classic one. These women as a whole ranked high on pleasure and low on mastery, the by now well-known portrait of a woman who has no objective measure of her function in life because her work is bound up in caring for other people. To no one's surprise, the mothers and wives who stayed home often felt worthless but optimistic. They could not gauge their effectiveness or measure their worth, and their self-esteem registered in the basement. But because they were involved in significant intimate relationships, they also had a considerable amount of happiness and hope.

The profile of single working women was just the opposite. They ranked fairly high on mastery and very low on pleasure. Of all the women in the sample, employed women who did not marry were the least happy, satisfied, and optimistic. The authors believe this very low pleasure index stemmed from the loss of intimacy in their lives and the difficulty they faced in maintaining relationships. Moreover, these were the best educated women in the sample. Many had surpassed their parents in achievement and had moved away from them. That meant they lacked emotional supports on two fronts and could not look to their families of origin for the ties they missed in their own lives.

The women at the top of both scales, with the highest overall measure of well-being, were married women in high-status jobs who also had children—the women with it all. My interviews with these forty-four professional women strongly confirm those findings. Working mothers were not only coping with both roles well but they probably benefited from a synergistic interaction, gaining energy as they moved from home to work and back again. It was the single women who paid a heavy price for the new world—and not all of them. In the *Lifeprint* study, those who expected to be single were happy with their lives; the women who suffered the most were those who wanted families. And there were many more women like that than there were working mothers in finance. It is too high a price to pay, to lose all family connections; yet there is no going back. That is the dilemma talented women have faced in one generation after another.

A few of the single women in the middle seemed to be suffering from another malaise in addition to the lack of intimacy in their lives. This group also contained some individuals who held onto their feminine identities, refusing to make the changes other women had done. Their working lives looked like a battleground because of it. To a greater extent than either the mothers or the women who rejected motherhood, some of these women in the middle held onto a feminine ethos that was maladaptive in the corporate world. They insisted on being themselves in an environment that classically shows little tolerance for emotional honesty or individuality. It was sad but true that women who showed their feelings, spoke their minds, or inspired anger or lust were in trouble in hierarchical power structures. In refusing to wear the mask of the new identity, they might as well have been soldiers going into battle without helmets.

And that was not all. In being the women they always were, such women denied themselves the opportunity to learn a new way of being in the world, as feminine people with power. That transformation came only to those who could allow themselves to pass through a sometimes difficult, angry, frequently awkward and isolating period when they put aside a large part of what they had been and learned to emulate the masculine ethos. Sometimes—and this was the hardest part—the change meant letting go of cherished feminine values.

12
Individualism
Versus
Image Making

From her office overlooking a major subway station in the financial district of San Francisco, Katheryn expounded on a paradox of the women's movement. Millions of women had been set free from the confining roles of mother and wife, only to be confined again in different roles, as bankers, lawyers, and stockbrokers—all wearing the same clothes, all affecting the same image. It was not supposed to be that way. The feminist movement had been about options and individuality, the freedom to be whatever you wanted. Now, women had thrown away the very thing they fought so hard to achieve: identity. The chance to be unique individuals.

At forty-five, Katheryn is a stunning woman. She wore her hair in long, blond curls around her neck, not the standard cut for a financial woman. Dressed in a nubby, purple suit, with a beautiful face and a powerful stream of conversation, Katheryn stood out absolutely. You couldn't miss her. Even if you didn't see her, you would hear her, digesting and serving up the world in a clear, articulated voice:

> Many of my friends are looking around and saying to themselves—and I have always been this way—"Look, dammit. I'm a human being first and then I'm a woman, and that's what I will always and want to be." How that fits into what I do . . . well, I want to just let that flow. I think women should stop fighting that. Just to feel your femininity. Don't attempt to disguise it by acting, looking more like men, melting into the woodwork, if you like. I think that's stupid.

Katheryn and her friends are disturbed by the price they see women paying for careers. They like the jobs, and the rewards that go with them, but they question the cost to personal life and a quality vaguely described as "femaleness." Katheryn wasn't quite sure what she meant by femaleness. Nevertheless, the experience was very real and concrete, even if the words were hard to find.

Among potential mothers, she is fortunate. Katheryn has not lost anything at the personal level for having a career. She could not have children and felt her thirteen-year marriage would not support an adoption. Divorced now and living alone, Katheryn loves being single. She revels in the bachelor life she never had when she was twenty, and doesn't want to be married again. Her professional rank is relatively new. An executive assistant for years, she moved into a line position three years ago where she began taking direct responsibility for production and budgeting. That move marked the transition from a feminine-type position where she supported other people's authority to a masculine-type position where she is in charge.

She remembers the change as both dramatic and traumatic. In her former job, Katheryn had a secretary, a receptionist, a chauffeur-driven car, a magnificent office, and almost unlimited access to the powers at the top. She knew the bank inside and out.

> But, no matter how bright I was, no matter how successful the project was, no matter how much energy I put into it, basically, what I was doing was making someone else look good. That's what those jobs are and there is no other way to cut it. It's not that I felt unappreciated particularly. I did not, but I just needed more. In fact, our chairman said, "You can do that job with your hands tied behind your back. You are too comfortable. It is time to move on."

Giving up the perks wasn't so bad, but taking responsibility for making decisions and designing her own career path was like jumping off a cliff. Nobody gave her any guidance or support. That came as a shock.

> I think I felt very angry, very let down. I resented the fact that there was really no one there to take care of me. Who is out there to tell me what is the next best step? Where do I go? Do I do two zigs and a zag or no zigs and all zags or what happens? Well, I was very unhappy with that and disappointed.

Eventually, Katheryn got angry enough to sit down, choose a course, and tell management what she needed. They said, "Fine. Go do it." Period.

Katheryn's assumption of authority did not come with an identity change. For one thing, she was already a fully mature woman in her forties when it happened; for another, she was well known at the bank after two decades of working there. But mostly, she has a special niche, a place where she is responsible only to herself, where she can be an individual. With a delighted laugh, she said: "I don't look like a banker and I love it that way. Customers constantly say to me, 'You're in banking?' It's a surprise to them and that pleases me. I don't want to be like everybody else." But in the next breath, she acknowledged: "It's very tough to find slots for people like me. I really don't think there are a lot of places in a large corporation where I could thrive and be happy."

She is right about that. Twenty-five hundred miles away from Katheryn's Montgomery Street office, a few women in the sample were holding onto their feminine identity and having trouble at work. In declining to learn masculine behavior patterns, they stood like feminine outposts in alien territory, prime targets of attack. It wasn't simply a matter of shunning the standard business suit that made these women stand out. They remained true to certain feminine values that were maladaptive in a hierarchical organization. They didn't respect political behavior, for example, because it was important for them to be authentic in social relationships. Karen, in Chapter 11, has that value. Extending friendship to people because she wants them as allies seems false to her, and she refuses to do it.

> I'm totally unpolitical in dealing with people. I've seen it work to people's detriment and I decided I wanted no part of it. I'm sure that has impeded me in the firm. I know it has. But that's the way I've chosen to do it.

Why does Karen hold onto behavior she thinks is hurting her, and what would she have to do to change it?

> I think you have to throw yourself in a lot more with people you don't care to be around. That is a very fake thing on my part. I wouldn't invite people to my house unless they were friends. It would never occur to

me to throw a cocktail party for the political knowledge I could get out of it. I just don't think on that level.

In Karen's ethical system, it is more important to be socially authentic than to be political—in spite of the costs, which she is mulling over. Single and thirty-seven, Karen would like to upgrade her professional status; she now thinks work will have to compensate for a larger share of her life than she ever realized. But doing that will mean a change in identity, because the feminine ethos Karen holds onto stands in her way.

There were other signs that Karen maintains an integrated system of beliefs and practices which she cannot change without feeling that she runs the risk of becoming masculine. Looking pretty is important to her sense of well-being at work, more important than looking authoritative, so Karen dresses in traditional feminine clothing rather than business suits. She thinks that if she changed any of this, she would be negating her basic sexual identity.

> I love to feel like I'm a lady. I wouldn't want it any other way. I think when you react negatively to [the idea] of being a lady, you're almost negating your whole sex. That's another problem with the people who wear the suits. I've never tried to change my act at all on that score.

The difficulty is that Karen often feels harassed at work by one of the partners in the firm, and she does not know how to stop these assaults. Being a lady, she likes to conduct herself always in a nice and accept-able way, almost as though she puts herself on a pedestal, so it would violate her rules of feminine behavior to confront the man who bugs her. Meanwhile, he goes around nitpicking and interfering with her clients when she's on vacation.

Karen is not by any stretch of the imagination a weak-kneed individ-ual. She manages millions of dollars in other people's money. She con-ducts professional meetings, heads committees, and, on the whole, accepts a great deal of responsibility for social action. Authentic, funny, and gallant, she can express the vulnerable childlike qualities that give life and spontaneity—the things that keep us honest. When Karen says she is not afraid to be emotional, she is expressing a value system that requires inner strength to carry out in a world where being emotional may draw attack. She has this to say about what it means to be feminine:

191

It's a different point of view than men express. It's a great gift that women bring to business. A lot of times they are more intuitive about things, more aware of the real feelings going on in the boardroom. We get more vibrations. I think I am able, because I am feminine, to really psych out when a client is unhappy. I listen and I can figure out a lot more. Feminine says you're capable of being emotional. And you are not afraid to be emotional.

Yet she is crippled by this gender identity, because it also lacks power. In Karen's mind, a feminine woman is not aggressive, and that belief means she cannot accept either what her life requires or what she has become. The feminine identity stands behind her like a shadow, undermining and diminishing her powers, causing her to say to herself:

Is this really me, doing all this stuff? How did I get here? Do I belong here? Do I deserve this? Do I really know enough?

It's weird. We [women] were never conditioned to accept all this responsibility. It's not that we can't. So there's a real struggle going on there.

To bring her old identity into line with the new, Karen would have to do something that feels completely wrong and undesirable, something that violates her ethics. She would have to do the symbolic equivalent of burning her bra, and through that act of eradication suspend the old identity, allowing her self-concept to float to new levels, trying out new skills, finding new powers. She wouldn't become a man if she did that, but she thinks she would, and the belief puts her out of touch with her own authority.

As the thousands of words from these forty-four women were transcribed and their answers compared, I found other women with attitudes like Karen's, not many, but a few who spoke of needing to be themselves rather than adapt in ways they felt were necessary for success. In each case, the statements came, not from women who were mothers, but from single women with frustrated desires to be mothers. These were the women who held on most strongly to a feminine identity that seemed to hobble them professionally. It was an unpleasant discovery at first: Women who expressed themselves as emotional, sexual, or authentic individuals had trouble in this professional world, especially in the New York environment.

Leslie looked like Everywoman: medium-sized, light-haired, nice-looking, and touched with a sense of weariness, as though she had coped with too many things. She wouldn't have stood out in a crowd, except for her voice, which rippled out strong and clear, vibrating in the lower registers. It was the kind of voice that could unmask the truth, the voice of a mature woman who had been working at a challenging job for years and had learned to trust herself. Quick and powerful, but not dominating. No big performances; just the truth. We sat in her Manhattan living room late into the evening. She hadn't wanted to talk in her office. In fact, she sounded downright dubious about the whole idea of an interview until she learned I would come to her apartment after work. Now she was curled up in a corner of the couch, with her shoes off, sipping tea while the voice rolled on, over the past, over pains and regrets, battles and betrayals—the self-examination of a woman caught at the crossroads of change, unprepared and so unfulfilled, but without self-pity.

Leslie is not happy at work. Upper management doesn't trust her; she believes they are afraid of her because she speaks her mind. The office recently went through a bloodbath in which many people were fired and Leslie was passed over. Now, although she is slated for promotion, she doesn't particularly want the job being offered. In fact, the man who wants to promote her and who thinks she is a real team player once called her a "hard-nosed broad from New York" and "volatile." The whole thing makes no sense—neither the initial attack nor the resurrection—because Leslie has not changed. She thinks it's better for her to leave than to try adapting to this environment. The people she enjoyed working with are gone anyway, most of them dismissed.

Leslie is an individual. She dresses in her own style, disdaining the Wall Street "cookie-cutter" look, the business suit in blue or gray. Moreover, she is open and friendly at work. She tends to react emotionally, from the gut, rather than hiding her feelings, and her face shows a lot. She knows she could change the way people deal with her ("Maybe I need a course in assertiveness"). But alongside this knowledge runs a consistent inner thread: Leslie is herself, with a strong sense of right and wrong, and a firm belief that if you do a good job, you will be rewarded—despite all the evidence to the contrary.

I think I react from a gut level a lot of the time and perhaps a professional doesn't do that as much as I do. . . . I've always been extremely honest, not only honest, but outspoken. I don't think I could ever be anything else. . . . I'm not good at manipulation. I shoot from the hip and look at it later.

Also, I was brought up to think that if you did a good job, you would be rewarded. Father said, "Change jobs if you wish, but as long as you're in one, do a good job." Those are the words I have lived by. I really do believe, and I know that's not true. But I hold onto the things I think are important. Often they hurt you, but somehow it's important to have a standard to live by.

Leslie changed her behavior once, to become more, not less, honest. She began speaking out about things she didn't like. The first time it happened, it was as if another voice came out of her mouth when she answered back to a superior who was acting like a bully. Everyone was shocked, including herself. Then she started doing it a little bit more. The honesty was powerful and it felt good.

From then on, when I didn't like the way things were going, about a company or what we were doing, I would stick up for my rights. . . . I have a quick tongue, and once you kill, it's easier to kill the next time.

Leslie has spoken up to a senior man in her department, a hatchet-man who fired several of her friends. The man has threatened Leslie, calling her a bad influence and demanding that she change her attitude.

I recognize that I represent some sort of power to this man. A negative force. I've spoken out when he has disciplined my peers. People in front of me. I've left the room. That kind of thing means I'm not on the team.

In hindsight, Leslie thinks she should have been more politically minded for her own good ("I should have been quieter"), but she still would have been loyal to her friends, no matter what the consequences: "I'm my person, not theirs." In those five words lies the will of the unreconstructed woman, who does not grasp the degree to which men surrender authentic expression to survive in hierarchical organizations. In the Army, good team players don't criticize the boss, no matter what he does.

At the same time that Leslie takes the risk of being powerfully honest in public, inside herself she doesn't feel very tough. She's afraid of being aggressive. She doesn't want to get the reputation of being difficult with men; she's sensitive and eager to please. She used to be easily hurt, which was hard to hide because her tears were close to the surface. Fortunately, that has changed over the years, as Leslie gets better and better at drawing on her own inner resources for reinforcement. "For all my hard-nosed broadness, I'm really not a very tough person. . . . Basically, it's my mouth that's gotten me into trouble. My sense of right and wrong."

In her private life, Leslie is running out the clock, with fear and longing about the idea of having a family. She won't bear a child outside of marriage and she won't get married just to have one. Soon the decision will be taken out of her hands. Leslie is thirty-nine. She delayed getting involved in the early years because she was eager to succeed, hopefully to win her father's approval. Also, she was waiting for the right man to come along to take her away from it all—the Cinderella syndrome.

Leslie is respected by her co-workers and maintains excellent rapport with clients in the field, but still she has this problem with upper management. For a while, she believed she was in truth volatile, as they said, but her faith in herself has returned. She thinks there is a place where she will fit without having to sacrifice things she feels are important and change in ways that seem dishonest to her, like learning politics and hiding her feelings. "They have beaten me to some extent, but I'm not dead."

K aren and Leslie are both women to whom being themselves is a primary value. They don't particularly want to change. Expressing their own authentic personalities is more important to them than projecting an image to manipulate the perceptions of other people. They tend to be honest and accessible as human beings. By all the ethics of the private sphere, where feminine culture predominates, these women are doing things right. The vast psychological literature on intimate relationships supports this theme: that honesty, loyalty, authenticity, and vulnerability are the keys to love and health. And they are. Relationships without those qualities become battlegrounds rather than sanctuaries. And yet, those admirable human traits are not particularly adaptive in a political environment, which includes corporations and most professional settings where the majority of people are masking their feelings

195

to protect themselves and projecting an image to win increased power and status. From the vantage point of feminine ethics, this seems wrong, destructive to individual happiness. It probably is destructive—to the individual, but not to the institution, which is what masculine culture is all about.

In their book *The Managerial Woman,* Margaret Hennig and Anne Jardim talk about the astonishment of female executives who watch two male colleagues sit down in a business meeting and exchange friendly chitchat, knowing that the men dislike and disrespect each other. How can they do it? Why do they do it? The answer is, because they need each other on the team and the product is more important than individual feelings. Or, to put it more opportunistically, they want to win and will play ball with whoever makes that more likely. Surrendering individual expression to the team is a price the man pays for economic success; without it he has fewer chances of becoming a husband and father. Even in liberated times, women have trouble accepting a man who ekes out a living for the privilege of being his own person.

If that sounds grim, it is not totally devoid of sense. The practice of extending friendship to people for political or professional reasons is the glue that keeps institutions operating, and the ability to move beyond personal feelings marks the individual as one capable of handling authority. There is a transformation involved for some women who move to this level, and who find that they must leave behind elements of their past, associated with the person they were. They make a deliberate decision to change the way they present themselves in the world, often symbolized by a radical change in dress (the act of eradication), followed by the conscious acquisition of new behaviors. Not only the clothes, but non-verbal gestures, interpersonal relationships, and mental attitudes all are trained and processed for one purpose: to project the right image. The right image, of course, being that of a go-getter, a star, a winner.

From the perspective of someone who has not gone through the process, image making seems wrong; yet that is the way women in this profession take control of their careers, particularly in New York, where they've learned, for better or for worse, that success depends on keeping up an expanded profile and an impregnable front. Said one young, ambitious woman in New York:

When you come to work, no one knows anything about the things that hurt. That's why you have so many people at work whose marriages are failing and you never know about it. At work, you are a star.

This woman wasn't going to tell people at work about her impending marriage for fear it would change their image of her, from that of a professional to that of a traditional woman.

Another financial woman in New York presents herself as indistinguishable from a man,

. . . because I want the same job and the same recognition. I like to have credibility. I like the fact that my work product is appreciated. It's only the man's way because they set it up. If women start doing it, it will be the woman's way. Until there is enough power and control, we have to play by the rules of the game. . . . I have no sympathy for someone who feels they haven't been accepted and they come in wearing a red dress or a shirt dripping with jewelry.

This woman once wore pants to a luncheon, shocking everyone into a new awareness of her personal identity. They told her they couldn't believe she dresses that casually. "That's the way they see me, and that's the way I want it. I'm seen only as a professional."

Image making is like putting on a mask that cuts down the flow of spontaneous, personal information, allowing other people to see only the professional identity. There is an individual behind the mask, so we are not talking about wooden performances, but about a limited projection of the self. People see only what they are supposed to see. Behind the mask, the individual stages the show with her own personal flair. No two masks are alike. Their purpose is not to convey uniformity but to manipulate the perception of an audience. In this sense, professional masks are like real masks displayed in museums. The actual articles, brought back by anthropologists from native peoples, were not stamped out by machines; they were made by individuals, and each is different. Small distinctions in color, style, and expression reflect the choices of the person who designed them. But all of them shroud normal human sensitivity and project an image.

Narrowing channels of personal information is only half the game. The other half is to feed out images of success, which the image maker does by dressing and acting in the role of someone with higher status. "I believe you don't get promoted until people already see you at that level," said one woman, who turned up one day at a business cocktail party dressed in expensive clothes. One of her superiors remarked innocently, "We don't pay you enough to dress like that," to which she replied, "No, but you will." This same woman once went through a difficult exercise in learning to dissemble. She had been an outspoken person, prone to letting people know what she thought of them. One man in particular she didn't respect:

> He was a dumb schmuck. No other word for it. Six foot three, broad shoulders, officer training, one wife, 2.2 kids, and dumb. He couldn't manage worth a damn, but he got promoted up the run. He could not communicate with anyone who was not in his likeness and image. But who could tell that, because when he walked in the door, people said, "Gee, he's got to be president or something!"

One day, this woman's boss walked into her office, sat down, and told her that by reputation she was not well liked. "Even people who don't know you, hate you," she recalled him saying. He advised her to take a course in management training that required her to visit people in their offices, sit down, relax, put her hands on the table ("So they are not white-knuckled"), and talk only about things of interest to the other person.

> I started with Mr. Anapolis: "Ahhh, that is a fascinating little baseball you have on your desk. Why do you have it there? Is that a big interest of yours? It is? You've had it since you were twelve? How interesting that you would have kept it all these years!"

Her voice was sticky with sweet sarcasm in describing this exercise, but there were serious payoffs for her both personally and professionally.

> After a while, you find out that even with really dumb people, there is some salvage point that you can find and relate to them. The next year I went to a manpower conference and my boss was congratulated on the terrific improvement in my behavior. And I did get promoted.

Because of her lessons in applied charm, this woman now makes efforts to reach other people on their home ground: How was your weekend? How was the girlfriend? How did you do in the race last night? But these communications occur within strict limits about what can be revealed. And others do the same with her. One young man who works for her will come in, sit down, and ask about her son, seriously listening for her reply. She knows he's trying to soften her up, but she gets excited anyway, because she loves to talk about her son. The technique works.

As opportunistic as this goodwill may seem, it has the positive effects of oiling the human machinery of an institution and overriding potentially destructive personal likes and dislikes that could tear a working group apart if they were allowed free rein. Moreover, the practice of extending friendship for political purposes does feed back into value systems. Over time, this woman's ambitious aggression—which had been patently selfish—broadened to include other people. She stopped trying to make other people look bad and ultimately came to the conclusion that there were no winners on a losing team. "The higher you go, the more you realize it is the success of the whole. You really have to bring the whole team along."

Many women wonder if all this manipulation and image making is necessary. They think it means masculinization and they rail at the suggestion that women must emulate men to be professionally successful. Why dress like the men do? Why change feminine behavior?

The simplest reply to this is that women won't make it in a male-dominated authority structure if they don't change to fit the prevailing culture, whatever the profession. At a sheer survival level, some aspects of feminine conditioning are maladaptive in public roles; to insist on staying the same in a changed environment is like choosing a form of glorious defeat. To some extent, we are like our fathers of one or two generations ago who moved from farms and factories into professions. They also experienced an identity crisis and picked up the rudiments of new behavior from books and seminars. Professional women have left the old feminine world as surely as Vietnamese immigrants have left Southeast Asia. There is no going back.

In striving for professional authority, women enter a culture in which some degree of masking seems essential. Image making is the process by which professionals grow in power and authority. They build themselves by constructing castles in the air and claiming they already live there. The public statement becomes an imperative to perform, and in

199

fulfilling the promise, the professional grows. All of this is directed, not by someone passing down job descriptions, but by the individual herself. She is responsible for her future. She stages the show. She provides the authority. To avoid the process is to decline responsibility for power. Only by submitting to change of this sort can professional women come out at the end of the tunnel with renewed strength and a more powerful sense of themselves as female.

The deeper reason for changing is that women need to train their innate power so that it can function beneficently in the public sphere. Females possess the elemental power of the mother, a charismatic authority capable of carrying both sexes back into childish states of mind. Men fear this power when they see women gaining positions of authority and equality on the job, and they are not the only ones. Quite a few women fear it as well. It's up to women to bring this power to the front in their own minds, acknowledge it, accept it, and recognize its effects on other people. The task is made more difficult when women are driven to deny their natural power, to suit non-aggressive ideals of femininity. Traditional culture enforces this blindness. Women are not supposed to be aggressive, but they are. Women are not supposed to have authority in the home, but they do.

Karen and Leslie both had powerful mothers who frightened and intimidated them as children, as did several other women in the middle. Yet, in their own lives, the feminine identity is weak or lacking in aggression, as if they must disown the example of their mothers. Exercising authority feels uncomfortable, fraught with the danger of being considered a castrating bitch, and when the power comes out—as it does from time to time—it comes out untrammeled and untrained, lacking in legitimacy.

Leslie's powerful voice was like that. When she stood up for what she believed, the sounds that came out of her mouth surprised everyone, including Leslie. She wants to give that voice free rein; it is, after all, the source of her natural power. But, at some level, she also wants to deny that, as evidenced by the fact that her personal definitions of herself as a feminine person lack strength. Until she alters her concept of femininity, her power will be illegitimate, something to be kept in the back room, to make its scary appearance at unplanned moments with the face of the bitch. To continue believing that a feminine individual has neither power nor aggression is to continue living a cultural lie that serves the purpose of crippling female authority. We have to embrace the bitch and train the mother. She's had a bad press for too long.

S uch an identity change is extremely hard on women—or anyone else. It's all most people can do to cope with a new culture, much less deal with the inner life, intimate relationships, and maternal power all at the same time. But, hard as it is, the process is not complete until women return to themselves in new form, exchanging weakness for strength at the heart of the feminine identity. It's not enough to have power in professional roles, because they are essentially lonely ones. Image making and masking behavior, for all their value in exercising public authority, are thoroughly destructive at the intimate level, where winning does not work. The need to be invulnerable, to have no loose edges, originates in distrust—the sense that feelings, openings, spontaneity, and sexuality will be used against you. Visions of feminine people as emotional wrecks or powerless victims drive many women to keep the image of invulnerability in place, not only at work but in their private lives as well. To open up those emotional places, to trust again, is asking a lot. But what choice do we have? The alternative is to live out singular lives with a level of independence most men couldn't reach and wouldn't want. It took strength for women to achieve positions of authority in this culture. It takes just as much strength to return to home ground, toughened but willing to be exposed.

Because they are alone, with fewer emotional outlets, single women experience more stress in dealing with the restrictions and inhibitions of the professional identity. They may try to combine their professional and personal lives, where married women keep them separate. They may vent their feelings at work and wish they didn't but lack the means of controlling their behavior because emotional support is not available. And they may be attracted to men at work, running the risk of involving their sexual lives in a political sphere that can be personally very dangerous. The chapters that follow spell out the rules being developed in financial circles to control sexuality among professional equals. Before, when men held the only power in the office, it didn't matter what they did. Now it does matter, and the interviews in this study indicate the appearance of a widespread taboo on sexual activity.

V

Sex
and
Corporations

13

The
Office Incest
Taboo

S tories of employers having love affairs with their secretaries are le-
gion in business—by far the most common type of sexual liaison,
or so it appears from the things that people say about sex in the office.
In the typical executive couple, all the traditional power relationships
between the genders hold true. Men wield public authority; women
stand behind them as intellectual and political assistants. For her personal commitment, a clerical woman achieves power and status in her
boss's name. The man carries the responsibility; the woman puts her
power and energy at his service. It is a familiar bargain, leading directly
to close personal bonds which may or may not become sexual. The
only thing that has changed about this classic relationship is that once
men just had love affairs with their secretaries; today, they are likely to
get divorced and marry them.

The professional woman, however, comes into the office as an equal,
either competitive or cooperative with men, but not ready to bond in a
complementary union. To hide her light behind a man by serving him
would be like giving away the keys to the kingdom after winning entrance at the gates. Moreover, she has control over her work life in a
way that a secretary can never have, since the secretary is vulnerable to
the power of one individual. She can decide whether to respond sexually and under what circumstances, without feeling that her job is on
the line or in the bed. If professional women have all this control, what
choices are they making? What are they doing about sexuality in the

office? Have they been overcome by the excitement of working with men toward a common goal, or are they acting out the myths of male behavior with a license for hunting? What is going on in the new, sexually integrated office of professional men and women?

The short answer to the last question is, not much. Far from taking license or being swept away, female professionals in finance have chosen to become the new Puritans. Their dedication to work, combined with their internal controls over sexual and emotional behavior, are impressive. And if the barriers they have erected seem a little high to men, who wish the women would act softer and more accessible, that is part of the transition toward sexual equality. The women have a point to make to themselves, the men they work with, and the world at large. They are there to work, not play around.

"I don't have much sympathy for that," said one woman in San Francisco, referring to love affairs at work. "When I was single, I wouldn't date anyone connected in any way with work—bankers, clients, people within the business."

And from a woman in New York: "I have no patience with a woman who mixes up her personal and business life . . . most women are not receptive to this at all. They would react as distastefully as I have. So [any woman who was involved with a man at work] would keep her mouth shut. I have no patience for it. I think it screws us all."

These were the hardest and most judgmental reactions I recorded to the subject of sex in the office. But they represent a common attitude among women that getting sexually involved with a man at work is not a good idea. The most liberal expression among the forty-four women came from a Wall Street broker who had moved from California to New York:

> It seems very natural to me. You spend a lot of hours at work, and it's quite likely that you would meet a man. Your sexual life is your own. There shouldn't be any consequences. Women feel they will not be well thought of. They're afraid of what the community will think. But I've seen men have affairs. Why shouldn't I?

Yet even though she had liberal attitudes, this woman behaved conservatively in many ways. She didn't think it was appropriate for men in the office to hug her or kiss her. She had learned to tolerate rather than reject being touched, but she considered it unprofessional behavior.

Professional women have erected a taboo against sex in the office. A majority of women I interviewed in New York and San Francisco share this taboo. Although some have broken it, they say things like "It's stupid," "unwise," "a bad idea," or, "I wouldn't do it again," about their actions. Married women are more likely to disapprove than single women, which is not surprising; they have less need for finding intimates. But the differences were not great. In San Francisco, when I asked if it was all right to have a love affair with someone at work, 75 percent of the married women said no, an opinion shared by 60 percent of the single women. In New York, the percentage saying no was only slightly lower: 66 percent of the married women and 40 percent of the single women. It seems that single women in New York were the only lenient ones in the group, but appearances are deceiving. Only one out of every two single women I approached in New York would even be interviewed on the subject. Talking about sex in the office was as taboo as doing it.

Their reasons for refusing an interview paint a picture of great concern and avoidance. "This is a very conservative company. Do you want me to get fired?" asked one contact. "I'm not interested in that subject," and, "That would not be appropriate," said two others. Two women mentioned fear of losing their jobs if they agreed to an interview. One said there is no such thing as sex in the office; it doesn't occur.

> A professional woman should not have such problems. Sex is absolutely out of place. If a woman is a serious professional, it should not occur. You have your work and you have your fun—outside the office.

Their reactions indicate that the single women I did interview in New York were selected for their willingness to talk about sexual behavior. Perhaps, if the New York singles had been as open as the women in San Francisco (only one individual refused an interview in that city), the vote against involvement at work would have been as high, or higher. Married women in New York were much more willing to be interviewed; unmarried women seemed especially careful—and threatened.

But even in a Puritan society, people fall in and out of love and some get married. Those things are happening among professional equals, although not at the rate people might expect who are unaware of the inhibitions and prohibitions that operate in the sexually integrated office. The taboo against becoming involved with a close working associate is so widely and firmly held by so many professionals of both sexes that anyone who breaks it does so in secrecy with their knees shaking, hoping they can relocate before their private life spills out into the public arena at work. A woman in San Francisco kept such a love affair secret for three years, and although people will say that can't be done, she seems to have succeeded by telling absolutely no one, not even her closest friends, about her budding relationship. "The hardest part was not being able to share my happiness." Even now, when the two work for different companies and there is no longer any need for discretion, she has a hard time talking about her personal life at work. It had become a habit to keep mum.

Margaret Mead suggested some years ago that, like the family, modern business and modern professions must develop incest taboos:

> If women are to work on an equal basis with men . . . we have to develop decent sex mores in the whole working world. . . . What we need, in fact, are new taboos that will operate within the work setting as once they operated within the household. Neither men nor women should expect that sex can be used either to victimize women who need to keep their jobs, or to keep women from advancement, or to help men advance their own careers. A taboo enjoins. We need one that says clearly and unequivocally, "You don't make passes at or sleep with the people you work with."

My interviews with financial men and women tell me that such a taboo has since developed. Understanding the taboo involves a tour through the social environment of financial institutions—an environment that had its rules about sexual behavior before women ever entered as equals, an environment that is far more political than it is personal, where love affairs are dangerous because they make people vulnerable to double doses of trouble when things go bad. A man or woman who, for whatever reasons, has trouble with a sexual or romantic union in a career setting runs the risk of being hurt professionally as well as personally.

Midway down the Wall Street chute stands a venerable American institution, its stone- and ironwork a monument to the glories of nineteenth-century capitalism—the bank built by J. P. Morgan. Morgan Guaranty is one of the last of the truly magnificent and opulent bank buildings. Most of the other banks have moved from their historic quarters into new towers, where mechanical elevators carry the bankers from empty lobbies to small offices high in the air. At Morgan Guaranty, the past is reflected in every burnished brass knob and gilded chair. The front gates open onto a cavernous room, hung with a glittering chandelier. The ceiling soars overhead, carved and decorated.

If there had been any sound in the room it would have echoed across the vast expanse of open, shining floor. In fact, there were many people working in the main room the day I arrived, but no sounds. Two smiling guards greeted me at the door and asked me to wait on a couch while they telephoned my arrival. I sank into the soft cushions and looked around. In the time I waited for the interviewee, about half an hour, not a single head looked up and not a word was spoken. I wondered how they could remain still for so long.

Morgan Guaranty represents a pinnacle in the civilized, reserved, traditional world of banking. In this realm, business is conducted with a great deal of charm and little revelation of feelings or information about one's personal life. Men make the social rules. They form the core of the authority structure. Often, they have social networks of friends in business that spill out in a continuous stream from the professional to the private life; but not always. Men in finance may separate their private and public lives, just as the women do. But by and large, these are people whose marital and professional relationships have lasted twenty years, and they know each other. Women have yet to break into the upper echelons in any numbers. A few front runners have succeeded, and they feel like sexual oddities at the top. If such a female senior executive participates in the social network, she may find that she is the only woman in the room with professional standing. All the other women are there by virtue of marriage, and she cannot identify with them socially or culturally. One top executive described the sensation as one of being the only member of a third sex.

Normally, the men are socially stable, although divorce is becoming more common, and their views on home, sex, and marriage affect the formal and informal rules for sexual behavior in the office. Married people are expected to be faithful to their spouses, for instance; and that value was mentioned more often in New York than in San Francisco. A man who breaks the rule may find his career snubbed off, either temporarily or permanently. "A man who cheats on his wife will cheat on the company," said one senior executive. It appears that in professional ranks, men get hurt as often as women do by an indiscreet love affair.

Formal rules governing sexual behavior are the rules against nepotism. Financial institutions ordinarily will not employ husbands and wives together in the same company, although big banks have less restrictive policies, and the rules are changing as professional women enter in greater and greater numbers. Company rules only mention marriage within the institution, not romance, but through social custom, the prohibition spreads to cover all sexual relationships. "Don't fish off the company pier" is one way to express the custom.

A tall and very well dressed man approached me across the shining floor. He was so gentle and personable, I had a hard time associating him with my image of Morgan as a hard-driving boss. William guided me to an adjoining room for an interview, where we sat at a baronial table, dwarfed at one end by the expanse of table and regal chairs. It seemed stunningly incongruous in those surroundings to talk about sexual behavior at work. If William had been an aloof executive, it would have been impossible, but he was surprisingly accessible as a human being.

All the men I interviewed were recommended by friends as people who would be interested in and able to talk about the subject, so the male sample is biased toward sensitive, aware individuals. I asked William whether he thought it was all right to have a love affair with a woman he worked with. The question, asked of everyone, reveals what social mores are developing to regulate sexual behavior in the office. It tells what people think they should do, not what they actually do.

He answered:

> From my own point of view, no, and I think, generally, no. I would be out of my mind to have an affair with somebody at this bank. I don't think I could isolate the affair from our relationship at work. There would be phone calls during the day. There would be—maybe not lunch at the bank because that would be too obvious—but longer lunches than you would ordinarily take. And if I saw her having lunch with somebody else or being particularly attentive, I know I would have jealous feelings. I think that compromises your ability to do a good job. It would be a mistake.

And for other people?

> If somebody I knew was having a love affair in the bank . . . well, you have to distinguish between people who are married and those who are unmarried. If two unmarried people fell in love and were sleeping together, I couldn't quarrel with that, but if somebody is married . . . that doesn't make any sense to me. It would be a reflection on his or her judgment. Professionally, if it were found out in management circles, it could compromise their careers.

William said he could see no reason why two unmarried professionals in the bank should not have a relationship, but there was a dubious tone to his comments.

> You hear stories of people who are inclined to do this sort of thing. I've heard of one-night stands from time to time on business trips. It's general knowledge that two bankers in [another region] spend all their spare time in bed when they go away on a trip. I just can't believe that doesn't have an effect on their boss. Maybe it's good for them, I don't know. But I don't think the bank would look favorably on it.

The wives of executive men often fear the growing ranks of female professionals because they bring so many talented women into close proximity with their husbands, especially on business trips. Bankers may have to reassure their wives or alter travel patterns so as not to make them jealous. In spite of these tensions, it has become increasingly commonplace for professional men and women to travel together. Gradually, the fear and gossip surrounding that custom are dying out as it becomes evident that professional women, and many men as well, function under a sexual taboo. Said William:

> People who travel together inevitably feel some sort of attraction, but I would say that most do not get involved. It's almost inevitable that if you are with somebody who's bright and a physically attractive person, that certainly there are temptations. But you just . . . It's a great mistake to get involved, and I think that 90 percent of the people here would react that way.

There were stories of men and women who traveled together for years without touching each other. One very attractive, vibrant woman

211

commented on her experience traveling with male colleagues by saying, "Most men, no way."

Nevertheless, the fears of what might happen still plague the lives of professional women. A highly placed financial woman told this story with a voice heavy with sighs:

> I was always traveling with men, so there were always lots of rumors. It didn't matter what I did or didn't do. There were going to be rumors anyway, so I just had to insulate myself from being hurt by it. Some men did indicate a sexual interest and a great many did not. But everyone speculated, whenever I went on a trip with someone, about whether or not we slept together. It didn't matter who it was.
>
> Now that [men and women are traveling] much more often, I think more people are willing to assume that nothing is there, which is a help. But it's still true in many cases that men are edgy about traveling with women because of how it will look or what they will say to their wives.

One man she traveled with stayed in another hotel for appearance's sake. On another occasion, an executive told her he couldn't hire her because his wife would be jealous at the notion of the two traveling together.

The taboo against love affairs often—but not always—includes flirting in a business setting. Defined as sexual seductiveness or as an invitation, flirting is considered offbase by the majority. Defined in broader social terms as teasing and banter, flirting is an important and positive aspect of working behavior. Several women were unaware that flirting could be used in playful social behavior without misinterpretation on the part of men. They had adopted a serious attitude because they thought if they didn't they would be encouraging a sexual overture.

But flirting has multiple uses. One male executive said he flirts only with the professional women who are doing a good job. It is a sign of his acceptance, not an invitation to bed. And there seems to be a level of flirting or rapport between the sexes that is positively valued in business. William said he would consider flirting right on the borderline of acceptable behavior, but

> If you have lunch with somebody, you like to have the feeling that you are an attractive man, and to a certain extent, that involves flirting, not suggestive remarks, but smiling and just trying to be an attractive man to

an attractive woman. If that's flirting, then, yea, I'm guilty of that. I think most people like to feel attractive to the opposite sex. To that extent, there is a certain amount of flirting that goes on. It's harmless, really.

A female banker in New York, socially adept and professionally successful, paused for a moment in confusion over the question. After saying that flirting was not all right at work, she went on to add:

> Yet, in some senses I suspect we do [flirt]. I think men and women talk differently. There is something personal going on. I don't know if it's male and female, or just me as a person. Maybe men and women talk differently because there is some rapport or trust, and it's not really flirting, but it is . . . I just realized what it is . . . I treat everybody the same. I treat service assistants with the same kind of bantering and kidding around that I do the senior people, and because of that, I'm not as reverent as a lot of people are.

Uptown in a huge, shimmering blue-glass tower, Citibank, one of the two largest banks in the country, sets the pace for contemporary trends. Filled with youthful, aggressive professionals, the Citibank environment has a reputation for being socially liberal, sexually active, and more brutal in its youthful dynamism than other smaller and more traditional banks. Compared to the formal procedures at most banks for announcing visitors, Citibank was casual in the extreme. The day I arrived, I found a Puerto Rican boy lounging at the front desk while the receptionist was away (to be fair, the area I visited does not normally serve the public). He waved me to the back of the building where he thought the man I was looking for was located. "You mean, I can just go back there by myself?" I asked, amazed. He smiled and shrugged his shoulders.

Citibank employs a high percentage of women and minority groups. It also makes a lot of money. The more traditional banks are looking twice at this success, trying to figure out the right formula. "Hire more aggressive women," was one solution being talked about in the latter half of 1981, the kind of women who can "chew nails and spit out thumbtacks," added one male executive.

Sexually and socially, Citibank more nearly fits the popular conception of what can happen when large numbers of young, energetic, single men and women get together in a supercharged working

213

environment. Friends and lovers are common; marriages blossom. People work long hours and may wind up sharing an intense and exclusive focus on business. According to one man:

> Lots of young, attractive, dynamite people are thrown together at Citibank. [The company] hires hoards of young MBAs who come in working very hard, committed to the same sorts of things, and who may be married to someone who doesn't think you ought to work seventeen hours a day. What you find is other women who do. Pretty soon, you are thrown together and . . . uh. . . . A fair amount of marriages occur at Citibank because of that.

But even here, in this high-powered and socially liberal working environment, the sexual restrictions operate. Two women who had worked at Citibank described spontaneous barriers that arose in their heads to prevent intimacy. They were simply not attracted to men with whom they worked closely. Both had made the decision that having a love affair in the working environment was a bad idea—personally too risky— and they formed platonic, not sexual, relationships with male colleagues. Their reactions acted as a powerful antagonist to sex in the office. Neither of the women, who were young and attractive, felt any romantic interest in the men. It wasn't as if they were trying to hold themselves back. In the case of one, a romantic interest developed after she had left the bank and started to date a man she had formerly worked with.

Citibank has formal rules governing marriage among its employees, rules that have changed over the past ten years in response to the increase in female professionals. Earlier, employees could not be married to anyone in the bank. Over the decade of the 1970s, that prohibition collapsed into smaller and smaller areas, until now it includes only the group known as the "direct reporting relationship," which varies in size from a handful of people to several hundred. These are workers with direct responsibility for each other in salary and promotion. That territory is out-of-bounds for love and marriage. If a relationship develops within the group, supervisors do something about it. Usually, they talk to the man and move the woman to another unit in the bank. Moving the woman may seem like sexual discrimination, but the choice is based on seniority, not sex. Ordinarily, the woman has inferior rank.

I wandered through the halls at Citibank, asking directions along the way until I found the office I was looking for. I was late and the office was empty. A secretary motioned me in to wait until my interviewee arrived, coatless and casual. He looked like the man next door. I had the sense I was sitting in the middle of a community, talking to one of the residents.

> I met my wife here. Lots of people I know have gotten married as a result of meeting in the work environment. It's only natural. You spend so much time at work. In fact, that's how our chairman met his wife. She was a lawyer for a firm that worked for Citibank.

He said the bank had changed dramatically over the past decade.

> It used to be, ten years ago, that the bank wouldn't allow any employees to be married. Then the rule changed to where you couldn't be in the same group. I guess this was in the early seventies. There were more and more instances of senior, talented, good people who were getting into this situation [involved with each other] and more and more women. It wasn't so much of a problem when there weren't many women in senior positions, but as women were added to the employee and executive base, it became more of a problem. We didn't want to lose good people for what was considered an outdated rule.
>
> They narrowed it [rules against nepotism] down to where you couldn't be in the same division. But we'd still be losing a lot of good people. Now it's just the direct reporting relationship, where you could influence salary and promotion. Even there, if the senior person did not review the status of a junior person, a relationship might be allowed. It's on a case by case basis.
>
> The guidelines only refer to married couples. There is no active effort to ferret out romances. What's business is business and what's personal is personal. It is expected that professional people will keep their personal relationships separate and out of the work environment.

When such expectations are not fulfilled at Citibank, the supervisor has a personal conversation with one of the couple. One man, friendly with his secretary, was spoken to and told that promotions would be affected by how he conducted himself in that relationship. "You should be aware of it and remedy the situation," he was told. The chosen remedy was to transfer the secretary.

* * *

Twenty-five hundred miles away, the brown-glass tower of the Bank of America Building climbs above the San Francisco skyline, rivaled only by the spire of the Transamerica Building. Inside this modern setting, the bank's interior still maintains some symbols of traditional banking: a cavernous main room gently lit by brass lamps on dark wooden desks. Bank of America has none of Citibank's reputation for a roiling social atmosphere. Six of the eight women I interviewed there have neither friends nor lovers at work. They maintain a separate private life and do not ordinarily socialize with co-workers. Said one:

> Bank of America people don't tend to socialize. Maybe you get together at lunch or when someone has a birthday party, but there isn't much real social interaction—really getting to know each other—outside of work. I haven't been able to figure this out. There is something here in the general organization that seems to [cut down on social interaction].

A male senior executive confirmed that impression:

> My experience is that while there are long-standing professional relationships, there are not that many social relationships. Some other companies are not like that, but I'm saying here in the bank. I think you'll find that around the Bank of America [people separate personal and work lives]. I do not single out people here and invite them to my house. I don't play bridge with them, go bowling or skiing. But I consider some to be very good friends of mine. So there probably is a dichotomy. If you have close associations with people from work, business can slop over. You're in a social setting and suddenly you're talking business again. I don't like to do that.

Nevertheless, marriages do arise from the bank. Sometimes entire families are employed, with the members in different branches following the long-standing rules against nepotism. The prohibitions against marriage, as in Citibank, apply only to the close working group. A woman who had watched the system operate described it this way:

> One couple just got married and she went into another department. In another case, they met outside, began working for the bank, and got married. The two are now in the same group and report up the same tree. That's an exception. Usually the couple is not in the same group, but the bank seems to feel they are far enough apart. He's on a slightly

higher level, but the number of tiers to their mutual boss is two, so they are equal. He could have no effect on her promotion.

What you see is that people are individually making the decisions. There's not a need for the bosses to come down and say, "We can't have that." When I was managing, one of my staff was going with a vice president. She came to me and said she needed to leave the area because she didn't think it was right for the two of them to be in the same area while they were getting serious. That's why she was out looking and I hired her. That was definitely her decision.

Love affairs within the group would be questioned, said my female informant. Both sexes accept the group as privileged ground, out-of-bounds for intimate ties. "You just don't work well when you're in that. . . . What if you have a fight? It just makes it hard to work."

Apparently, love affairs do occur among professionals within the group, but far less frequently than at Citibank. On many occasions at Citibank, supervisors acted to break up a romance or move the partners to different areas, away from the close working group where emotional, relational ties could interfere with business. At the Bank of America, the senior man I interviewed had experienced that only once in his tenure. A love affair was going on at the moment I interviewed him, much to his chagrin.

> Quite frankly, I don't like it. There is one going on here now, and I don't like it. In this office where we all walk around and see each other, it's tension on the job. You get into a fight with someone and you have to face them the next morning at work. There's no issue of promotions here, but I'm concerned. She was angry once. She took some time off and came back. But suppose they have another fight and she says, "Well, I'm going to leave." Then, I've got a problem and I have nothing to do with it. She just doesn't want to see the guy anymore.
>
> You have a husband and wife combination in an office and it can be destructive. If I see that happening, I will tell one of them to leave or break it up, because I don't want the whole office to feel uneasy because of them.

If the couple should decide to marry, their procedure would be to tell the supervisor, George, who would consider moving one of the couple. Until then, the affair falls under the informal rules—an expectation that men and women will keep their private business out of the office. Professionals are expected to be discreet. As long as a romance is handled with discretion, it will be ignored as much as possible. Whatever makes the relationship public will tend to make the couple vulnerable to social censure. Such behaviors as expressing emotion, whether in anger or affection, make the affair public and therefore indiscreet. Once marriage is announced, however, the affair must become public and then officers have to do something about it. George was waiting. "Maybe they'll come in. I don't know. I don't know if they plan to get married."

So far, the social environments I've described are all from banking. But there is another, very different setting in finance, so different, in fact, that it could be considered the opposite of the discreet, civilized, decorous world of banking and investment. If banking is Dr. Jekyll, the other environment—the world of trading and selling, the stock market in the raw—is Mr. Hyde. Financial women in New York call this environment the "snake pit" and the "zoo." Several referred to men there as animals.

Working under high pressure with the sound of a tickertape in their ears and open lines to any city in the nation at their fingertips, gambling in the millions and crowded into close quarters with no walls to separate them, financial traders act like John Belushi and his fraternity brothers in the movie *Animal House*. A female institutional trader with ten years' experience on Wall Street said the only thing that prepared her for the business was learning how to drink at fraternity parties without falling down. She detested and at the same time enjoyed the raw macho environment. One thing she did to protect herself was to keep absolutely silent about her personal life. She was never seen walking from the office with a business associate at night, for fear it would be broadcast around the office in the morning. But that didn't stop the speculations about her personal life in the wide-open locker-room atmosphere of a trading desk.

A few weeks after I came, they would start making cracks as I walked by: "Is it true you're sharing an apartment with Larry?" or something like that. If someone came from out of town and we were going out to discuss business, I left alone while there were still men around who saw each other. I always made it very clear that I went home alone. I didn't open up about my private life. They thought that was strange.

Anna, who was raised in the Midwest to respect manners and people's feelings, was tough enough to put her training aside and adapt, but the going was rough.

> For the first six months I was upset, under pressure, and I didn't perform all that terrifically. I used to make mistakes in math, especially when I was working for this one guy. [She made an ugly sound in her throat] I was his assistant and he used to insist at the end of the day, when I was madly trying to fix up my tickets and figure the positions and profits, he would insist that I stand in front of him and read off the long and short positions, while he talked about my underwear. He would imagine what I was wearing: "Why do you wear a bra?" Things like that. If I didn't react to one of his dirty little jokes, he would tattle on my mistakes. That one! He was hopeless! I hated him so much. You . . . cannot . . . believe . . . how . . . much! I mean, I really hated this person. Let's say despised. He didn't deserve to be hated.

Anna was getting wound up. She leaped from one story to another— laughing at times—with hardly a pause between the anecdotes.

> By and large, this is just a zoo business. You have to be careful not to be too intellectual. Now, I'm talking about trading. If you talk to a retail broker who goes into a beautiful office instead of into a trading room, and the air conditioning works, and they have lunch like normal people, it will be different. But in trading, I mean, it's *uncivilized.* Some of it's funny, if you can get over the shock of the first six months.
>
> People come in very relaxed. They don't worry about how they look or how they are dressed. If the tie didn't come from Tie City, you're considered a good dresser. Or if you even wear a tie. If a young woman came through on a tour, there would be yells and wolf calls: "Would I!" or, "Did you see that pair of . . . ?" Even strangers. They didn't care.
>
> Or they'd do things like put a hit on somebody, either because he was well liked or not well liked, and it was his birthday. What you do is hire a guy for fifty dollars who comes in with a huge cake and hits the guy in the face and then runs for the hills. That goes on quite a bit.
>
> We had one guy who used to get crazy. He would turn red and yell vile things at anyone for tiny reasons. A lot of people yell, but he would just turn around and say such horrible, cutting, critical things that it would

kill everybody. Three of us bought a cake and hit the guy. The messenger wouldn't do it unless we held open the elevator door for him. That's the kind of thing you do, and you don't care.

One day a group of visiting Japanese businessmen came through. This guy got up wearing a helmet, like from World War II. I swear he was dancing around the whole trading room holding up a headline about Pearl Harbor and screaming, "Die, you American dogs!"

Have you ever seen these soft rubber, squiggly things, like little heads? Well, the guys would pretend they were breasts and pass them around.

We told terrible sick jokes . . . black humor. You're under so much pressure that you love black humor. The funny part [of the business] was hysterical, but I wasn't so crazy about people trying to find out about my private life and telling stories on me.

Women rarely mentioned the word "nepotism" as a reason for staying away from male co-workers, but concern for work was mentioned often in their reasons for keeping sex out of the office.

It colors your objectivity.

It conflicts with your ability to be professional, which is judgmental, independent, and strong.

It's wrong to interfere with the merit system.

It's OK if you can handle it—as long as it's not in the immediate office.

It's too messy; things are political enough.

It's an unwritten law not to go to bed with anyone in business.

Not with people in the immediate office.

I don't want it to interfere with work. It's not good for your business sense.

I would date men from other banks, but not men in my office; it goes back to the time I was passed over because the boss was having an affair.

But there were many other equally persuasive reasons why women shied away from sexual involvement. They thought it was personally dangerous:

It's uncomfortable when you are emotionally involved, because when it's over, you have to quit your job.

It adds strain. If the affair ends in marriage, you have to find another job. If it doesn't, your former partner makes life difficult for you.

It's too close for comfort. If you get into a disagreement at night, you're going to run into him all day long. There's no extra space.

If it's with a superior, you're going to get the shaft. Down the road, it's him or you.

Their comments reflect the obvious fact that many love affairs end badly, with animosity, and at work former lovers can begin slugging through professional channels. But even if the two hide their feelings and conduct themselves with polite discretion, there is an emotional price to be paid every day they walk into the office and have to face the person with whom they once shared a dream. Women, in their wisdom, are separating love and work. Men, in their institutions, agree that is a good idea. The workplace is no place like home.

These are the rules for sexual behavior in the office. The behavior is something else. The taboo is not exactly honored in the breach, but more than a few women become romantically involved with men at work, in spite of their self-made promises to stay aloof. In the next chapter, we see them exploring the consequences—or lack of them—of mixing love and work.

14

Mixing
Love and
Work

I n this study, roughly half the women in each city—New York and San Francisco—said that they had broken the taboo against having love affairs with men at work. Their experience gives much-needed information on the costs to women of exercising their sexual preroga- tives in business. On the whole, the costs were not high. Most of these women carried out love or sexual relationships without significant neg- ative effects on their careers—as professionals. But several of the women began their working lives as secretaries, and they tell very different stories from that era. The secretary is much more vulnerable to profes- sional damage from a romantic interlude than is the woman of higher rank.

Five of the forty-four women said they had had love affiars with sen- ior men they considered mentors; in all cases, they identified positive effects on their work. The men were advanced by one or two levels compared to the women, but they were located outside the group the women reported to, so these love affairs had no effect on promotions or salary. What the lovers did was function as informal mentors to the women, who learned something about the business they were in.

That kind of relationship was more common in San Francisco than it was in New York, according to these women, and usually they were acknowledged by single women. One young, ambitious financial officer in San Francisco expressed a common theme when she said:

Ummm, yes. There were a couple of relationships. I was not helped in my ability to get ahead, but I might have learned some things. Eventually, the conversation would turn to work and I would pick up information that became valuable to me. [She thought some more] I would say these people were almost mentor-like to me. In each instance, in fact, they knew much more than I did and I learned a lot that way.

Told that it was not uncommon for women to learn from a mentor-lover, she said, with relief, "Oh, good. Great!" All of her relationships were quiet and discreet, if not secret. "You have to be careful of the people who think it's wrong," she said.

Mentor love relationships occurred as a natural extension of the work relationship. One woman learned the corporate ladder from a mentor-lover; another learned political behavior. None of the women acknowledged any material benefit from the affair, but a male banker in New York talked about that. While he was single, Joseph was a special conduit for women. Sexually active and ready to help, he had, in his words, "a fair number of physical relationships with women in the same organization." I asked him if it was dangerous. He answered:

Yes, sure.

But I was very straight. I was single. I was an endangered species. I was a single, straight, reasonably nice male; therefore, a fair number of women pursued me. A lot of time I helped them get jobs. Sometimes it was just useful I was there for them to come and talk to, because I understand organizations.

I don't think anybody got hurt from a career point of view; I think a number got helped. There were a number of liaisons; probably 25 percent got helped. In a place like this, people need help. They need a job. I could pick up the telephone and help them get one. Or if they needed help with a business problem or an interpersonal problem, I could clear it away. I could get them to talk to that person.

I asked Joseph how many women got promotions or jobs as a result of his connections. He said:

Let's see . . . I would say six or seven. I like doing that. I would probably make an effort to do that anyway. I generally believe everybody ought to work and there's a place for everybody. I've had a number of mentor relationships with women, both with intimate relationships and without. If there is an intimate relationship, that makes it much better.

I think sex is terrific. My view is, I will jump into bed with anybody who is willing to go to bed with me. . . . Although I've been so well behaved lately, I can't believe it.

Two of the relationships, however, could have cost the women in terms of their careers, and they define the ways in which sex and work create social consequences. Said Joseph:

I did have an extended relationship with a woman here which was out in the open and which didn't work. It may have been more difficult because everyone knew we were going out and then everybody knew we weren't going out. From a career point of view, that didn't hurt her. But it didn't help her either.

The other was with a woman in his close working group.

It was not OK. It was the wrong thing to do. It didn't hurt either one of us, but . . .

We spent three years on the road without ever coming close. We were working very hard, to get an organization turned around. I can't tell you how; it just happened one night after a very pleasant dinner. One night I didn't get up and go home. She may have made a decision. I don't know. In four years I never touched her, but as I remember, she took my hand. Maybe that was it. The relationship was extraordinarily advantageous from a business point of view. I am a thinker of great thoughts; she is a doer of great deeds. We had almost complete trust. I would trust her to do anything and she felt comfortable enough to tell me I was full of shit when I was. No one really had an idea this was more than a close friendship. It was short-lived. She's very successful now, and some of that was due to me. I pushed her.

Joseph's relationship skirted the dangerous waters of nepotism, where both partners in a romantic liaison can get hurt. That happened in an account he gave of someone else.

She had an affair with her boss. He tried to push her ahead at the expense of another woman. It was generally understood that the guy was having an affair with her, which nobody cared about, until he tried to do something for her. A competitor went to the controller of the division, and they got him, because he was entertaining this woman on the bank's money. He lost his job, not for having an affair, but for entertaining on the bank's money and lying about it. Her career was not helped. She was put off on the side with nothing to do.

These were the stories I collected of women who benefited professionally from love affairs, or thought they did. What stood out was the innocuous, even benign character of the affair when nepotism was not involved. It was hard to identify any damage to anyone. There was nothing wrong with a woman learning from a more knowledgeable lover; nothing wrong with a man going to bed with a woman he helped at work. The work roles, in fact, may have charged the personal relationship with special feeling. In several cases, the partners remained friends for years after the sexual affair was over.

But the fact that professional benefits were involved means that the affair could never really be separated from the achievement game. The potential that the romance would turn against the less powerful player was always there. That it didn't suggests these women were finding good men, rather than men who might exploit their positions for social gain. Not all women are so lucky. Love affairs that become confused with professional gain carry both personal and social risks. At the personal level, the issues can be intense. One professional woman, not in the study, carried out a love affair with her mentor for years—until she discovered that he had other mentees and other lovers, and was thrown into a crisis. Suddenly feeling like a whore, she believed that everything she had done professionally was cast into a doubtful light. The mentor relationship fits into traditional patterns of American sexuality associated with status and male dominance; although it can be rewarding, it can also turn belly side up and reveal the basic power issues.

But I was concerned in this study with the social consequences of love affairs, and from the stories these women told as professionals, I couldn't see major costs. I came away from the interviews thinking that from a career perspective, it was a good idea for a new professional to find a senior man (or woman, in those cases where the status relationship is beginning to be reversed) to nurture his or her professional skills. There was, however, another set of stories these women told, which came from their histories as secretaries. In that situation, the social consequences were very different.

225

A number of women now in their thirties and forties started their working lives as secretaries. They clearly remembered the passage from clerical into professional ranks, sometimes with the help of an employer who was also a mentor-lover. Some heavy price tags were attached to these relationships, including social ostracism, sexual harassment, and mental abuse.

Marlene told me this story with a mixture of love, pain, and disgust. She didn't seem to know how to feel about her former mentor-lover, and I could see why.

> I was working for a firm when six of us left to form another division. We were working together as a team, and I got to be friends with one of the men. We were together constantly, day after day. The attraction grew and we became intimate. I was still a secretary, but basically I was running the profit-sharing program and doing all the account supervision.

During the early stages of the affair, Marlene's lover used the relationship to control her decisions at work.

> There were times I would be coerced into doing things at work by sexual means. I don't know if "coerced" is the right word, because I was not pressured into having the affair. I was a willing party. But he would use sex to get me to do things, like telling me I should do certain things or he wouldn't see me that night. That to me was major sexual harassment.
>
> We were both dissatisfied with the firm. I knew I wasn't going anywhere, so I went job hunting. He did too, and we both got good offers, but he offered me more money to go with him, so I went.
>
> Two weeks later he asked me to marry him. I was flabbergasted. He was nineteen years older than I was. I couldn't say yes, so I never really gave him an answer and started looking for another job. I wanted desperately to get out of this.

Marlene found another job only days before her boss gave notice himself. She offered to stay with the firm, but that night they told her she was out of work. The next day when her new employer called for a reference, the company said she was no longer employed. With a few words, whether out of censure, indifference, or spite, the firm put Marlene's new job in jeopardy.

They said that because I was filling a position for a man who was no longer with them, that I didn't have a job. I didn't get two weeks.

The price I paid . . . I won't say it was too high. But it really faded the goodness.

The power imbalance between Marlene and her lover was overwhelming. In addition to an emotional inequality—the ideological power difference between masculine and feminine which Marlene believes at fundamental levels—she shared other sources of inequality with her lover. He had real power over her; he was her boss. And he had the authority and prestige of a professional; she was a secretary.

A stockbroker in San Francisco recalled the affair she had with her boss when she was in clerical ranks, and the social censure that followed:

> I shouldn't have done it. I didn't get fired or anything. There was no power play, no coercion. But it was a stupid thing to do. There was some talk among the women that I had gotten half a step above because I was sleeping with the boss. It wasn't true, because I was there before he came. No one said anything directly to me, but after [the affair] was over, I found out there had been numerous comments. I isolated myself because I didn't like any of those people, but had I been seeking their approval, I would have been ostracized. It made life damned unpleasant. I moved away from that city.

A professional woman in Philadelphia, now a boss herself, remembers the night her employer called her eleven years ago. She was twenty-eight and naive. She was a secretary; he was married.

> When he called, I was dumbfounded. I thought to myself, "Oh, my God! How do I handle this? Do I really have a choice?" I didn't think so. I wasn't nearly so attracted. I could have done without it. I had no way of knowing what to do, so I just fell madly in love and it grew into a very special relationship.
>
> I really liked him as a person, and in some ways I am grateful that he forced the relationship on me, but I also knew that if it didn't work out, I was the one taking the risk. I would have been the one to leave the job, not him. What if he'd had his fantasy and said, "Yuk!"

227

This woman refuses to believe she was sexually harassed. It is not part of her belief system to think she could have been victimized, so she turned the event into a positive experience. Others might disagree, and the story illustrates how intertwined are the concepts of "sexual harassment" and "sleeping your way to the top." In one case, the man is blamed, in the other the woman; yet the event may be exactly the same.

Throughout these interviews and the stories men and women told about sex in the office, it was the secretary who paid the highest price for breaking the sexual taboo, the secretary who lived out the realities of male dominance at a personal and social level. The status difference, more than the gender difference, was what counted in the outcome. Only one woman in this sample had been involved as a professional woman with her boss. She suffered long-term anxiety anticipating the repercussions, which never came, even though her working associates knew about the relationship. She was very discreet, and the relationship, which was very strong, continues now while the two are employed in different companies. But as it was going on, the woman recalls,

> It was a very hard thing to do . . . like the Mary Cunningham thing . . . that whole issue. Oh, it's awful! Maybe it was good for me, because I had to strengthen inside, know who I wanted to be with and what I really wanted. Before that, I think I had been too easily swayed by other people.

This doesn't mean a professional woman can have a love affair with her boss with impunity. Nepotism is politically and socially dangerous, no matter who does it, and one case doesn't prove otherwise. But it does raise the possibility that professional women pay a lower social price than do secretaries when they break the rules, that increased rank on the part of the woman changes the outcome. A senior executive in New York told of a professional woman who fell in love with and married her superior. Both were high-ranking members of the firm. Both are still there, in the same jobs.

If the suggestions in this preliminary study truly reflect social reality, it means that much of the social disregard women experience as sexism is really elitism, the unequal dumping of social grief and responsibility on the individual of lower status. Because women as a class have been of lower status through their economic dependency on men, they have suffered the same negative consequences as other depressed groups. And there were further indications that status and rank were the more important factors in determining who paid the price for breaking the rules.

The rumors and stories people told followed a common pattern. I heard very few stories—almost none—of professional women being forced out in the context of a love affair. But those rumors that did exist involved women in relationships with the head of the company. There were two of them. In one case, the woman was fired when a new person took charge of the company. In the other case, the woman was forced out when her liaison with the married man who ran the company began to cause social disorder. The man's wife was becoming involved; friendships were being broken; the chairman thought things were getting too nasty, and the woman had to leave. Both instances involved major status differences between the lovers.

In contrast to the rare story of the professional being forced out, there were many of secretaries following typical scenarios: the clerical woman who was promoted by her lover and fired when he left, or simply fired because he left, with no promotion involved. Said one high-ranking man in the brokerage business:

> If we fire him, *she's* got to go. I don't want somebody staying behind, feeding him with what's going on in the office. When we fired the manager in [one office] and then found out his secretary is married to him, we fired her right away! 'Cause when she goes home at night, she's going to tell him everything that's going on, and he's managing another office. . . . It's a highly competitive business. You just can't trust them now. If she won't leave, we'll assign her to a job that is not any good and she won't like it.

I asked this man what he would do if the woman were a professional rather than a secretary. He replied: "I don't think we'd fire her. It would depend. If he went to another firm, we probably would. On the other hand, we have people here [whose spouses work for competitors]."

The other source of evidence that status differences rather than gender are paramount concerns the question of who had to leave the job when a love affair erupted into the open. Professional women were rarely fired or publicly forced out, but many were transferred or asked to leave in order to avoid conflicts. It was usually the woman who moved, not the man, ostensibly because she tended to have lower status. Throughout financial institutions, men and women quote the same rules for anyone who breaks the sexual taboos: The junior person is the one who moves. Since women are usually junior in any rank differences, they are the ones who have to leave a unit or organization when issues of nepotism arise.

"I know plenty of stories about women having an affair and it becoming public knowledge within the company, then the woman has to leave because she was in a lower position," said a woman in San Francisco. Said another in New York, "I know half a dozen cases where women changed jobs [in the course of a relationship]. You rarely see people make public their relationships and stay at the same firm."

Many women don't like the fact that it is the female who always moves, or seems to. An experienced woman in New York said she knows too many women whose opportunities have been limited for the sake of an office romance.

> We have a young lady now. She was terrific, a real rising star. And he was a good guy. She got taken out of the job. I swear! You can't move John, but you can take Mary and move her to Timbuktu. Someday, I'll hear one of these stories and the woman will not have been removed from her job!

Most people I talked to seemed to accept this as a status issue. But there was no proof of that, because women had not advanced high enough in the hierarchy to reverse the pattern, and if they did have the opportunity, it wasn't clear they would take it. There was always that old tendency of American women to seek out men of higher rank. From the perspective of women, it hardly matters whether rank or the double standard determines this inequality—in either case she pays for getting involved with a man at work. But for society as a whole, it matters a great deal that the individual of lower status pays all the social costs. The office love affair is a paradigm for social injustice on a broader scale, in which people of high rank pay nothing for breaking the rules, while people of low rank bear harsh criticism and heavy consequences. Through social injustice, we create winners and losers, and that builds an uglier and more permanent wall against equality than sexism could ever erect by itself.

Having a love affair with a peer would seem to be safe. There are no status differences with the man to undermine a woman's position at work, nothing the lover can provide that carries the stigma of nepotism. Moreover, the peer relationship is an equal one, so that neither partner has to deal with the insidious effects of mixing professional advantages with personal life. So far, so good. Unfortunately, it isn't true. A peer relationship in the office is no safer than one with rank differences, and understanding that fact brings women face to face with the political realities of the working environment.

Most women who broke the sexual taboo broke it with a peer. The outcome for them was equally split between no effect and a negative effect on their professional lives. Twelve women had love affairs with men they considered peers. In six cases they said it had no effect on their work or career potential, but five described a negative impact. Only one thought the relationship benefited her working life by making a job she didn't like more tolerable.

Compared to the mentor relationship, which was always described as positive in a career sense, the peer relationship brought more headaches. This is an interesting twist because it suggests that when women become involved with an equal at work, they take more risk than if they become involved with a man who can help them. The reason, however, may only be that the peer relationship is less likely to be hidden and more likely to be carried out in spite of the often unknown and unanticipated political consequences. Because they tended to be more overt, especially if both partners were single, peer love affairs exposed personal vulnerability in an environment that had a low tolerance for it.

Carol welcomed me into her midtown office, shut the door firmly, and proceeded to give me a blow-by-blow account of the political scene at work. She is a veteran of the New York financial world. Manhattan sweeps beneath her window, with a view the length of the island to the Statue of Liberty. At the age of thirty-five, she has achieved a commanding position in her field, and everything in her bearing expresses that.

She moved her short body around with great energy, her heels hitting the floor with a determined click. She spoke as definitely as she walked, with a positive upbeat cynicism. I could tell she cared about people—especially other female professionals—but she was quick to put them into win-lose categories. "This one is together; this one is not," she said as she moved down the list of female colleagues, ticking them off as though they were petals on a daisy.

Carol thinks it is crazy for any woman to become involved with a man at work. But she did it successfully. Her experience proves "that you cannot go through this sort of thing." Married now and separated professionally from her husband, who works in a different institution, she recalls the anxiety she felt in making herself politically vulnerable. There was nothing intrinsically wrong with her choice. The man she liked was not her boss; he wasn't even located in her immediate office; and he was single. It should have been all right. But Carol's decision to break her taboo concerning love affairs immediately complicated her moves within the organization, even though there were no professional conflicts of interest.

I had always behaved in a very careful fashion. I never dated anyone I worked with, and although I went out with lots of people outside and was close friends with people at work, they were buddies. I had always maintained that sexual relationships are not the thing that can occur at work. You don't make your career and your bed in the same place.

So, this was the first time I dated someone at work. I could rationalize getting to know him by thinking of it as a friend date. He was single; we were on the same level and I decided he was really interesting. I remember the night we went out for dinner. I excused myself, went into the bathroom, and held my head. I said to myself, "Oh, brother, what have you gotten into? This is irrational. You've been out with him for two hours and you think you've gotten into a mad love affair. You'll simply go back out there and say nothing. Talk about the weather and stop this personal stuff. This is nonsense."

I can remember my whole body withdrawing from the table and me saying, "Listen, I don't do this. I don't do this."

He kept saying, "What's the matter with you? We don't have to worry about that."

I said, "Yes, we do."

It was just terrifying. You could see he was a lot less concerned than I was.

I got good at not telling anyone, but all the interesting jobs were under [the man she was dating]. Friends would say to me, "Why don't you go work for ____?" I thought to myself, "Shit. I don't want to do that." But neither did I want to stay where I was. I knew of a woman in the bank who had a terrific job uptown, which would put distance between him and me. I didn't really want to work for her because she was a real witch on wheels. She was the kind of woman who would shoot you in the back if she knew you were violating any of the rules. But I said to myself, "Listen, now that you've broken your rule, this is better." So I went up and worked for her.

It was a marvelous assignment, but Carol's new boss and her lover were enemies. She reasoned that it was only a matter of time before the woman found out and then she, Carol, would suffer the consequences of a negative shift in perception.

Perception of you is skewed by the way they view the guy. There's no question that people look at me and say, "But he's not your type."

I went to the personnel guy and said, "Listen, I want to look outside the group for a job."

He said, "Wait. There's a big reorganization coming. You don't have to leave."

I said, "Yes, I think I do."

He said, "Well, we wouldn't like you to leave."

I said, "That's all right. I'd like to leave, for personal reasons."

He said, "Now, Carol, that's not good enough."

So I said, "All right. I'll tell you, but you've got to swear you won't tell anybody. I'm going out with someone in the group."

He was relieved. He said, "Oh, no big deal. Lots of people go out with others in the group. That's all right."

But I knew it was not all right. He couldn't figure out who the guy was at first. When he found out, he said, "Holy shit! Does your boss know about this? Where do you want to go?"

It was perfectly clear to him. I left the group. This is the evidence that you can't go through this sort of thing.

Carol added that it was not good for their personal lives to work together. Too much of their time was taken up with work. And the decompression at night was filled with the emotional wear and tear of processing hot strategic issues in the office. Moreover, she is convinced that perception of the woman is changed when they see her in a personal as well as a professional light. "I see this with all the people who have these relationships. And there have been a lot of them."

Many women fear that negative shift in perception. It is an ancient, gut-level fear that once the lover, mate, or husband is known, the world will judge her in his shadow. Suddenly, there will be questions raised about the work: Who actually did it, anyway? Was *he* really responsible for the ideas, the push, the creativity? And if he is not well liked, she will be tarred with the same brush, because women by tradition are perceived as extensions of the man. They are absorbed into the union and held responsible for his behavior. Professional women must cope with the debilitating effects of these traditional biases if they allow the personal, familial side to show at work. The anti-feminine bias is passing as women demand and achieve higher positions at work, and especially as they outperform men, which they do when driven by the need to overcome prejudice. Nevertheless, that bias remains a potent force in evaluating women who become personally associated with men at work.

The high-ranking couple at the brokerage firm, for instance, were the targets of two kinds of social reactions when they began publicly to acknowledge their union. Staffers at lower levels were immediately suspicious of anything she wrote: "Is he writing it? Is he giving her favored treatment?" "People talked about it, and it may have affected her," said the senior executive, who insists that the woman never lost her credibility. Toward the man they were critical on moral grounds. "They questioned his judgment, as in 'Why didn't he make an honest woman out of her quickly?' instead of taking two years. For a period of time, it may have slowed their careers down, he more than she."

Just as a woman's talents are attributed to the man, so his bad behavior is attributed to her, in the distorted reasoning of traditional sex roles. Carol unabashedly judges the woman by the man's behavior.

> I interviewed somebody yesterday, and I can tell you, I didn't hire her, in part because of her husband. I know he did something on an interview. He tried to price himself up in the marketplace. He dragged people along and turned them down after they'd done cartwheels to get him. I think she wouldn't have taken the job in a hundred years. Now, am I applying her husband's behavior to her? Obviously I am. I don't know that about her.

One female executive put it very simply as she reviewed in her mind the cases of women she'd known who found lovers and mates in the working environment. "The women were probably viewed less favorably in the environment where they met. I think I know that for sure," she said reflectively. "They experienced a loss of prestige."

In New York, some women experienced negative political effects when the men they picked were not doing well in the system, and the guilt spread by association to the woman. "It may have hurt me," said one woman who had relationships with two men, one of whom was fired. She was forced into a lateral move which reduced her commissions. Later, she learned that secretaries were making comments about her to her boss, who called her a "bad influence." She believes it was guilt by association.

> If either of those two people had been married, I would have made more of an effort to hide it. Because they were not, I felt there was no problem. I seem to pick the wrong people to be friends with. But I have ultimate respect for those two people and much less respect for the people who might have been condemnatory. Being me, I didn't take that into consideration, and I would not, if I had it to do over again.

In another case, a young woman fell in love with a man who was later fired for expending so much energy fighting for custody of his children at the expense of work. She began by saying there were no effects on her position at work; but as the anecdote continued, its tone became more hostile, loaded with potential repercussions. She told the story with a don't-you-dare-question-my-private-life attitude, so I knew she had felt threatened. She ended by saying she wouldn't do it again.

> I didn't set out to do it. But you spend so much time and you work that closely with someone and you get to know them. You do. You get to know them better than their wives in many ways.
> I was in love. I was feeling very, very good. And generally I don't think the relationship affected my work. My office is very discreet. People do have affairs there, usually long-lasting, and they're terribly discreet. He was not in my reporting relationship, more of a peer.
> When I came into the situation, it became very messy. He decided to go for a divorce and custody and he became so entangled in that venture that his work suffered. He was fired.

At one time, I wondered if . . . quite frankly . . . if anything had happened. . . . Our attorney [at work] was probably more paranoid about my taking them to court should they want to fire me. He was very sensitive to that whole question.

The man I was working for at that time was a sonofabitch. A paranoid man with a temper. He got fired and the next week I got a poison pen letter from him. [She read it with relish.]

"Dear Jackie: It did not make me happy to hear you classified me as 'burned out' before I was out of the building. It's ironic since not only was I most tolerant with your extensive problems with your job, but I supported you when others were quite upset with your rather tacky and certainly unprofessional interoffice personal involvement."

She put the letter down and laughed. The man had never said a word to her about her affair. In strong tones, she repeated the hoary phrases about privacy of her own time: " 'Criticize my work, not my personal life.' And I believe that. But for myself, I would not do it again. It does put strains on you in the office."

Anna, who knows the world of trading better than most, encountered more serious dangers when a man she was close to was forced to resign and she was caught in a tense intraoffice schism.

This guy who had the power used to walk by my desk and wait until the people next to me had moved. Then he'd say, "Just remember. I'm an Italian and we never forget anything!" I was scared silly. I'd wake up in the morning with dry heaves. My stomach was empty but turning over. I told myself, "This is wonderful. You're going to wake up in an alley, dead for breakfast." I don't think he meant anything would happen, but in this city, you never know who knows who.

This went on and it kept getting worse and worse. I said to myself, "Let's be realistic. You don't have a future with this firm." It was a political thing. I was forced to pick sides and I knew my side would not win. I quit.

Stories like that did not occur in the San Francisco sample, perhaps because the environment there is politically less intense. There were no stories at all of political alliances or schisms where the woman's position was compromised by having the "wrong" lover, and very little discussion of the political consequences of mixing private and work lives. The San Francisco interviews seemed apolitical compared to those in New York. Nevertheless, there were disadvantages to romance in the office. Two of four women who had had love affairs with peers described negative effects on work, and both spoke of personal consequences. One woman couldn't work well with her lover around; the other couldn't work well with her lover when the affair was over.

> It wasn't a heart-splitting separation or anything. It wasn't even a long-drawn-out affair. It just soured me on the idea. Because relationships in the office will normally end, and it's very difficult to work with that person, I found. For a while, it made me very uncomfortable and it hurt our relationship professionally.

In San Francisco, as anywhere else, people suffer from the ego-crucifying effects of continuing to work with a former lover. One San Francisco woman told this story of a woman she knew—a story that could be told of anyone who suffers publicly from sexual rejection.

> I know of one [public affair]. It stifled her growth. Yes. It hurt her. I don't understand why she stayed. She was given a small promotion, nothing more, considering her years and background. The relationship is over now and she's still working with him. And he's getting married to someone else. The general tone is that people don't respect her. Let's say they don't think highly of her. She's of no consequence to other people. She's enclosed herself in a shell and she's isolated. As a result, she's not as assertive or direct. She does not command respect—all of those things that make you a more successful, professional person.

So, these are the dangers of sex in the office—the political, social, and personal consequences of having a love affair in the working arena. In terms of the consequences to women, two points stand out.

The first is that a woman can have a love affair with no real cost, as long as she keeps it quiet. The woman's image was more important than her actual behavior. Discretion was the better part of virtue. Several people reiterated this point, that it doesn't matter so much whether you become involved but how you conduct yourself in the process. If the affair becomes public, however, then women have to deal with all the social baggage of having introduced themselves in a feminine role at work. But even if the anti-feminine bias were to pass so that women are no longer judged in the shadow of their men, there would still

237

remain a fundamental tension between the politics of the office and the loyalties of love and friendship.

The second point is that the dangers to women of having love affairs at work have less to do with traditional attitudes toward women than with the political environment and the structural relationships of people in a hierarchy. Sex is dangerous. Friendships are dangerous. Family ties are dangerous, in a place so powerfully oriented around rank and status.

Alliances, schisms, rising stars, falling stars—the office is a hotbed of shifting allegiances involving every single individual. It is not the place to make personal commitments.

15

Conclusion:
A Modest
Proposal

M any women harbor the not-so-secret hope that someday they will be able to humanize the working environment, if they don't give up their values as women. As Becky in Chapter 11 said, "I think we should be adding our humanity, emotion, and softness to the world, rather than turning into men. That doesn't do us any good." She was talking about a softer, more cooperative approach to handling authority than men are used to. But other women voiced similar opinions, holding out the promise that someday women can be the kind of people they want to be on the job as well as at home. Yet the reality of their lives in this professional financial culture is that they don't gain the authority they seek unless they learn to act like men, and that seems to set up an absolute paradox: In gaining power, women lose feminine identity, as well as any hope they have of changing the system. Coincidentally, they validate a male attitude that the way men have been doing it all along is the correct way. In other words, the fault lies in the roles, not in the gender. Women, given the power, cannot do it any differently. Like all broad generalizations, the statement is both true and false. There are areas—considering the competitive, political nature of these roles—in which women need to learn masculine behavior. But there are other areas in which we can change the system.

But to do so, we have to know what we are fighting for. What feminine behavior? What values and traditions? What do we stand for as a gender, if anything? Are we all so different as individuals that there is no pattern worth preserving that arises from our sexual natures? Are we just like men in positions of power? The realization that women in finance lose traditional feminine identity seems to suggest that we are just like men, and that once the cultural restrictions keeping women in domestic labor break down, we splinter into our individual patterns, shaped by the environment we're in and the roles we choose to play. From this perspective, feminine identity is a cultural artifact rather than a part of our biological and spiritual guts. When the scene changes from kitchen to office, we are transformed into beings who differ only in genital equipment from the men we work beside.

But to draw that conclusion misreads the evidence. Women as a gender are so different from men that the effort of adapting to unadulterated masculine roles is leading to widespread loss of reproduction. Nothing identifies a pattern as maladaptive more quickly than a substantial decline in the rate of reproduction. When women can't have children, something is wrong, and the fault lies not in the genes nor in the bodies but in the cultural patterns. Professional roles, as they are presently conceived, threaten female fertility, and that phenomenon has been evident since the latter part of the nineteenth century.

In 1982, the typical corporate female executive in the United States was single and without children. More than half of these women were unmarried and almost two-thirds—61 percent—had no children, according to the study done by the UCLA Graduate School of Management and Korn/Ferry International. Lack of families among the women compares with the opposite picture among male executives, of whom only 3 percent had no children and only 4 percent were unmarried at the time of the interview. The sample of three hundred women included corporate vice presidents, financial officers, lawyers, and senior level officers, drawn from Fortune 1000 companies. And they are not unusual among professional women.

Some analysts, viewing these statistics on the modern-day American Amazons, explain them away as representative of a transitional generation. These were pioneers—women who made the difficult transition from feminine to professional roles. Many of them grew up with sexual inhibitions, or they were women who bought the idea that they had to be very, very devoted about their work to be taken seriously. As a result, they lost the families. But that's in the past. It's all different now.

Women can have their families and their jobs too. Yet history tells us a different story.

Every generation of new women is a transitional one. The historic division in the spheres that puts parenting in the hands of women and productivity in the hands of men means that every woman who wants both roles has to cope with cultural problems, making the merger difficult. And, while the barriers are falling, many problems remain. Fifty years ago, women were laid off when they married, never mind having children. Ten years ago, it was acceptable practice to refuse to hire women with children. In the 1980s, prejudice against family women has finally become illegal, but that is only a beginning. Untold numbers of women still go home to rear their children, surrendering their career ambitions and putting themselves at economic risk, because alternative patterns of child care are so poorly developed. Those who stay on the job continue to surrender their family lives, and this has been true since women began moving into masculine work roles in the early nineteenth century.

In his history of women and the family entitled *At Odds,* Stanford historian Carl N. Degler traces the movement of women into the labor force from 1820 to the present, paralleling these economic transformations with data on the number of women who remained single or childless. The statistics are overwhelming. In 1890, 88 percent of the working women (in non-agricultural occupations) were single, widowed, or divorced. Thirty years later, in 1920, that percentage had declined to only 78 percent. According to census data, only 12 percent of all professional women in 1920 were married. Nor are we talking about small numbers of women. The first great transformation in women's work occurred in the nineteenth century, when thousands of women moved into traditionally non-feminine occupations such as manufacturing and began making inroads into elite professions. By the end of the century, virtually every occupation and profession had been integrated to some degree, and the question of how women could have both jobs and families had become a pressing social issue. In 1919, a publication of Smith College strikingly anticipated the outraged sentiment of women sixty years later: "We cannot believe that it is fixed in the nature of things that a woman must choose between a home and her work, when a man may have both. There must be a way out and it is the problem

241

of our generation to find the way." Two generations later, women are still struggling with the same issues, with glacially slow progress in the meantime. A 1913 sample of 880 prominent, mostly professional, women revealed that the great majority—about three-quarters—were childless. When the Korn/Ferry–UCLA group did their study in 1982, 61 percent of the women were childless. Not great progress, considering that the better part of a century has passed since society began grappling with the issue in earnest.

The 1920s marked an era of energy and optimism on the part of women, who saw themselves integrating the two spheres. Women were moving rapidly into the higher levels of male authority, earning PhD's, gaining entrance into the professions, intent all the while on maintaining their options to marry and have families. A 1926 book by Virginia Collier asserted that the question was no longer "Should women combine marriage with careers?" but "How do they manage it and how does it work?"

The Depression buried this ebullience along with any public effort to give women equal access to love and work. The pendulum swung in the opposite direction, as thousands of married women were fired or laid off from their jobs. States and cities passed laws barring women with husbands from paid work. Even school systems fired women who married, leaving the job market open only to women who surrendered their family lives by choice or necessity. In 1934, a Vassar alumna looked back, almost wistfully, on the dream that had been: "Twenty years ago, we all believed in the economic independence of women. Domesticity was regarded with impatience. . . . We all expected to have careers and we all hoped to be distinguished. . . . It was part of the doctrine that we should marry and have children, but that these incidents should not stand in the way of our work. Marriage does not interfere with a man's work. A woman, too, should have both a rich personal life and a useful public career."

As the country headed into World War II, professional and other working women faced the same agonizing choices they had faced forty years before. The great majority of them were single and few had any children. The point of summarizing Degler's history is not to prove that integration for women is impossible, but to point out that the problems women cope with, at great personal cost, are deep and recurring, and they're not over.

Managerial studies of women discover many times over that marriage and motherhood do not interfere with careers. Women take on the average three months off work to bear a child. Mothers are not absent more often than other people; they don't work fewer hours. Having children does not dilute a woman's attention to the job, nor cause her to drop out of the labor force. But what these studies don't mention is that women, on the whole, maintain their competitive position with men by sacrificing reproduction. Only a minority are fortunate enough to have the right constellation of factors coming together—familial support with child care or the money to purchase it, a husband who believes in and knows how to practice equality, control over the conditions and hours of work, and a mind-set influenced by a strong female role model, so that a woman doesn't have to stumble on the field of weakened feminine authority. Working mothers in this sample often—but not always—testified that women can have both spheres. They don't have to surrender one for the other. These women do have families without career sacrifice. But the fact remains that most of their female colleagues have no children and only a bare half are married. Some of these women don't care and have rejected motherhood voluntarily, but the greater number do care. Their loss of family connections says that something is wrong. What is that something? What lies behind the low reproductive rate of professional women?

The ethics and practice of the workplace are a major part of the explanation. Modern professions were born in one of the most patriarchal centuries the Western world has ever known. The nineteenth century saw the institution of a radical separation in gender spheres, and with it came a profound devaluation of feminine work and ability. Men, separated from their families or any responsibility for nurturing intimates, generated values that are in many ways inimical to the creation and maintenance of life. Exclusively focused on achievement and performance, these values leave very little time or energy for maintaining relationships or doing the other things that contribute to family health. Sexuality, sensitivity, time to play, willingness to care for other people, and other traits associated with the feminine ethos all become casualties of the value making work the most important thing in life. Men, whose role in reproduction can be limited to twenty minutes, remain fertile. Women, who must put their bodies on the line for a year or more and figure out how to maintain that life after birth, do not. No matter how sanguine working mothers may be about the ease of combining the two roles, being a parent does change the singleminded focus of a professional, not only because of the time it takes but because people care less about their work. The pleasures and responsibilities of having a familty restore the balance between love and work. But our present definition of careers requires an imbalance.

So many women have heard their fathers and husbands put career first that it's only natural they would pick up the same ethos when they become professional. If they didn't, the organizations they work for would instill the value by creating an environment where it is natural to be excessive about work. When colleagues work ten hours a day as a matter of course and promotions are given to those who display a devotional level of commitment, the effect is to strip the professional staff of any other significant activity in life, including hobbies, home, and family. Military and religious organizations demand and receive this level of devotion from people who choose to forsake other things in life for their mission. The same singlemindedness shaped career ethics defined by men who could, with money and status, purchase the humanizing relationships they didn't have time to develop. In the lives of women—the childbearing sex—we see the true dimensions of what has been forfeited.

When parents work eight to ten hours a day, as these mothers did, they barely have enough time to take care of themselves, much less someone else. These women managed by hiring full-time maids, which means their solution is limited to wealthy people. There is nothing culturally new about women with money assuming a role in the public sphere. With hired help to take care of the children, wealthy women have long been able to develop their artistic, mental, and political abilities. But not all the women in this sample were rich, and some—particularly in San Francisco—rejected the idea of hiring maids. They put their children into day care instead. Their experience more nearly matches that of the bulk of American women, who must scramble like hell to find adequate day care and possess the insight of a wizard to pick the man and the employers who will help rather than hinder their ambition to have a family. (Corporations were blind to these issues until the early eighties, when they began to make strides on two fronts, parental leave and support of child care facilities.)

While women maintain the masculine ethos as a ruling value system, they tend not to reproduce. We can see this ethos operating in the lives of women from patriarchal backgrounds who reject motherhood and sometimes marriage as well. Influenced by the career values of their fathers, they are living out a masculine cultural identity, with negative concepts of what it means to be feminine. In many ways, they are running from the image of femininity they saw enacted in their families. The only way to avoid the cultural legacy of male domination expressed through such family patterns is to avoid feminine roles.

The same awarenesses and fears influence other women, who do not permanently reject feminine roles but simply delay them in the drive for professional success. They think that if they give in and marry, they will wind up serving other people while losing their own autonomy and professional movement. Indeed, the risks of doing that are very great in women who for whatever reason believe that being feminine means being weak, soft, and conciliatory to men. There is no way to carry this feminine identity into a relationship without risking personal autonomy, which then begins to threaten professional life.

In seeking to change the feminine legacy of subordination in our own lives, many of us have been left with a dichotomous split between feminine and professional identities. In the professional role, we are strong and independent. In the private role, we continue to fall into relationships that undermine our strength, either because we are ridden with doubt about how to behave or because the men we choose haven't changed their expectations of what men and women do for each other in a marital arrangement. Either way, the conflict leads to loss of reproduction. It is easier and safer to delay relationships while shoring up the professional life than to fall back into a condition we know doesn't work. Integrating the two identities means taking the power home to fight for a more equal partnership, even though such a move carries the risk of divorce. Thousands of women have done just that, accepting the pain of divorce rather than continue to subordinate their needs in an unequal partnership. The earlier it's done, the better. All of the working mothers in this sample were first married in their twenties. Several had marriages the first time around that stunted their growth toward autonomy. But the women had time to divorce and remarry more equal partners before time ran out on their reproductive lives. Indeed, a quality that marked the mothers in this group was their willingness to change and the speed with which they carried it out.

But taking power home is only part of the answer. The other part lies in humanizing the professional identity with the qualities of a strengthened feminine ethos. We suffer from a cultural heritage that devalues things done by women, including child care, teaching, domestic labor, and most other productive work shaped by women—no matter how difficult it is or how important in the life of the society. Collecting the garbage, work done by men, is more highly paid than rearing a child, and that inequality permeates all the layers of our culture, from the meanest physical labor to advanced scientific thinking. If men do it, it must carry more weight—a skewed valuation that is worse, if less overt, at the highest levels of achievement than at the lowest. The threads of nineteenth-century patriarchy form a tighter weave at the top than they do at the bottom, where they are unraveled by the harsh realities of life. If we as women cannot examine and uproot this value system from our own lives, we rob ourselves and society of a perspective it badly needs for social balance.

The feminine perspective is different. Whether by nature or culture, or both, it differs from, and is sometimes better than the world seen through the eye of the masculine ethos. We need to value what our bodies can do and trust our intellect. Sexuality and mind. Inseparable qualities, one the source of love and rejuvenation; the other the means of knowing and evaluating the world. They operate together. Men project their sexuality upon the world. Their fantasies and passions, childhood dreams, needs and longings inform all the products of their minds. Women can do no less. If we are to be equal, we must love our bodies in feminine form—the miraculous source of life—and project that love onto the world, knowing that its expression is true, no matter how it may stack up against the received wisdom. When we succeed in doing that—over and over again—the masculine ethos will change, and is changing, because it is a product of divided gender cultures.

Such cultures create ugly consequences—war, personal aggression, abuse of women, and threatened, desensitized men. Beginning in the late 1950s, anthropologists prominent in the study of culture and personality began to see that the divided sex sphere in which men remain aloof from their children or any responsibility for nurturing seems to create a warrior ethos. Distanced from their families by gender role, men generate values and beliefs that elevate male over female abilities. Unable to acknowledge their own human sensitivities, they become hyperaggressive and hypermasculine, denigrating everything feminine and inclined to seek out the exclusive company of men. Not surprisingly, such cultures are particularly warlike.

But why? What accounts for the emergence of a warrior ethos in cultures that give fathers only a minimal role as parents? A Harvard team, led by anthropologist John Whiting, first glimpsed part of the answer in 1958, when they realized that the painful, often sadistic initiation rites that boys in some primitive cultures went through at puberty occurred primarily in societies where men lived apart from their wives and children. Typically, the men neither ate nor slept with their wives, except on visits, and the children of both sexes were reared with women, producing in the boys an original feminine identity, which was thrown into reverse gear at puberty. At that time, senior men took the boys away and subjected them to incredibly painful ceremonies, sometimes involving circumcision, but often abuse alone. In this way, they broke the link with the mother and inculcated a masculine identity associated with brutality, as well as a range of "manly" traits set up in cultural opposition to the feminine.

Achieving such dramatic shifts in personality required a fair degree of repression and denial. The boy's new identity was based on defense mechanisms, with insecurity at the core. Newly aggressive and violent, anti-female in orientation, the young men in these cultures achieved masculine identity through a forced rejection of their prior personalities.

The Iatmul are not the only example of such practices. Of fifty-six cultures reviewed by the Whiting team, eighteen of them had puberty rites for boys involving either severe hazing by adult men, genital operations, seclusion from women, or tests of endurance. Among the Thonga, a South African tribe, the boys were severely beaten on the slightest pretext, made to sleep without covers in the cold, forbidden to drink a drop of water for three months, fed the half-digested grass from an antelope's stomach, and punished by having their fingers almost crushed. If a boy revealed any secrets to women or tried to escape, he was threatened with death. After the *rite de passage,* the boys moved into the men's house with personalities far removed from the children they had been.

In later studies of these gender-divided cultures, other characteristics emerged, particularly male domination of women. It wasn't simply gender separation that created the hypermasculine syndrome, but that plus cultural values giving more prestige and power to men. "The conflict will develop in those male children who move from a world dominated by women and children into a world dominated by men. It will be a problem for those boys who have formed a strong identification with women only if people in the world make it very clear that being a man is very different from being a woman, and that men are more important and more powerful," wrote Beatrice Whiting in 1965. The greater the contrast between the power of men and women, the stronger the sexual conflict for boys, and the more elaborate the defenses protecting masculine identity.

But what purpose is served by doing violence to masculine identity? The process is certainly not innate, since boys reared in intimate company with their fathers had no such initiation rites. Able to identify with males from birth, the boys experienced less conflict and no dramatic shift in personality at puberty. The Whitings and their colleagues proposed that such customs may have arisen from the need for warriors to protect capital investment. The practices were much less frequent among hunters and gatherers, who had no land, than among farmers and herdsmen.

Gender relations in nineteenth-century Europe bear an unpleasant similarity to these male-dominated tribal societies. Across the nations of Europe and into America—where it was attenuated but still present—spread a masculine ethos that was threatened by female power and intent on keeping women in bondage. Rules of patriarchy stripped women of any power or authority in the public realm. Women could not own property, manage their own money, appear in court, open their own bank accounts, or incur debts in their own names. Nor could they claim legal responsibility for the children they spent their time rearing. In the event of a divorce, men claimed custody. "Even the most scandalous, neglectful and brutal of husbands could obtain custody of his children. . . ." writes Peter Gay, author of *The Bourgeois Century*. "Throughout the bourgeois century, all across the western world, women remained virtual chattels in the hands of their fathers and later of their husbands." Family life was crystallized by the epigram: "My wife and I are one and I am he." The domination by men was accompanied during the nineteenth century by a division in gender cultures that had not been present before. Although there had been an ideology of feminine submissiveness in prior centuries, the reality of life for men and women was far more equal. The sexes worked together in small industries still associated with the domestic realm. Women played important roles as midwives and were not prevented from taking control of businesses or other activities in the public realm. The ideology of the woman as a dutiful wife had little impact on the way people lived their lives, noted William H. Chafe in *Women and Equality*. That changed with the rise of modern professions and large-scale businesses. Men left home, creating a domestic ghetto for their wives, and the gender cultures diverged. Patriarchy was entrenched in law and in practice.

Women fought for entrance in the emerging professions and industries against enormous male resistance. Men disparaged the female intellect as part of a cultural campaign to limit feminine consciousness to domestic topics. The art and literature of the age reflected the theme of the dangerous woman—destructive, frightening, and castrating, a vagina with teeth. Theories about "natural" masculine and feminine temperaments, perpetrated through young medical and social sciences, reduced feminine psychology and mentality to the level of a child. The mental condition of hysteria, for example, exemplified to Freud the weaknesses of the female mind. But to twentieth-century thinkers, it appears increasingly as a political disease, the only way that individual women could exercise power—manipulative and indirect as it was—in homes where adult females could be locked into a room to force compliance.

As for the men, they lost contact with their children during the nineteenth century. The disciplinary function remained, but the close, immediate daily contact of father and son that provided a role model for masculine identity was gone. Boys were raised by women, and then in dramatic and traumatic ways were introduced to a masculine ethos that was the opposite of what they had known and inculcated as part of their personalities.

At the first feminist convention in the United States, held in Seneca Falls, New York, in 1848, women pointed directly to the division in gender spheres as being responsible for their suppression by men. In their final declaration, the women at Seneca Falls called for the elimination of all barriers separating the activities of the two sexes. An ex-

249

tremely radical proposition for its time, the declaration tells us that from the beginning women recognized that their subordination could be traced to the segregation of the sexes.

Men are not to blame for the insensitivities of the masculine ethos, any more than women are to blame for the weaknesses of the feminine ethos. Both represent cultural personalities that seem to arise in tribal groups threatened by endemic war or some other harsh condition of life that exerts pressure on populations. The genders divide because their purposes in life become diametrically opposed: women to create and nourish life, men to kill and preserve. It's an efficient use of gender differences. Although individuals suffer from having to serve a gender system that stifles personal freedom, the people survive. They can tolerate the loss of male life with no effect on reproduction. All of the humanizing traits devolve on one sex, allowing the other to function in an arena defined by personal risk and death. Increased aggressiveness, insensitivity, denial of feelings, loss of contact with unconscious processes, and a number of ways of externalizing and projecting pain emerge as character traits in the male personality, in sufficient numbers for it to become an ideal and a standard for masculine identity—the masculine ethos.

Culture pulls from the male repertoire a particular constellation of traits, denying all the other capacities for nurturing and sensitivity that men have in full measure in other environments. Those behaviors become defined as unmasculine, off bounds, outside the male identity. And the same is done for the feminine ethos. Traits associated with the masculine identity are forbidden to the feminine. She cannot be tough, aggressive, destructive. She should not be insensitive to her children (if she's a feminine woman). She should admire the men, reward them for their sacrifice, make them heroes.

In explaining sex role conditioning, many people look to the very early years of childhood. They analyze the effects of playing with certain kinds of toys and, led by Freudian thinking, locate the trauma of masculine identity at the age of two. According to Freudian theory, that is the time when boys recognize that their sexual form is different from their mother's and they make a leap in gender identity from mother to father. Differentiating from the loving figure that gave them birth is a difficult process—and boys achieve it by denigrating everything feminine. Anything associated with the mother is tagged unacceptable in the

250

boy's mind, including many aspects of his own personality. The original, primary loving relationship must be broken as a source of identification; thus, masculine identity depends on a process of breaking bonds and losing relationships. Denial and repression are normal to masculine identity in ways that are not true for feminine identity. Forbidden aspects of the personality must be projected, and the obvious people on whom to project traits men cannot accept in themselves are wives, mothers, and close female figures. But the fragility in this process, the inherent weakness in masculine identity, creates a need to control and dominate the feminine component.

As the dimensions of the nineteenth-century patriarchy come to light, historians of both sexes recognize how deeply men feared women's power and sought to contain it. They look for explanations in "normal" male psychology. Men "naturally" fear the power of their mothers, who were so overwhelming in their childhood. Men naturally want to form all-male groups antagonistic to the inclusion of women. It's the male bonding instinct. And the theories go on reflecting nineteenth-century thinking from the perspective of an exceedingly vulnerable masculine identity. The historian, Peter Gay, for instance, looks for the roots of patriarchy in a primitive fear that grips men in the presence of female power. Women's equality represents the intimidating power of their mothers, and men do what they can to control, contain, and suppress that threat, a threat which for unexplained reasons reached epidemic proportions in the nineteenth century. "No century depicted women as vampires, as castrators, as killers so consistently, so programmatically, and so nakedly as the nineteenth. . . . The little boy concealed in the 19th century man looked up at his powerful, unpredictable mother and was afraid."

But if these qualities of masculine identity are natural, why have they not been evident in all centuries of the Western experience and in all cultures? On the contrary, many tribal societies show no inclination on the part of men to fear and oppose women's power. Exclusive men's clubs do not exist. Relations between men and women are friendly, not hostile. Nor do the men in these cultures have an ethos that stifles emotional life and expression.

To locate the roots of gender personality solely in infant development (or nature) ignores the evidence of cultural anthropology and recent psychology as well, both of which point to adolescence and pu-

251

berty as times of critical change in personality. So crucial is this period, when hormones flood the body and the adolescent is faced with an entirely new set of gender issues, that childhood personality may bear little or no relationship to the adult personalities of men and women. This is the time when boys must fit into the adult masculine culture however they can, as standard bearer, rebel, recluse, or dropout. In Iatmul society, boys were taken into the men's house and subjected to a brutal ritual that went on for days, changing their personality. The feminine ethos the boys had been reared with was driven out; the masculine personality that emerged was insensitive, bullying, and hostile to women. In nineteenth-century English society, boys entered special schools where, in all-male company, they were subjected to brutal discipline for the purpose of creating a personality capable of handling authority. Meanwhile, on the Continent, military training became widespread among common men. Prior to the nineteenth century, the military had been an elite occupation. In France, after the Revolution, and in Germany in the early nineteenth century, military conscription was introduced along with the concept of the "citizen-soldier."

From the perspective of masculine identity formation, all of these activities share the common theme of "turning boys into men," boys who were originally reared by women separated from the world of men. Moreover, the process in all cases involves an experience with abuse associated with masculine identity. It changes personality. In gender-divided cultures, the distance between the boy's early personality and his later adult role is so immense that a cultural event operating at puberty is needed to maintain the divisions. This is the time when the Freudian mechanisms of denial and repression come prominently into play.

American society is no longer segregated by sex, but neither is it completely integrated. Throughout the sixties and seventies, women achieved what integration exists by moving into the public sphere, largely at the cost of their reproductive lives. Now we face the problem of integrating men into the domestic sphere, and beyond that, of changing the institutions that arose in the nineteenth century with no room for children. Professions and corporations took their shape from a masculine culture separated from the family; in fact, they may have been responsible for creating that division. In explaining why patriarchy overwhelmed the Western world during the nineteenth century, Peter

Gay makes a tentative link with the rise of modern business: "In earlier centuries, women had participated in running small family shops, helped to direct draftsmen's enterprises, and played highly visible roles as midwives. Then came, gradually but irresistibly, the modern professions and large-scale manufacturing and merchandizing in which women were denied any posts of command; and the diffusion of prosperity allowed many respectable couples to exempt women from the workplace." Thus, the dual forces of size—removing work from the domestic arena—and prosperity created for us a professional world with few traditions involving family life or even making allowance for its existence. The effect has been steadily to undermine the social bonds we all need for mental, emotional, and spiritual health.

Women's thorough integration into business and professional roles presents institutions with a critical choice. They can either move in fundamental ways to balance their requirements with family life, or watch reproduction dwindle among the daughters of the middle class.

Some social scientists, seeing this dilemma, have called for a restructuring of the work environment to accommodate families. Often they speak only of the woman's special role, arguing that industry must recognize that women cannot be expected to follow out the male pattern of work without sacrificing their ability to reproduce. But if we accept this solution—that women are uniquely responsible for child rearing—nothing will change except the career aspirations of women, who will continue to be kept in subordinate positions, filling two roles with difficulty. Something more profound is needed than a change in work patterns for women.

The experience of men and women in other cultures holds out the hope that if men are brought close to their children as nurturant parents, the entire system will reflect a change in the masculine ethos, with far-reaching effects on the social order, including our patterns of work. A warrior ethos does not survive well when men have the same rights and duties as women in the family sphere.

Equalizing the gender spheres means that corporations offer fathers the same privileges they offer mothers, with the exception of disability leave for childbirth. It also means that women give up their primary rights over children, sharing not only the responsibility for rearing them but the legal preference at gaining custody in a divorce suit. And it means that the priorities of the workplace change significantly, to allow both men and women the time and energy to rear families. Parental leave of one to three months for infant care is not enough. To be closely involved with their children, parents need consistently more time, on a daily and weekly basis, as well as more flexibility in hours and greater stability in the location of work. Work should be altered to fit the needs of family, argued Kenneth Keniston in a 1977 Carnegie Corporation study on children and the family. "It should no longer be assumed that families are not the business of employers or public officials."

Will men accept this alternative? Will they integrate the gender spheres, as women have struggled to do for two centuries, and complete the social transformation toward a sexually equal society? There are reasons to think so.

In nineteenth-century Europe and in tribal cultures where the rules of patriarchy prevailed, men claimed ownership of their children whether or not they had anything to do with rearing them. Distanced from any nurturing role, still men retained rights to the children by virtue of their position in the social order. That is not true in modern American society, where women claim the offspring, but claim them on the basis of their dominant role in nurturing. The crux of the issue is the child's welfare, not the mother's right, and it makes sense that in a time when women must relinquish their domination of this sphere to pursue careers, men would increase their participation, not because they are altruistically motivated to make things easier for women but because it is the only way to reach equality with women in the divorce courts. American men have no choice but to become better parents or let their children go. Just as women know in their guts that they can no longer depend on men for economic support throughout life, men know in the same basic way that they cannot hold onto their children when women have the right and the means of taking them away. It is just this kind of personal experience with the basic issues of survival and continuity that motivates mass cultural change.

As a sign of the times, the overwhelming majority (83 percent) of companies in a survey of corporate attitudes expressed the belief that men increasingly feel the need to take a larger role in parenting. That survey, done by the Catalyst research group in 1980, also found that only 9 percent of those same companies provided paternity leave of any sort—in spite of their perception of men's needs. Four years later, Catalyst did the survey again. This time, the percentage of companies offering paternity leave had exploded to 37 percent. In the same period, corporate support of child care leapfrogged from a few hundred to more than a thousand companies.

The researchers also found, however, that few men were taking advantage of the new benefits; but that may be a temporary lag. With the need and the opportunity coinciding, fathers may well decide that the time has come to build the bonds they seriously need, if they are going to become central rather than peripheral in the lives of their children. And that one small step could change the world.

16

The Nineties:
New Perspectives on
the Two-Gender Workforce

In 1986 the American media discovered that working women could not "have it all," meaning full-time careers and an involved family life. Until that time, there had been an ebullient belief that women were somehow managing to solve the career/family dilemma if they wanted to. Stories of women making salaries in the upper registers while raising families appeared ad nauseum in the women's magazines in the first half of the decade. Whenever the subject came up—in print or on the air—it was cast in the framework of "choice." Women were *choosing* to have careers instead of children, or children instead of careers. Rarely was their true dilemma described, nor did these stories recognize that polarized tendencies of the culture had come together and made a battleground out of women's lives.

During the early stages of writing this book, I also was impressed with an overly optimistic point of view. Working mothers in my study, particularly those in New York, made it plain that their life-style was entirely feasible.

"There are two points of view in the women's movement. You can have it all, or you can't have it all. I believe you can have most of it," said one. "It's not difficult per se, but very time-consuming."[1]

Another working mother in New York explained that the only time she took for herself was during the walk to the subway in the morning. But she was successful—and happy.

It was OK, I thought. Working mothers had full lives, but they were doable without fundamental shifts in our way of life.

But the statistics told a different story.

Sixty percent of executive women in the U.S. had no children. Fifty percent were single, compared with only 3 and 5 percent of executive men in the same positions.[2] This was not sexual equality, but a new form of inequality—the opposite side of an old coin.

Moreover, the single and childless women I interviewed had another story to tell. They described lives in which they had inadvertently surrendered a home life, including children. It wasn't a conscious choice, for the most part. The surrendering came in a million small decisions along the way to delay personal life, or wait for the next promotion, or more money, or more time, or a better man. Very few were aware soon enough that they would have to fight determinedly and bargain courageously for a family life—if that was what they wanted—given the career environment they were in.

In the words of one thirty-nine-year-old woman on Wall Street: "I am sorry that I gave up so much... children, a home life... I don't want you to believe that I consciously at age twenty-five, as girls do now, made the decision that I wasn't going to marry or have children. I was not that definite. It just sort of happened that way. And, now that I look back on my thirties and see that I did give up an awful lot in terms of a home life, I'm not very far along in my career for having done that."[3]

Said another woman, thirty-two, in the financial district of San Francisco, "I keep thinking, I'll wait, make all my money and if I'm not married by forty, I'll adopt. That's what I keep telling my parents. But I still think that some day I'll marry and have children.... I don't want to spend the rest of my life alone."[4]

The truth I came away with was this: Yes. A woman could have both family and fulfilling career, but a very high percentage—perhaps even a majority—had not achieved that blessed state of integration. The task of combining these two roles was difficult enough that large numbers of women were losing access to one or the other of what Freud once said were the two pillars of a healthy life: love and work. Many were paying a high price for careers.

A review of *The Third Sex* in *Business Week* magazine carried the headline: "Corporate Women Have It All—But a Family."[5]

On the other side of the fence, American women who did have families were frequently carrying a double load, doing most of the domestic work in their households while holding down a full-time job. As Hochschild demonstrated in her 1989 analysis of how domestic and childcare work was allocated within marriage, women were exceeding the workloads of their husbands by a full month of twenty-four-hour days.[6]

Unfortunately, the working mothers in my sample had no generally applicable solution to this problem. Most had hired full-time, live-in help—a time-honored pattern of elite levels of society, but not one that would be available to the majority of women.

In the face of these obstacles to a fully realized life of love and work, if women could have retreated into the domestic nest in the 1980's, as they did after World War II, no doubt many would have done it. But the economy of 1986 was not the economy of the early fifties. In the later era, only one in five jobs paid a wage high enough to support a family of four on one salary above the poverty level. Two incomes were needed to maintain a middle-class life-style. A mother had to work.

All well and good. But without systemic change involving both men and women, the 1980's rhetoric of new career options for women concealed the fact that most women were being confronted with the same old dilemmas in reverse.

Let it be said, at the outset, that this societal debate is not whether women will work and also bear children. They have always done that—except for women in the middle and upper classes. The debate is about whether working mothers will be kept in dead-end, low-status, low-paid jobs as a tradeoff for a personal life while other women are induced to surrender reproduction.

It is also about the kind of leadership we have in this country. The entrenched masculine model is a stripped-down version of humanity—a model requiring sacrifice of personal and family life, including any experience with caring for the young and vulnerable or any time to nurture the self or develop friendships. This antisocial model of the leader derives from a warrior culture and the special experience of men in a gender-divided society.[7] It does not work in a two-gender labor force.

Special career tracks have traditionally been available for working mothers at the low end of the job scale. These have not necessarily been simple jobs in educational or skill requirements, but they are "women's work" and therefore identified as non-professional or quasi-professional. Along with low status and low pay, women have also had in these jobs greater freedom to follow a cyclical or periodical career pattern, entering, leaving, and returning to work in relationship to personal life.

In 1988, news surfaced from the business world to indicate that the practice of creating women's work had spread to the professional level, this time affecting women who had all the educational credentials and potential for challenging male rule. It was called the "mommy track."

The phrase first came to national attention in a *New York Times* article describing how law firms were dealing with motherhood in their female professionals.[8] The firms were setting up barriers to advancement for women who chose to take maternity leaves and more flexible working hours. If they cut back on their hours at all, the women were losing a chance to become partners. Some firms, according to the article, were even thinking of making the mommy track a formal option, a two-tiered system that would separate out women with children (who took time for them) from women without children.

Working part-time in this environment meant working not twenty but forty hours per week. Full-time was literally all the time. According to the article, lawyer mothers were cutting back to forty hours.

Five months later, a woman who had been a powerful force for generating new ideas about women in the business world proposed such an option for the majority of career-minded professional women. In an article published by the prestigious *Harvard Business Review*, Felice Schwartz, head of the Catalyst research group in New York, suggested that corporations take a good look at the women in their managerial ranks and recognize that they can be classified into two types: career primary and career family women.[9] The first type is, like many men, willing to put careers first, wrote Schwartz:

> They are ready to make the same trade-offs traditionally made by the men who seek leadership positions. They make a career decision to put in extra

hours, to make sacrifices in their personal lives, to make the most of every opportunity for professional development. For women, of course, this decision also requires that they remain single or at least childless, or, if they do have children, that they be satisfied to have others raise them.[10]

Schwartz recommended that corporations recognize these women early, accept them, and clear the path for them to the top.

The career family women, on the other hand, should be offered numerous inducements to stay on the job after childbirth—inducements such as part-time work, job sharing, and other, more flexible working arrangements that would allow them to balance responsibilities in two spheres. Without ever using the words "mommy track," Schwartz stated that the majority of women would be "willing to trade some career growth and compensation for freedom from the constant pressure to work long hours and weekends."

Catalyst, although funded by corporate money, had maintained a progressive attitude about the new two-gender work force, so this proposal literally knocked the props out. Forty-four women's organizations protested the terms of Schwartz's article.

In an editorial, the *New York Times* inveighed:

> Ladies, take your choice. The big time belongs to the single, the childless, or the woman with a 24-hour nanny. Others must settle for less pay and just possibly a dead-end job.
>
> ...where, by the way, is that new world in which male and female were to work side by side, not only on the job but in the home? It's not here yet, nor will it ever be while women are required to make a choice that is never asked of men and not until society acknowledges that men can be as ambivalent as women about what they owe their jobs and what they owe their families.[11]

The public response to the Catalyst article was so intense that the words "mommy track" were soon buried, not to be heard of again except by those willing to take the risk of sounding dated.

But while the business world stopped talking about a two-track system for women, it didn't stop employing one. At least part of the furor was due to the fact that Schwartz had openly identified and endorsed a system that was in fact the traditional historical response to female labor. The new difference was that most companies had not yet provided the flexible options that Schwartz suggested would keep many working mothers on the job. Instead, they were forcing such women to quit by offering no alternative to excessive work demands.

At a deeper level, there was fury over the intolerable choices women were being forced to make. Schwartz argued that career primary women could be identified early. But attitudes and goals change over time and the choices people make are shaped by the rewards they receive in the workplace, among other places. Most professional women are career primary in their early years and only as the consequences of that choice become clear do they develop a sense of urgency about their private lives and seek to make changes toward having families.

A concerted effort to single out women willing to forfeit family ties could only have a chilling effect on their reproductive lives. When promotions, status, and equality in the workplace are based on a woman's willingness to remain childless, many women would do just that and many would regret it later. It is a very high price to pay for careers.

Moreover, it bears the mark of encouraging women to make what are essentially unhealthy decisions to forfeit family connections and personal life for work. This is not to say that an individual cannot have a rewarding and happy life in a single life that is devoted to career. Some women (but very few men) have done that. The human condition, however, is that most men and women experience isolation and alienation when they are not bound together with others in bonds of mutual dependency. A single life is a very difficult one to maintain over the years. The individual must spend a great deal of time finding emotional outlets, support, and companionship.

Finally, the model of an ideal corporate manager is notorious for exploiting the labor of professional people. Burnout is an ever-present risk and the end result—more often than not—is failure to achieve the few top rewards held out as inducement.

But no matter how abnormal this system might appear from the perspectives of women's lives, it represents everyday reality in the history and culture of corporations that evolved out of the labor practices of men in a sex-divided culture. In this culture, a balanced work and family life are *not supposed* to exist. The normal expectation for men, particularly ambitious men, is to sacrifice personal life.[12]

The conservative 1980's represented a step backward in the quest to bring fathers more thoroughly into the lives of their families. During the early part of the decade there was hope that if employers would give men the opportunity to take family leave, they would do it. By the end of the decade that was apparently not happening, although there had been a great increase in the number of companies offering paternity leave.[13]

The way corporations offered the leave, however, made it plain that there would be a price to pay in careers and probably also in masculine image if men took the leave. It was disguised as "personal leave" and often companies did not tell their male employees about it, or else they might describe it as a benefit for men who had no ambition in the company.

In resisting change in the status quo, companies were able to play on classic themes of masculine identity: Men always put career first. Men don't leave work to take care of babies. Men are naturally more aggressive and less nurturant than women. These and other dictates of the masculine ethos resurged in backlash fashion to keep men on a straight and narrow path defined by culture as the male gender role.

This occurred in spite of an evolutionary movement on the part of millions of individual men away from stereotypical masculine themes. There has been, for instance, slow growth in the amount of time fathers spend in domestic chores.[14] Between the years 1975 and 1981, men increased by 20 to 30 percent the time they spend in childcare and housework—not a huge difference, but a movement toward greater participation in the work of maintaining their families. A more dramatic sign of change occurred during the decade of the eighties when the number of single-parent households headed by men almost doubled to more than one million homes, according to the 1990 census. There were 616,000 male-headed single-parent households in 1980, compared to 1,153,000 in 1990. Women still carry the lion's share of single-parent households, heading up 6,599,000 in 1990, but the male proportion grew from 10 percent to 15 percent during the decade.[15]

But acting like a brake on these evolutionary changes among men, the institutions of the culture exerted an increasingly regressive force in the five years since this book was written, keeping men in their place at work and on the front lines. Affecting not just men in their family roles but women also, resurgence of traditional male values dominated the cultural environment.

The professional advances women have made are typically seen as a victory—and a victory they are. But the system has the power to utterly subsume women's lives, shaping them into a male pattern. It is male culture that defines the professional world, determining its level of aggressiveness, competition, and tolerance for personal life, just for a start. How men view their inherent nature sets the mold for the institutions within which women work. The institutions in turn feed back an ideology of masculine behavior that supports their existing structures and habits. This tight fit between male behavior and institutional practice creates enormous resistance to change and is accompanied by an ideology which says that men—and therefore human institutions—possess a "killer" instinct, the product of millions of years of evolution. Such an ideology props up the system of male dominance, defining it as genetic rather than cultural, as anthropological studies have shown it to be.[16] These attitudes were very much in evidence at the turn of the decade.

One telling example from the scientific and lay press in 1989 demonstrates the powerful ways in which this traditional view of men as aggressive and militaristic directly affects contemporary life. From stories of apes and baboons, early man and remote tribes, Western scientists have constructed an enduring image of a highly aggressive, warlike human male. The image is highly selected, meaning that it is pruned from the wondrously diverse array of male behaviors—both peaceable and aggressive—that occur naturally in the wild and in human culture. Nevertheless, this construction of masculinity spreads from academe to a vast general audience via the media, almost never subjected to a sustained or critical evaluation.

Such an image appeared prominently in 1989 in the nation's premier scientific journal, *Science*, mirrored in the extraordinary aggression of a group of Amazonian warriors called the Yanomamo.[17] In a major, lead article in the weekly journal, anthropologist Napoleon Chagnon set up this depiction of violence as a crucible for the evolution of the human male:

- Forty-four percent of the adult Yanomamo men have killed someone in repetitive blood feuds among kin groups usually focused around sexual competition for women.

- Seventy percent of all adults over the age of forty have lost a relative to violence.
- Warriors among the Yanomamo make continual raids on neighboring tribes to capture wives or exact revenge for the killing of a relative. No one is free from the threat of homicide since the raiders don't take care to kill just the perpetrators of a blood feud; anyone from that tribe will do as a victim of retribution.

So why should society take this small and remote Amazonian tribe as representative of male human evolution? Chagnon's answer is that the killers among the Yanomamo have more children than the men in that tribe who don't kill. From his twenty-three years of research among them, Chagnon was able to track the histories of some thirteen hundred individuals to discern a reproductive advantage among the avengers, who win the most prestige and, in this polygynous culture, the most wives. He claims, without evidence, that the tribal period of human prehistory was more violent that we know about. He also neglects to mention that the Yanomamo practice female infanticide because they value men over women, setting up a scarcity of females that is the main impetus for continual warfare. There are few examples in the anthropological literature of a more self-destructive culture than this one.

Chagnon's article was picked up by major newspapers and his example of aggression in the jungle was expanded to men in business suits. The *Los Angeles Times* and the *Washington Post* both ran stories on the Yanomamo, distributing the article through their syndicates to dozens of small papers throughout the country.

Boyce Rensberger of the *Post* wrote that the so-called male blood lust (or whatever behavior did evolve; Chagnon wasn't clear about that) could be expanded not only to all people, but to economic and political realms:

"Although Chagnon's theory on the causes of social violence applies to all peoples, the effects may be quite different in societies where a strong police force and judicial system deter violence. Male sexual competition may then be channeled into other arenas such as the pursuit of wealth or power."[18]

Thomas H. Maugh II of the *Los Angeles Times* also expanded the example of this very remote and unrepresentative tribal group:

"Chagnon's findings reinforce an emerging consensus among anthropologists that violence is continually present in primitive societies," he wrote. Quoting Chagnon, the story demurred that "'I'm not saying that man has genes for warfare or violence, but that the strong will take advantage of the weak whenever it benefits them. That principle is as applicable in arms control negotiations as it is in primitive tribes.'"[19]

No one wondered why thirteen hundred men still living in the Stone Age in 1987 could represent four million years of human evolution. Moreover, far from being representative of tribal men, the Yanomamo actually represent only a minority of cultures. Warrior systems like the Yanomamo have been found in one-fourth to one-third of the roughly 150 tribal cultures ever studied by anthropologists, a small fraction of those that populated prehistory. *Their behavior does not fit the majority of men in tribal societies that are known to science.*[20]

Moreover, Yanomamo social customs include brutal puberty rites that are believed to raise the level of male aggression to abnormal heights, what could be called pathological in American society. Chapter 3 of this book describes the harsh rites of passage used by warrior cultures to traumatize and brainwash young boys to enter an adult world where they will be called upon to kill other people. A division between the genders, separation of fathers from children, suppression of women, and other social patterns work to produce these violent men. Genes you don't need. The social system is purely violent enough to turn young boys into killers. Nor are polygamy and female infanticide common occurrences in tribal society.

The reoccurence of this killer image of male behavior during the late 1980's offered testimony to its endurance. When society needed the labor of women, the ideology of women as passively feminine and relatively incompetent fell quickly. But the ideology of masculinity is maintained by a powerful complex of business demands, social custom, and national aggression. It is being challenged, but slowly.

Along with the resurgent themes of the warrior culture came setbacks in efforts to design a new family policy that would help families deal with the two-gender work force. In 1990, President George Bush vetoed the nation's first federal family leave policy passed by Congress.* The most conservative family leave policy in the Western

---

*As this book went to press, The Family Leave Act was reintroduced in Congress for the sixth time, passed in both chambers with large majorities and was forwarded to the president.

world, the act would do little more than require companies of more than fifty employees to provide twelve weeks of unpaid leave to their employees for medical or family reasons, so perhaps little was lost in the veto. Most large companies already have such a leave policy.

Passage, however, would represent an important national statement that some changes are needed to cope with the conflict between an immovable wall (the notion that business interests always come first) and an irresistible force (the crying needs of children and families). Today, under prevailing conditions, an employee can be fired for taking three months off work to care for a newborn or a sick parent.

A s the debate over work and family developed through the turn of the decade, fundamental differences emerged between those who thought the system could change and those who thought it wouldn't. Although both sides were seeking answers, their solutions differed radically, depending on whether they felt the system was a permanent given.

At the end of 1989, nearly a year after the Schwartz article, the *Harvard Business Review* published a counter view by Fran and Charles Rodgers of Work/Family Directions, Inc. in Boston. Calling for corporations to be more "family friendly," the Rodgerses wrote that the forty-hour work week is nothing more than a sacred cow. "Employers cannot imagine that anyone working fewer hours could be doing anything useful," they said. Arguing that most companies have not looked seriously at the options in connection with work productivity, the authors challenged the axiom that supervisory and managerial personnel must always be full-time.

"It takes a lot of ingenuity and cultural adaptability to devise meaningful part-time work opportunities and to give employees individual control of their working hours.... But if adaptability and labor-market competitiveness are the goals, then the usual definition of fast-track career progression needs modification."[21]

In February 1990 the magazine carried the debate further by publishing an extensive assortment of letters to the editor, including ones from Schwartz and the Rodgerses.[22] The latter wrote: "Rather than try to rethink careers designed for men with wives at home, Ms. Schwartz's entire prescription seems to be to remove all barriers, so as to give the competitive edge to those (increasingly few) men and women who can live as though work were the only thing in their lives."

Schwartz answered that a forty-hour week may be enough for those up to midlevel management, but for anyone aspiring to more:

"In the corporation as we know it and in the face of our faltering position in the world economy, those who want to participate at higher levels of management and in leadership positions cannot confine their work commitment to a 40-hour week. ...I see little prospect of reducing this time requirement or the demand for relocation and travel."

Reportedly distressed by the intensity of the public reaction to her original article, Schwartz also clarified in her letter that the mommy track need not be permanent:

"Employers must learn how to provide such flexibility for finite periods, which can be *as long as three or four years* [italics added] without derailing people who want to start families and then get back on the fast track."

The notion of a finite period or a parenting phase within an upwardly mobile career stands worlds away from a mommy track, which has connotations of permanent divergence for women only. It may be, as the pessimists insist, that nobody can have it all at the same time, but a lifetime is a long time. The idea of cycling in and out of career-family and career-intensive phases makes it possible for many to combine the two. The appearance of those few words in Schwartz's letter changed her proposal fundamentally, from a special track for women with children to a parenting phase for both sexes.

The problem at this time in history, on the threshold of the twenty-first century, is to bring the idea of cycling into the male-dominated workplace. An even more radical problem is to make it acceptable for men. And out on the fringes is the notion that all people, single people included, need freedom from the excessive demands of the professional role to make rewarding personal lives for themselves.

Schwartz's article contained the kernel of an important idea, that fundamental changes in working hours are needed to accommodate working parents. The shame of it was its conservative framework. Fathers were barely mentioned as working parents, and the notion of an upwardly mobile career as all-consuming was challenged not at all. It was—like water that carries cholera—an essential idea in a contaminated form.

Sex and Corporations

European nations recognized and dealt with the two-gender work-force much earlier and more fully than the United States. According to some observers, Europeans have been motivated by an acute labor shortage that arrived there earlier than its predicted appearance here during the 1990's. Whatever the reason, England, Sweden, and West Germany (among others) have adopted the notion of career cycles that give parents time away from work and welcome them back after extended leaves.

English companies call their parenting cycles "career breaks,"[23] which may last for up to five years on top of an initial maternity leave for a childbearing woman. Either men or women may take the career break—a one- to five-year period when the employee works part-time or not at all before resuming his or her career. In practice, however, the breaks are usually taken by women, only occasionally by men.

Employees who take the leaves are not sidetracked into dead-end jobs when they return; in fact, many are promoted, according to research by Ellen Galinsky of the Families and Work Institute in New York. Moreover, the company continues benefits for the employees on leave and encourages them to continue their training as well as attend staff meetings and parties. Job guarantees accompany the shorter leaves, but even without a guarantee, the employee retains an identity with the company and is more likely to return, Galinsky discovered. English national law provides, in addition, a ten-month maternity leave for women at childbirth during which time the woman receives part of her salary.

Commenting on the differing attitudes and practices in England compared to the United States, Galinsky wrote: "Only a handful of the most progressive employers [in the U.S.] even approach this amount of time off—AT&T has a one-year leave, IBM's is three years, with part-time work required the second and third year." She continued: "In England, all those I interviewed thought that children must get a good start in life. No one questioned the length of the leave. In fact, when I mentioned that American employers would find this length untenable, that we even have intense opposition to ten weeks off as proposed by Congress, the British employers were astonished. They couldn't understand how a society could ignore the need for mothers and babies to be together."[24]

Sweden, widely recognized as a leader in the arena of family leave

268

policy, offers new parents the option of a year's leave from work with 90 percent of their salary. (By contrast, the family leave bill vetoed by President Bush would have provided a three-month leave without salary.) Swedish parents have had this and other family options since 1974.

As another option, parents are allowed ninety days per year to tend a sick child, a generous benefit that seems to offer much room for abuse. But Swedes do not abuse the option; Galinsky found that they take on the average six to seven days per year for a sick child. Men and women take these days equally. A parent may also reduce working hours by two hours per day until a child is eight years old, a benefit taken mostly by women.

In Sweden, as in England, employers' attitudes toward family issues are stunningly different from those in the United States. In a 1989 paper on European policies commissioned by the National Academy of Sciences,[25] Galinsky observed these attitudes on the part of employers: "It is positive for employees to want to have children"; "The company must adapt to work/family needs"; and "There is a time for career and a time for families."

She wrote: "Rather than portrayed as an interruption, a hindrance, even a problem, a family's desire to have children was talked about in positive terms by male and female, executive and factory worker alike."[26]

These forward-looking attitudes do not mean, however, that childcare is borne equally by men and women in Sweden. Especially when children are infants, women are considered the essential primary parent. While men do take parental leaves, their average time out is only a month and a half, and they tend not to work part-time, while 65 percent of the women do. Nevertheless, male involvement in childcare has grown steadily over the past two decades. In 1974, only 2 percent of Swedish men took a parental leave. Today, that number has risen to 22 to 30 percent.[27]

Galinsky also observed that there was a sense of greater tolerance for interests other than childrearing: "Swedes seemed to endorse more adamantly [than in the U.S.] the idea that people should be multidimensional. In general, the Swedish executives described all employees as expecting and even demanding a good quality of life on the job and off the job. As one put it, people want 'to develop themselves.'"

Sex and Corporations

As in England and Sweden, West Germany offers a very generous government-supported leave policy for parents. Women receive a three-and-a-half-month paid leave around childbirth, and either parent may take up to a year and a half leave after birth—leave that is partially paid by the government, and job-protected. Part-time work is becoming increasingly common and is frequently taken by men for educational reasons, less often for family reasons.

West German workers also describe a growing disenchantment with the workaholic culture. "People want multidimensional lives. Fathers are also more concerned with forming relationships with their young children."[28]

In spite of these changes, West Germany's more traditional sex roles are strongly reflected in industry. Men with wives at home remain in charge at the top and, as in the United States, frequently do not understand the family/work conflicts that people lower in the hierarchy experience. Such men do not take family leaves. Nor have women broken into the upper ranks, even as much as in the United States. It is widely believed that no one can combine a career and a family, and women remain disenfranchised in either their private or their professional lives.

As in the United States, Galinsky discovered that a few companies have moved far ahead of the pack in terms of grappling with work/family issues. These pioneers have created far-reaching policies on part-time work, childcare, and extended leaves with a guaranteed return. The Shering chemical and pharmaceutical company, for example, surveyed its workforce and found out that an astounding 85 percent of all its jobs could be divided into part-time work.[29]

In the United States, the current state of affairs could be described as one of uneven, slow change. Employers are increasingly confronted with work and family issues, as their valued female employees threaten to leave or ask for new flexible working conditions so that they may have families. Usually, however, arrangements are being made on a special, case-by-case basis rather than through general policy. It is rare for an American company to have considered these issues in depth or to have looked at the work culture which requires professionals to put jobs before families. Moreover, the general cultural attitude in corporations is to discourage upwardly mobile women from taking any time off for family reasons.[30]

On the opposite side of the ledger, efforts are being made to identify "family friendly" companies by listing them in a hierarchy from best to worst.[31] The fact that this can be done, with effect, is testimony to the fact that companies care how they look on the work/family issue. It has impact on their ability to attract and retain both men and women. So there is a growing consensus for change. But the nature of that change remains murky.

The issues for one elite profession—law—were crystalized recently in a *Harvard Business Review* article titled "The Case of the Part-time Partner."[32] In this fictional case study, created by a professor at the Harvard Business School, a female lawyer is poised on the brink of partnership. She is an exemplary employee, among the best in the firm, with top-notch legal knowledge, courtroom performance, and ability to attract new clients. She has also been working reduced hours since her child was born three years earlier. Working as necessary to meet the needs of her clients, the lawyer bills about half as many hours as her colleagues who work a standard *seventy hours per week* in this company.

In the scenario written by Gary W. Loveman, four partners meet to consider the lawyer's promotion and they split down the middle on whether to accept her into their ranks. Two of the partners (one man and one woman) argue against promotion, saying that the reduced hours reflect a lack of commitment, or at least an unequal standard. Two (both men) argue for promotion, commenting that 40 percent of the firm's new hires are female and unless a more flexible environment is established, they will continue to lose associates. One of these men points out that all of them had paid a high price for working excessively, a price that included family separation and divorce.

There is no conclusion to the tale; such case studies are meant to stimulate discussion, which in this case gives insight into American attitudes toward these issues. The responses of five experts inside and outside the legal profession were published along with the story, their answers covering a range of attitudes which tended to cluster in three areas.

1. Prevailing work standards should be changed. Three of the five experts commented on the killing pace of a seventy-hour work week. They recommended that this standard be reassessed for everyone. Said a vice president at Merck and Co.: "Given the reality of pressures from an increasingly stressful world outside the office, including, but not limited to family obligations, is this firm (and other businesses) really benefitting from a tradition of working its employees 70 hours a week?"[33]

Others questioned the accepted relationship between hours worked and "commitment" to the company. A career-management expert at Boston University thought that service rather than hours should define commitment. Indeed, eliminating hours as the major criterion of service would represent a revolutionary change in the workplace, opening up the whole issue of productivity to new evaluation. Advocates for change argue with evidence[34] that people who work reduced hours are more productive in their allotted hours than are the people who work full-time. That applies even more strongly to people working longer hours, who may be tired, burned out, and ineffective.

2. Anyone who wants to be a member of the club should pay their dues (i.e., it's unfair to give the same perks and privileges that full-timers get to people who work fewer hours). This is arguably the most significant source of resistance to change. Workers already accepted into the upper ranks of their professions sometimes find it extremely difficult to accept new people who are not making similar sacrifices. And a sacrifice it is.

The process of becoming a full-fledged member of an elite profession (a doctor, lawyer, or academic, among others) is so all-encompassing that it reshapes attitudes, values, and emotional life. One aim of this kind of experience (born out of male-gender culture) is to expand the identity of the professional at the expense of any other identity, such as father, husband, son, friend, or independent self. People get lost in the roles. Because their waking hours are dominated by work, their consciousness and personal development are dramatically limited.

Women, in particular, may have made an enormous sacrifice to gain membership. Not all women want children, but of those who do, many have surrendered reproduction in a process called "choice" and they may be emotionally unwilling to recognize the cost to themselves or the injustice of asking other women to pay it.

In an unusually candid response, a female partner in a New York law firm spelled out the terms of the sacrifice. She voted against partnership for the fictional lawyer, named Julie Ross.

272

Without a doubt, making someone a partner who has not "suffered" as much as his or her peers creates resentment in the partnership...most women who have attained a level of professional success have done so by consciously sacrificing other aspects of their lives—whether it is marriage, children or community involvement. They have discovered that they can't have it all and have had to choose what they want most. Creating a new set of partnership criteria for part-time associates, most of whom will be women, risks alienating women who have earned their status in the traditional way and have made the sacrifices Julie Ross was unwilling to make.[35]

Other sources of resistance come from men who have benefited substantially from traditional sex roles. With wives at home to maintain the family side of their lives, they may have little emotional understanding of the problem and no sense at all of sacrifice. The majority of major businesses in America are still headed by men with these kinds of advantages, although their ranks are increasingly penetrated by men whose wives also work and who are asked to take a more active role at home.

Interestingly, no one in the article argued that it was necessary to work such long hours to get the work done. In fact, studies of productivity that would prove such a necessity are hard to come by. One such study comparing the publication rate of academic scientists showed that there was no difference between mothers and women without children. In other words, women who had to take time for family care published just as often as women who had no such responsibilities.[36]

Not everyone in elite ranks, however, maintains a hard-nosed attitude about tradition. Some want to see the system become more flexible but are sensitive to the equity issues involved, which brings up a third common attitude among respondents in the Case of the Part-Time Lawyer.

3. *Career goals should be modified while people are actively involved in parenting.* This set of attitudes recognizes that amount of time at work *does* matter in setting the income, responsibilities, and sometimes the status of a worker, but not in any permanent way. Some respondents thought that the part-time lawyer should be promoted more slowly, or they recommended that firms develop new kinds of partnerships with different levels of compensation or investment in the company. This last alternative may look like a mommy

track unless the system is open to the top at some point and unless there is a prevailing sense of equal status.

Central to this point of view, which seeks to change the prevailing rigid work standards, is the notion that people working reduced hours should be given more time to achieve membership in the club. But never should they be barred from membership or kept in a subordinate and insecure position.

"Hours worked may be relevant to the size of Ross' piece of the pie, but not to her ability to sit down at the table," wrote a member of the American Bar Association's Commission on Women in the Profession.[37]

The kinds of accommodations being made (or not being made) for family responsibilities are specific to each profession. The University of California, for instance, offers an extra year to achieve tenure for a professor who has a young child and needs the time. In business it is widely believed that managers cannot work part-time, an idea that effectively bars promotions for active parents. The Merck vice president, for instance, commented on the strengths of part-time workers and noted that these employees frequently focus more on getting the job done than on just putting in hours. But then he added, "Nevertheless, it is only non-managers that work part time at Merck; we don't have managerial part-time work...because...let's face it, supervising is a full-time job. The only possible way managers could work part-time is on a job sharing basis. The rules here are still emerging. Merck has not yet dealt with this."[38]

Those last few words from Merck sum up the common theme in the United States: Most companies have not yet dealt with the basic issues posed in the work/family dilemma. In the aftermath of his article's publication, Loveman received many calls, but few callers talked about promoting the woman. In his analysis, "The position of women (with children) is still pretty tenuous. Progress in the past five years is not startling at all."[39]

In the absence of national or professional progress in the work/family area, women must forge their own individual paths through the cultural wilderness with little societal help or guidance from those who have gone before. One consequence is a pervasive sense of anxiety about time—trying to get it all in before reproductive age runs out. One academically talented young woman in California who aims to be an actress spoke of this anxiety one night over a cappuccino in a Berkeley café. She said she had the feeling she was start-ing too late on a career and may never have a chance to have chil-dren, which she wants. She was only twenty-four.

The public debate over women and work has richocheted from one polar position to another, only rarely engaging solutions that lie at a cultural level, involving both genders. In one era, women are told that they "can do it." Problems are swept out of sight; sacrifices are over-looked, and selected images focus on individuals who, while making lots of money, also rear children. In reaction, the next era ushers in all the problems. Sacrifices are still overlooked and women are told they must choose between career and family.

Meanwhile, women's lives continue their inexorable confrontation with the workplace, in a largely mute struggle with enormous com-promise. Men often ask the question, Why shouldn't women make compromises? Men have had to do so for generations. But the plain fact is that men have not been making compromises on the scale expected of women. Male sacrifice of the family is psychological. Onerous, yes, but not absolute. There is always the possibility of change, of coming to a different set of priorities and balancing one's life. The family, however neglected, exists. For women the sacrifice is total, not psychological.

It is a subtle form of outrage that ambitious young women are led to contemplate a future without families, as though it doesn't matter, as though the single life is a fully equivalent choice for women. It is not. And that does not distract at all from the freely adopted choice of some women to forego marriage or reproduction.

Equity, however, is not the only reason for advocating basic change. The dream of a more humane world enters through the por-tals of sexual equality. The anthropological record of past and present cultures tells us that male power must be balanced with equally significant female power if it is not to become abusive power.

I do not argue that women are inherently better people than men are. Either gender can abuse power, if given exclusive access to it. We know from the example of many female leaders that they will wage war just as readily as men will. We also know that mothers can be abusive in their own domain. The memories of childhood that some grown men and women carry around with them is a major source of misogyny.

Such memories may also be a primary mechanism underlying the psychological structure of patriarchy. As many authorities have observed, men develop an inordinate fear of female power when they either are dominated by their mothers or lack close fathers to provide masculine models for growth. The child's fear engenders an adult male need (under certain cultural conditions) to suppress and dominate women. One could add that women also develop that same misogyny when their mothers have loomed too large or too destructively in their lives.

So I don't advocate a matriarchy. The solution for the evils of male dominance is certainly not female dominance. A balance of male and female power offers a very different kind of society, a different view of the world. Only through such a balance do men and women have the capacity to check the excesses of the other gender, which they are uniquely suited to do.

Men and women, intimates of each other and capable of forming marvelous bonds of trust and cooperation, have the capacity to enlighten and alter the behavior of the other, so long as each is mutually empowered. And this empowerment must be vested, not just in individual women, but in the emotional and social sphere women have been responsible for.

We need proud and loving women who can confront men in close encounters of the revolutionary kind.

We need women who are not afraid to acknowledge their distinctiveness and women who are totally unwilling to concede male superiority.

And we need men wise enough to take a good look at their own culture with the courage to see it change.

Through overlapping responsibilities and systems that hold each accountable to the other, men and women working together can create a more stable world. For that, there are some models. Among the Iroquois Indians of North America, women, who were the farmers, had a culturally accepted power to stop wars they didn't agree with by refusing to supply food to the fighters.[40] Such power on the part of women is often viewed as too much simply because it represents greater power than contemporary women have in American society, but the Iroquois pattern reflects an egalitarian society, not a matriarchal one.[41]

Finally, I'd like to answer the people who say that fundamental change is not possible; that the feminist vision of an equal society is pie in the sky. It's too costly to slow down the pace of work for family concerns, or too dangerous to risk losing a competitive position in the global market. I'd like to suggest that it's too costly and too dangerous not to take these risks. To the extent that America has inherited a warrior culture, it has also inherited a division of labor that places primary responsibility for maintaining the human realm in the hands of women. Young children, old people, the poor, the ill and dispossessed—women traditionally have taken care of these people, as they have maintained the churches and most of the community links. Altruism, spirituality, nurturant and cooperative values—all necessary for this kind of work—cluster in the female realm, not because women are naturally that way or any better than men, but because that's the part of the sky they've been holding up.

With the masses of women now in the labor force, striving to do the same things that men have done and changing in ways that give them the same privileges and opportunities, the female sphere is collapsing. A society cannot function with only half a sky, and we feel the effects in the deepest parts of our lives. We feel it in disorientation, loss of love, increased aggressiveness, and lack of mutual caring, not to mention lack of childcare. That's only a part of the problem and the most obvious.

If we buy into the conservative argument that ambitious career women should remain childless, we help maintain a warrior cultural pattern, and the transformative power of an equal society is lost. Inevitably, women in their full sexual identity offer revolutionary changes in the way society is run. They can't help it. As the childbearing sex, they bring the family with them wherever they go. And the family is the essential humanizing force in any culture—the lack of which gives impetus to warrior tendencies.

It will not be cheap to balance the worlds of work and family. Maintaining the human realm is costly, but perhaps not as costly as a continuing succession of wars. And anyway, one can always ask, as a female business writer once did, "What's an economy for?"[42]

Questionnaire

1. Age.

2. Where are you from?

3. Married _____ Single _____ Divorced _____ Children _____

4. College attended: Coed _____ All women's college _____

5. Current position and type of work.

6. How do you feel about your current work?
   enthusiastic _____
   satisfied for the time being _____
   not currently enjoying the work _____
   working too hard (separate dimension) _____

7. How do you feel about the future potential of your work?
   very good; committed to company _____
   good enough; committed to company _____
   plan to look for better (or different) position _____
   feel stuck; dead-ended _____

8. How do you feel about your working environment and colleagues?
   like it very much _____
   like it all right _____
   don't like it _____

9. Do conversations with male and female colleagues go beyond business to personal levels?
   yes _____
   no _____

10. Birth order _____ Sex of older and younger siblings _____

11. Was your mother a professional?
    yes _____
    no _____

12. How would you characterize your father in terms of personal power/authority in the family and emotional warmth?
    high power _____
    low power _____
    high warmth _____
    low warmth _____

Questionnaire

13. How would you characterize your mother in terms of personal power/authority in the family and emotional warmth?
high power _____
low power _____
high warmth _____
low warmth _____

14. Did you perceive a difference between your parents in terms of general competence?
both competent _____
mother more competent _____
father more competent _____
single parent _____

15. Did you experience either parent as punitive or controlling; i.e., were you afraid of either one?
neither _____
both _____
mother _____
father _____

16. Which parent did you feel closest to?
mother _____ father _____

17. Which parent did you take as a sex role model?
mother _____ father _____ neither _____

18. When you were young, were you taught what females should do in life and what they should be like? If so, what?

19. When you entered the professional world, did you have the sense that your background growing up female provided you with appropriate behavior at work, or not?
appropriate _____
not appropriate _____

20. Is there a conflict in your mind between yourself as a woman and as a professional? (Do you feel like yourself at work?)
yes _____
no _____

21. Did you change your behavior at some point to protect yourself against being treated like a woman?
yes _____
no _____

22. What does being feminine mean to you? You may think about this concept along several dimensions: dress, demeanor, values, attitudes, personality traits, or mental and emotional abilities. Please name all the connotations you have for the concept of being feminine.

23. What does being a woman mean to you? (Same explanation as for "feminine.")

24. What does being a lady mean to you? (Same explanation as for "feminine.")

25. Do you think of yourself as feminine or not feminine? Is that concept relevant to you?
    feminine _____
    not feminine _____
    not relevant _____

26. Do you think of yourself as being a lady, or not a lady? Is that concept relevant to you?
    lady _____
    not a lady _____
    not relevant _____

27. How do you dress for work?
    the primary objective is to be serious and businesslike _____
    looking businesslike and looking feminine are equally important _____
    the primary objective is to look feminine _____
    neither is important _____

28. Do you think women in your type of work should eliminate feminine qualities and signs of sexual attractiveness at work?
    yes _____
    no _____

29. Do you think it's all right to flirt at work, or not?
    all right _____
    not all right _____

30. Do you think it's all right to socialize with male colleagues outside of work, or not?
    all right _____
    not all right _____

31. Have you ever experienced sexual harassment at work?
    yes _____
    no _____

32. Do you think it's all right to have a love affair with a man at work, or not?
    all right _____
    not all right _____

Questionnaire

33. Did you, or do you, find men to date at work?
    never _____
    once _____
    more than once _____

34. In office love affairs, has there been a power differential between you and the man?
    yes _____
    no _____

35. Did the love affair (if any) help you at work? Did it hurt you?
    help _____
    hurt _____
    no effect _____

36. Have you ever heard rumors in the office about love affairs, indicating that someone is getting hurt professionally, or is paying a price for mixing romantic entanglements and work life?
    yes _____
    no _____

37. How were you socialized to be a professional? Were you strongly influenced by books or magazines?

38. How do you feel about being a mother?
    interested _____
    not interested _____
    good _____
    not good _____

39. Do you think that women are discouraged from being a mother and a working woman at the same time—by friends, relatives, working associates, and more impersonal sources?
    yes _____
    no _____

40. Did working contribute to a divorce?
    yes _____
    no _____

41. To what extent have you surrendered your desires for children and a home life for work?
    a great deal _____
    slightly _____
    not at all _____

42. How is your health?
    good _____
    chronic disease _____

43. Have your ideas about sex and morality been strongly influenced by religion?
    no _____
    at one time _____
    still are _____

44. Do you think women are capable of doing the same work as men?
    yes _____
    no _____

46. Do you think women should be prepared for a lifetime of employment or for a largely home career as wife and mother?
    work _____
    home _____

46. Do you think women can exercise power and authority while retaining their femininity?
    yes _____
    no _____

47. If yes, describe such a woman, in whatever thoughts and images come to mind.

Notes

Chapter 1 (pp. 21–37)

1. Complementary sex roles in which the masculine and feminine personalities represent opposite types are characteristic of cultures with a strong division in labor. According to Sanday (1981), "Sexual separation is so extreme in some societies that almost all work activities are defined as either male or female, with the result that the sexes form sexual ghettos" (page 80). In other cultures, where tasks are relatively sexually integrated, "distinctions by sex, though present, are less important in social life" (page 83). See also Martin and Voorhies (1975).

2. Mead's comment on the Manus, Toda, Arapesh, and Dakota Indians is from the Introduction to *Sex and Temperament* (1963).

3. From Bateson (1958), page 14.

4. From Bernard (1972), page 39.

5. Levinson (1978), whose work on the midlife transition has provided important information on personality change in adulthood, says that stagnation at midlife is vital to a man's development. "To become generative, a man must know how it feels to stagnate, to have the sense of not growing, of being static, stuck, drying up, bogged down in a life full of obligations and devoid of self-fulfillment. He must know the experience of dying, of living in the shadow of death" (page 30). From that point, the individual moves on to empathy and compassion for others. But not everybody moves on.

6. Among the Kaulong tribe of Papua New Guinea, women are the sexual aggressors and may attack a man to initiate courtship. Men are afraid of both sex and marriage. From an unpublished paper by anthropologist Jane C. Goodale of Bryn Mawr College.

7. Men drive stakes through the feet of women in the New Guinea highland tribe, the Kuma, studied by Marie Rhey (1959).

8. Men win prestige through generosity and by throwing large feasts among the people of a Solomon Island society called the Siuai, studied by Oliver (1955).

285

9. Fatherhood is exalted among the Manus tribe of New Guinea studied by Margaret Mead (1956). Strong ties between father and child are established when the mother goes into seclusion with a new baby and the father takes over the care of older children. Boys remain devoted to their fathers until about the age of six or seven when they join peer groups.

Chapter 2 (pp. 38–49)

1. See Goodenough (1963, 1971) for his theory of social identity as a program of rights and duties. The theory is discussed further in Chapter 4.
2. The quotes are from Komarovsky (1946).
3. Women supply 80 percent of the food in hunting and gathering cultures, a fact recognized by the authors of *Man the Hunter* (Lee and DeVore, 1968). But their awareness of the central role of women in providing food in the ancient environment did not cause them to modify their thesis that male hunting has shaped the genetic evolution of humankind—all of which has provoked strong challenges from female anthropologists. See Slocum (1975).
4. The quote is from Smith-Rosenberg (1972).
5. A division in labor, including separation of the sexual spheres, does not necessarily mean low power for women. There is a pattern Sanday calls "dual-sex systems" in which each sex manages its own affairs and maintains its own political and religious institutions. Women have power and may make decisions affecting the male sphere; ultimate authority rests in a female monarch, who rules in a complementary fashion with a male monarch. Examples of the dual-sex system abound in West Africa. Sanday (1981), page 88.
6. Women were held as chattels by male relatives in the nineteenth century. From Gay (1984), page 174.
7. Women fought the spread of gender ideologies, according to Chafe (1972).

Chapter 3 (pp. 50–65)

1. The fantasy and the quote are from Kaye (1974).
2. Few sex differences survive the test of cross-cultural analysis. Martin and Voorhies (1975) examined aggression, intelligence, dependency, ambitiousness, and nurturance, finding all of these traits to be culturally variable. Anthropologists do, however, recognize that endemic warfare is a virtually exclusive male activity. According to the theories advanced in this book, the masculine role as warrior has systematic effects on personality, reflecting both the effects of masculine conditioning and the structural position of boys in a family. Cross-cultural patterns in gender personality do exist, but they are neither innate nor universal.

3. In a few cases, women have been known to assist men in battle, but they rarely do the actual fighting. In one instructive example, among the Kapauku of the New Guinea highlands, women run in among the fighting men to retrieve fallen arrows, but with the understanding that the enemy will not harm them. From Friedl (1975), page 59.

4. In an analysis of the division of labor by sex, Murdock and Provost (1973) list fourteen activities that are done almost exclusively by males in most known societies (from a sample of 186 cultures). Those activities include hunting, smelting, metalworking, lumbering, fowling, boatbuilding, and stoneworking. Explanations for this male work domain vary and are a source of considerable debate in anthropology. Murdock believes the division of labor is due to the greater physical strength of men. White, et al., and Friedl believe that danger and long-distance travel are more important factors, that cultures do not want to expose childbearing women to potentially dangerous work. For a fuller discussion, see Sanday (1981), Chapter 4.

5. The common explanation for female infanticide is that people need warriors and place a higher value on male than on female life. But the underlying purpose of this practice may be quite different: Killing some female infants has the effect of limiting population growth in regions and periods of scarce resources. See Harris (1977), page 17.

6. Sanday's description (1981) of sexually equal and unequal cultures identifies male proximity to children as a significant variable. The closer the fathers to their children, the more equal the society. The more distant, the more unequal. Such a correlation does not prove that this variable is a *causal* factor in the creation of male dominance and a warrior ethos, but the hypothesis is supported by psychoanalytic reasoning. See Whiting, et al. (1958), and Whiting and Whiting (1975).

7. Descriptions of the Lepcha are from Sanday (1981).

8. For a fuller discussion, see Bateson (1958).

9. Slater (1964) argues that the strong sex-role differences in parents from traditional father-ruled families sets up the father as a potential scapegoat. Barred by role from nurturing or indulging his children, the father in these families may become a target of hate.

10. Galbraith's quotes are from *The New York Times Magazine* column "About Men" (1984).

11. For a fuller discussion of the growth of rationality in organizations, see Rosabeth Moss Kanter (1977).

12. The figures are from the Catalyst publication "Corporations and Two-Career Families: Directions for the Future" (1981), based on a 1980 survey of *Fortune* 1300 companies. Twenty-nine percent of the companies queried returned the questionnaire. Responses on the upward mobility of parents were based on a sample of 355 companies.

13. The Korn/Ferry–UCLA survey included presidents, senior officers, vice-presidents, financial officers, and corporate counsels of *Fortune* 1000 and 50's companies. Fifty percent of the executive women surveyed returned the questionnaire.

Chapter 4 (pp. 66–85)

1. Rosabeth Moss Kanter (1977) explains the work personality of executive women as a product of tokenism. The token individuals, whether a racial or sexual minority, develop defense mechanisms and personal strategies that allow them to survive in an environment where they are being watched and judged by people of the dominant culture. Assuming a neutral, businesslike personality is a significant part of this defense strategy.

2. For a psychoanalytic description of the masculine syndrome in women, see Horney (1967).

3. For a contemporary discussion of feminine identity in the psychoanalytic tradition, see Nadelson (1983) and Notmen and Nadelson (1981).

4. For a major new theoretical discussion of feminine identity in the psychoanalytic tradition, see Chodorow (1978).

5. Goodenough (1971, 1965) proposes that culture be studied as a series of rights, duties, and privileges conferred on individuals in given social roles. These rights and duties define the limits of behavior and establish priorities among individuals for distributing resources and satisfying competing wants. No human community is without such rules, and social relationships can be analyzed therefore as "an ordered distribution of rights, privileges and duties among well-defined categories of persons." The ideas people have concerning what wives, husbands, fathers, and mothers should do under various circumstances offer a direct means of studying these cultural rules. The professional woman lives by rules established primarily for the male gender, which are frequently in conflict with the rights and duties of feminine roles.

6. For an excellent summation of research on gender behavior and gender identity, see Money and Ehrhardt (1977). Basic gender identity is established by the age of eighteen months and is highly resistant to change thereafter. In the first months of life, the gender of an infant can be changed with surgery, hormonal therapy, and conditioning. The child will come to see himself as having the gender he was given, regardless of the chromosomes he inherited. Thus, basic gender identity is malleable but subject to deep imprinting. After the first year and a half of life, it cannot be changed without serious psychological damage. Even a flood of hormones from the opposite sex at puberty will not change the basic identity. Girls, for instance, who are masculinized at puberty by male hormones (caused by the adrenogenital syndrome or by tumors of the adrenal cortex or ovary) feel

stigmatized by the virilization (page 213). It runs counter to their basic female identity. By the same token, men treated with estrogen continue to see themselves as male, even though they may develop breasts.

7. Cultural changes requiring a change in identity are apt to traumatize the individual whose sense of personal worth and integrity are grounded in the existing social order. For this reason, people will resist such changes unless the system leaves them compromised and humiliated. In the process of change, bitterness and misunderstanding are inevitable. See Goodenough (1963), Chapters 8 and 9, for further discussion of identity change in developing nations.

8. A few of the twelve men interviewed for this study made a point of separating their professional and private lives. They did not have friends who overlapped the two spheres. But generally, this split is less characteristic of men than of women, a point supported by Hennig and Jardim (1976) in their study of managerial women.

9. Hennig and Jardim (1976) describe this midlife switch among women managers who began to retrieve aspects of feminine behavior after the first decade of work. During this period of change, half of the sample of twenty-five executives married. All of them married men who had children from a previous marriage. None of the women bore children of her own.

Chapter 5 (pp. 89–100)

1. All twenty-five women in the Hennig and Jardim sample (1976) had extremely close relationships with their fathers and had been involved as children in tomboy activities with their fathers. The presence of an influential father is so common in studies of executive women that it has become an expected attribute of high-achieving women in business. Nevertheless, the women who recovered feminine identity at midlife were the ones who advanced to senior levels of management, while the women who retained the masculine style stayed at the level of middle management (pages 178–179). In the present study, women were not graded by managerial level. All the women were considered professional by virtue of their membership in professional financial women's organizations. They were not ranked by career status within that broad category.

2. Sociologist Talcott Parsons believed that in all nuclear families, power and authority gravitate to the father while emotional and supportive functions gravitate to the mother. Families with this kind of sharp differentiation in parental roles along an instrumental (male) and expressive (female) axis were considered by Parsons to be normal (1955). But rather than providing a normative standard for families everywhere, the pattern most likely represents Euro-American middle-class culture of the past two centuries. (See Slater, 1964.)

Notes

Chapter 6 (101–111)

1. For a description of the traumatic emotional reidentification of pregnant women with their own mothers, see Bibring (1959) and Bibring, Huntington, and Valenstein (1961).

Chapter 7 (112–122)

1. Slater (1955) found no pathological consequences of the cross-sex identification. His subjects—all Harvard male undergraduates—were no more nor less psychologically adjusted than other young men of their age and background.
2. How the children perceive their parents is crucial. Those who see a high degree of role differentiation are more likely to have conflicts in self-image than children who see their parents as more similar. From Wecksler (1957).
3. In Horney's (1967) analysis of the flight from womanhood, she commented on the cultural subordination of women: "In actual fact, a girl is exposed from birth onward to the suggestion—inevitable, whether conveyed brutally or delicately—of her inferiority, an experience that constantly stimulates her masculinity complex. . . . It seems to me impossible to judge to how great a degree the unconscious motives for the flight from womanhood are reinforced by the actual social subordination of women" (page 70). The stories of these financial women suggest that cultural factors play a major role, as Horney suspected.

Chapter 8 (pp. 125–140)

1. Historian Carl Degler points out that the "great values for which the family stands are at odds, not only with those of the Women's Movement, but also with those of today's world." Democracy, individualism, and meritocracy are "conspicuous by their absence from the family." As one difference, families accept members simply because they are born into them, not because of what the members may achieve or contribute. Subordination of individual interests to group interests is the hallmark of family life, and altruism, far more than egoism, is its central operating value. The family, in other words, lives by the Communist motto "from each according to his abilities, to each according to his needs." All of these values and principles stand diametrically opposed to those of the American marketplace. Women, as the carriers of family values, therefore face enormous conflict in reconciling these opposing principles—a task that goes to the heart of Western history. From Degler's concluding chapter, "Women's Dilemma."
2. The large investment of women in child rearing is a product of the last two centuries of Western experience. Prior to the nineteenth century, chil-

dren were seen as miniature adults, who could be sent away at the age of ten to work in other homes. From Degler (1980), Chapter IV. In many non-Western cultures, small children are reared by older children, while adult women work. From the *Six Cultures* study, Beatrice Whiting (1963).

Chapter 9 (pp. 141–150)

1. Ulanov (1971), influenced by Jungian psychology, gives an excellent description of the feminine principle. In her writing, it has two aspects. One is static: "receptive, dark, ingoing, moist and enclosing. . . . The elementary aspect of the feminine gestates new drives, images, fantasies and intuitions and is thus associated with the unconscious and with the dark mysteries of God." The other aspect is transformative, associated with elements of the psyche that urge change and break conventions. Through this second, transformative power of the feminine principle, people experience divine madness, ecstasy, and moving out of the self to merge with others. Creativity, feelings of zest, excitement, and vitality all emanate from this principle. Men as well as women have feminine capacities. See pages 157–162.

2. Chodorow (1978) believes that women want to be mothers because their sense of self is more continuous with others and more imbedded in relationships. This happens because they are females, reared by females, do not break identification with the original mothering figure—a break that boys must make and which separates them in lasting ways from feeling, empathy, and intimacy. "As a result of having been parented by a woman, women are more likely than men to seek to be mothers, that is, to relocate themselves in a primary mother-child relationship and to have psychological and relationship capacities for mothering" (page 206). This theory, however, does not take into account the sometimes severe break in identification that some career women make as they seek to follow a path that is very different from the one followed by their mothers. Reproduction of mothering is not automatic when women have career options.

3, In Bibring's clinical study (1953), fathers tend to be passive and compliant or too busy to be involved with their children. Mothers are often disappointed in their husbands, a feeling they communicate to their sons.

4. From Slater (1955, 1964).

Chapter 10 (pp. 151–161)

1. From Kagan, Kearsley, and Zelazo (1978).

2. From Rutter (1981).

3. Kagan (1978) advises a child-staff ratio of no more than three to one and discusses separation anxiety on pages 266–267.

4. Data on the two-career couples is from Catalyst (1981).

Notes

Chapter 11 (pp. 165–183)

1. The low rate of reproduction among financial women is documented by Korn/Ferry International and the UCLA Graduate School of Management in their 1982 survey of three hundred executive women. Sixty-one percent of the group—presidents, vice-presidents, financial officers, senior officers, and corporate counsels—had no children.
2. See Baruch, Barnett, and Rivers (1983) for their study of mastery and pleasure among contemporary women.
3. Changes in identity are often major crises for the individual. The person feels confused, anxious, and self-conscious in the period of transition. He swings back and forth between his old behavior and his new model and may surprise himself unpleasantly. During the act of eradication, the individual turns from his former self with a sense of finality. He can never go back, whatever happens. His bridges have been burned. Goodenough (1963), page 229.

Chapter 12 (pp. 184–197)

1. In the Hennig and Jardim study (1976), women were much more likely than men to take the posture: "This is who I am—like it or leave it." They felt it was more important to be true to themselves than to adopt a style to please the boss. "There is no sense of a game being played, of a temporary adoption of a different style for reasons of self-interest. It is all for real. The investment in oneself is specific, the vulnerability to criticism and to personal hurt is consequently greater" (page 51). Men, in other words, have a larger capacity for dissembling.
2. The process of identity change is not complete until women retrieve a sense of feminine strength. In Hennig and Jardim's sample (1976), the women who got stuck at middle management were by and large women "who clung to self-concepts and behavioral styles which were masculine in orientation and they possessed few human skills to bring to bear on their work. In short, this group of women continued to accept that their sexual identity and their careers were necessarily in conflict and they sought to cope with that conflict by evading the fact of femininity" (page 179).

Chapter 13 (201–217)

1. In her monthly *Redbook* column, Mead wrote that traditional rules for sexual behavior have broken down; at the same time women have entered a new realm in the office where there are no traditions defining acceptable sex behavior between men and women. In this new equal environment a taboo is needed. "Like the family, the modern profession must develop incest taboos" Mead (1978).

292

2. In cultures studied by anthropologists, incest taboos frequently cover not just close blood relatives but large groups of people, such as the several hundred members of a clan. These enormous extensions of the incest taboo obviously have a socio-cultural rather than a biological purpose. Moreover, the kin-based group in primitive cultures has a productive function not unlike that of modern corporations.

3. Some authorities believe that even among close family relatives, the purpose of an incest taboo is not so much to preserve the gene pool from inbreeding as it is to preserve the social organization of the family from a violent upheaval in roles. From a discussion of the incest taboo by Harris (1968).

Chapter 15 (pp. 235–251)

1. The authors of *Lifeprints* (Baruch, et al., 1983) believe that single women of the current generation are transitional. Brought up with the feminine mystique, they expected to be married and they suffer from unfulfilled dreams. Future generations of women may find it easier to be optimistic about their futures as unmarried women (page 211).

2. The war years of the early 1940s marked a turning point in the history of working women who married. Before that, women were systematically laid off when they married. But the enormous need for female labor during World War II led to the abolition of governmental and industrial rules against the employment of married women (page 146). After the war, some of those rules were reinstated (page 180), but never again on the scale of the prewar days. The position of married women in the labor force was permanently altered. From Chafe (1972).

3. The statistics and the quotes are from Degler (1980), pages 383–385 and 421–424.

4. In the Catalyst survey of 815 two-career couples, 69 percent of the mothers were employed when their babies were born. The median time taken for childbirth was twelve weeks.

5. Sex-identity conflict lies at the source of the hyperaggressive syndrome in males. See John and Beatrice Whiting (1975) and Beatrice Whiting (1965).

6. See Gay (1984), page 169, for a description of the spread of patriarchy in the nineteenth century.

7. Whiting, et al. (1958) published their original study under the title "The Function of Male Initiation Ceremonies at Puberty." They theorized that brutal initiation rites would occur primarily in cultures where husbands and wives roomed apart so that the boys developed a strong primary identification with the mother and an unusually powerful form of the oedipus conflict. That theory was confirmed and extended in later publications to explain the psychodynamics of warrior cultures.

Notes

8. Aloofness between husband and wife goes hand in hand with warlikeness. Building on prior work, John and Beatrice Whiting demonstrated that husbands and wives live in separate quarters in cultures with a high need for warriors to protect property. The rooming apart has the effect of producing hyperaggressive men via a conflict in sexual identity that is resolved at puberty with brutal initiation rites. "The custom may have been invented and have diffused as a concomitant of the need for warriors.... The social behavior of children brought up in cultures with the rooming apart pattern is less intimate and more aggressive than that of children brought up in cultures in which the fathers are more involved in domestic affairs." Whiting and Whiting (1975).
9. The quote is from Beatrice Whiting's paper on sex-identity conflict and physical violence (1965).
10. The quotes are from Gay (1984).
11. Codification of Roman law in the Code Napoleon consolidated the inferior status of women across Europe. The code classified women and children along with "persons of unsound mind" as being legally incapable of entering into contracts. From Deckard (1979), page 216.
12. See Chafe (1977).
13. Chafe (1972) interprets the Declaration at Seneca Falls on page 6.
14. Gay's quote (1984) on the male fear of female power appears on page 192.
15. For information on the relationship between early child experience and later adult personality, see Brim and Kagan (1980).
16. See Degler's discussion (1980) of potential solutions, page 464.
17. The Keniston quote (1977) is on page 122.
18. Catalyst repeated its survey of paternity leave in 1984. The original survey was published as part of its 1981 study.

Chapter 16 (pp. 252–274)

1. Patricia McBroom, 1986, *The Third Sex: The New Professional Woman*, William Morrow & Co., New York, p. 139.
2. Ibid., p. 64.
3. Ibid., p. 32.
4. Ibid., p. 181.
5. "Books" section, *Business Week*, June 2, 1986, pp. 12, 16.
6. Arlie Hochschild, 1989, *The Second Shift: Working Parents and the Revolution at Home*, Viking Penguin, New York, p. 3.
7. McBroom, 1986; see chapter 3.
8. *The New York Times*, August 8, 1988, p. 1.
9. Felice Schwartz, 1989, "Management Women and the New Facts of Life," *Harvard Business Review*, January–February, pp. 67–76.
10. Ibid., p. 70.
11. *The New York Times*, March 13, 1989, p. A18.

12. McBroom, 1986; see chapter 3.

13. Catalyst staff, 1986, "Report on a National Study of Parental Leaves," Catalyst Career and Family Center, New York City, pp. 28–31, 59–61.

14. N. Radin and R. Goldsmith, 1983, as quoted in *Fatherhood Today: Men's Changing Role in the Family*, Phyllis Bronstein and Carolyn Pape Cowan (eds.) 1988, John Wilely, New York, p. 324.

15. Current Population Report, March 1990 and 1989, Series P20, #447, "Household and Family Characteristics," Bureau of the Census, Washington, D.C.

16. Peggy Reeves Sanday, 1981, *Female Power and Male Dominance: On the Origins of Sexual Inequality*, Cambridge University Press, New York, pp. 163–175.

17. Napoleon A. Chagnon, 1988, "Life histories, blood revenge and warfare in a tribal population," *Science*, February 26, Vol. 239:985–992.

18. Boyce Rensberger, 1988, "The men who will kill for women," *San Francisco Chronicle* (from *The Washington Post*), March 27.

19. Thomas H. Maugh II, 1988, "Remote tribe shows streak of violence," *Los Angeles Times*, February 26, p. 34.

20. Sanday, 1981, found that unequal male-dominant societies occurred in 28 percent of tribal cultures, defined as societies where women are excluded from economic and political decision-making and where men are aggressive, particularly to women, as measured by five traits: the presence of exclusive men's houses, frequent quarreling or wife beating, the presence of rape, and raiding other groups for wives. In 32 percent of the cultures, women had political or economic authority and men were not aggressive to them. Sanday defined these cultures as equal societies. The remaining 40 percent were called "mythical" male-dominant, a mixed form in which women had some power and men expressed aggression against them (pp. 164–5). For further information on the psychological and cultural underpinnings of warrior cultures, see John W. M. Whiting et al, 1958, "The function of male initiation ceremonies at puberty," in *Readings in Social Psychology*, 3rd ed., E. Maccoby (ed), Henry Holt, New York; and Whiting and Whiting, 1975, "Aloofness and intimacy of husbands and wives," *Ethos*, Vol. 3, No. 2:183–207.

21. Fran Sussner Rodgers and Charles Rodgers, 1989, "Business and the facts of family life," *Harvard Business Review*, November–December; Vol. 67, No. 6:121–129.

22. "Letters to the Editor," *Harvard Business Review*, January–February 1990; Vol. 68, No. 1:194–199.

23. Ellen Galinsky, 1990, "The relevance of British career break schemes for American companies," a paper published by the Families and Work Institute, New York.

24. Ibid., p. 7.

Notes

25. Ellen Galinsky, 1989, "The implementation of flexible time and leave policies: observations from European employers," a paper commissioned by the National Academy of Sciences, published by the Families and Work Institute, New York.
26. Ibid., pp. 29–31.
27. Ibid., p. 19.
28. Ibid., p. 9.
29. Ibid., p. 30.
30. The federal family leave bill exempts the top 10 percent of a company's wage earners from the provisions of the legislation. The prevailing attitude among conservatives is that company executives can negotiate personally for family leave. But without the law to help set new standards of behavior up and down the hierarchy, executives continue to be exposed to the prevailing work ethic, leading to a stratification of the workforce into parents (lower-level workers) and nonparents (higher-level workers). Also see Schwartz, 1989, and Galinsky, 1990, p. 5.
31. Ellen Galinsky and Dana Friedman, 1991, *The Corporate Reference Guide to Work-Family Programs*, Families and Work Institute, New York.
32. Gary W. Loveman, 1990, "The case of the part-time partner," *Harvard Business Review*, September–October.
33. Ibid., p. 21.
34. Women with flexible work schedules or reduced hours generally say they learn to be more efficient and to use their time more productively. A cutback may occur, however, in the time available for politics and socializing on the job. See Galinsky, 1990, p. 9, and *Beyond the Parental Leave Debate: The Impact of Laws in Four States* (in press) by James T. Bond et al., Families and Work Institute, New York.
35. Loveman, 1990, p. 20.
36. Jonathan R. Cole and Harriet Zuckerman, 1987, "Marriage, motherhood and research performance in science," *Scientific American;* Vol. 256 (February): 119–125.
37. Loveman, 1990, p. 24.
38. Ibid., 1990, p. 21.
39. Loveman, personal communication.
40. M. Kay Martin and Barbara Voorhies, 1975, *The Female of the Species*, Columbia University Press, New York, pp. 226–227.
41. Sanday, 1981, pp. 114–118.
42. Irene Pavey, 1986, *Business Week*, June 2, pp. 12, 16.

Bibliography

Banner, Lois W. 1974. *Women in Modern America: A Brief History*. Harcourt Brace Jovanovich, New York.

Baruch, Grace, Rosalind Barnett, and Caryl Rivers. 1983. *Lifeprints*. McGraw-Hill, New York.

Bateson, Gregory. 1958. *Naven*. Stanford University Press, Stanford, Calif.

————. 1972. *Steps to an Ecology of the Mind*. Ballantine Books, New York.

Beach, Frank A., ed. 1976. *Human Sexuality in Four Perspectives*. Johns Hopkins University Press, Baltimore.

Bernard, Jesse. 1972. *The Future of Marriage*. World Publishing Co., New York.

Bibring, Grete L. 1953. "On the Passing of the Oedipus Complex in a Matriarchal Family Setting." In *Drives, Affects and Behavior: Essays in Honor of Marie Bonaparte*, ed. Rudolph M. Lowenstein. International Universities Press, New York.

————. 1959. "Some Considerations of the Psychological Processes in Pregnancy." *Psychoanalytic Study of the Child,* Vol. 14:113–121.

Bibring, Grete L., Dorothy S. Huntington, and Arthur Valenstein. 1961. "A Study of the Psychological Processes in Pregnancy and of the Earliest Mother-Child Relationship." *Psychoanalytic Study of the Child,* Vol. 16:9–72.

Brim, O., Jr., and Jerome Kagan. 1980. *Constancy and Change in Human Development*. Harvard University Press, Cambridge, Mass.

Brownmiller, Susan. 1984. *Femininity*. Simon and Schuster, New York.

Campbell, Bernard. 1966. *Human Evolution,* 2nd ed. Aldine Publishing Co., Chicago.

Catalyst. 1981. "Corporations and Two-Career Families: Directions for the Future." Catalyst Career and Family Center, New York.

————. 1984. "Preliminary Report on a Nationwide Survey of Maternity/Paternity Leaves: A Position Paper." Catalyst Career and Family Center, New York.

Chafe, William H. 1972. *The American Woman*. Oxford University Press, New York.

————. 1977. *Women and Equality*. Oxford University Press, New York.

299

Bibliography

Cheney, Dorothy L. 1978. "The Play Partners of Immature Baboons." *Animal Behavior,* Vol. 26:1038–50.

Chodoff, Paul. 1982. "Hysteria and Women." *American Journal of Psychiatry,* Vol. 139:5:545–51.

Chodorow, Nancy. 1978. *The Reproduction of Mothering.* University of California Press, Berkeley, Calif.

Chowning, Ann. 1973. *An Introduction to the Peoples and Cultures of Melanesia,* 2nd ed. Cummings Publishing Co., Menlo Park, Calif.

Colegrave, Sukie. 1979. *The Spirit of the Valley; The Masculine and the Feminine in Human Consciousness.* Virago Press, Great Britain, distributed by Houghton Mifflin Co., Boston.

Dahlberg, Frances. 1981. *Woman the Gatherer.* Yale University Press, New Haven, Conn.

Deckard, Barbara Sinclair. 1979. *The Women's Movement.* Harper and Row, New York.

Degler, Carl N. 1980. *At Odds.* Oxford University Press, Oxford.

Dinnerstein, Dorothy. 1976. *The Mermaid and the Minotaur.* Harper and Row, New York.

Dowling, Colette. 1981. *The Cinderella Complex.* Summit Books, Simon and Schuster, New York.

Fraker, Susan. 1984. "Why Women Aren't Getting to the Top." *Fortune,* April 16:40–5.

Frank, Harold H., ed. 1977. *Women in the Organization.* University of Pennsylvania Press, Philadelphia.

Friedan, Betty. 1962. *The Feminine Mystique.* W. W. Norton, New York.

Friedl, Ernestine. 1975. *Women and Men: An Anthropological View.* Holt, Rinehart and Winston, New York.

Galbraith, John Kenneth. 1983. *The Anatomy of Power.* Houghton Mifflin, New York.

———. "Corporate Man." In *The New York Times Magazine,* January 22, 1984.

Gay, Peter. 1984. *The Bourgeois Experience,* Vol. 1: *Education of the Senses.* Oxford University Press, New York.

Geertz, Clifford. 1973. *The Interpretation of Cultures.* Basic Books, New York.

Gilligan, Carol. 1982. *In A Different Voice: Psychological Theory and Woman's Development.* Harvard University Press, Cambridge, Mass.

Goodale, Jane. 1971. *Tiwi Wives: A Study of the Women of Melville Island, North Australia.* University of Washington Press, Seattle.

Goodenough, Ward H. 1963. *Cooperation in Change: An Anthropological Approach to Community Development.* Russell Sage Foundation, New York.

———. 1965. "Rethinking Status and Role." In *The Relevance of Models for Social Anthropology,* ed. M. Banton, Tavistock, London.

———. 1971. *Culture, Language and Society.* Addison-Wesley Publishing Co., Reading, Mass.

Harrigan, Betty Lehan. 1977. *Games Mother Never Taught You.* Warner Books, New York.

Harris, Marvin. 1968. *The Rise of Anthropological Theory.* Thomas Y. Crowell Co., New York.

————. 1977. *Cannibals and Kings.* Random House, New York.

Hennig, Margaret, and Ann Jardim. 1976. *The Managerial Woman.* Doubleday and Co., New York.

Hockschild, Arlie R. 1977. "A Review of Sex Role Research." In *Women in the Organization,* ed. Harold H. Frank. University of Pennsylvania Press, Philadelphia.

Horn, Patrice, and Jack C. Horn. 1982. *Sex in the Office.* Addison-Wesley Publishing Co., Reading, Mass.

Horney, Karen. 1967. *Feminine Psychology.* W. W. Norton and Co., New York.

Johnson, Miriam. 1975. "Fathers, Mothers and Sex Typing." *Sociological Inquiry,* Vol. 45(1):15–26.

————, 1977. "Androgeny and the Maternal Principle." *School Review,* Nov. 1977:50–69.

Jolly, Alison, 1972. *The Evolution of Primate Behavior.* Macmillan Publishing Co., New York.

Jonas, David, and Doris F. Jonas. 1975. "A Biological Basis for the Oedipus Complex: An Evolutionary and Ethological Approach." *American Journal of Psychiatry,* Vol. 132:6:602–6.

Jung, Carl G. 1959. *The Archetypes and the Collective Unconscious.* 2nd ed. Princeton University Press, Princeton, N.J.

Kagan, Jerome, Richard B. Kearsley, and Philip R. Zelazo. 1978. *Infancy: Its Place in Human Development.* Harvard University Press, Cambridge, Mass.

Kanter, Rosabeth Moss. 1977. *Men and Women of the Corporation.* Basic Books, New York.

Kaye, Harvey E. 1974. *Male Survival: Masculinity Without Myth.* Grosset and Dunlap, New York.

Keniston, Kenneth, and the Carnegie Council on Children. 1977. *All Our Children: The American Family Under Pressure.* Harcourt Brace Jovanovich, New York.

Komarovsky, Mirra. 1946. "Cultural Contradictions and Sex Roles." *American Journal of Sociology,* Vol. 52:184–9.

————. 1950. "Functional Analysis of Sex Roles." *American Sociological Review,* Vol. 15:508–16.

Korn/Ferry International. 1982. "Profile of Women Senior Executives." 277 Park Avenue, New York.

Lee, R. B. 1972. "Work Effort, Group Structure and Land Use in Contemporary Hunter-Gatherers." In *Man, Settlement, and Urbanism,* ed. Peter J. Ucko, et al. Schenkman Publishing Co., Cambridge, Mass.

Lee, R. B., and I. DeVore, eds. 1968. *Man the Hunter.* Aldine Press, Chicago.

Bibliography

Levinson, Daniel G. 1978. *The Seasons of a Man's Life.* Knopf, New York.

Lips, Hilary M., and Nina Lee Colwill. 1978. *The Psychology of Sex Differences.* Prentice Hall, Englewood Cliffs, N. J.

Lurie, Alison. 1981. *The Language of Clothes.* Random House, New York.

McBroom, Patricia. 1980. *Behavioral Genetics.* National Institute of Mental Health, Washington, D.C.

MacKinnon, Catherine A. 1979. *Sexual Harassment of Working Women.* Yale University Press, New Haven, Conn.

Malloy, John T. 1975. *Dress for Success.* Peter H. Wyden Publishing Co., New York.

Martin, Kay M., and Barbara Voorhies. 1975. *Female of the Species.* Columbia University Press, New York.

Matthiasson, Carolyn J., ed. 1974. *Many Sisters: Women in Cross-cultural Perspective.* The Free Press, Macmillan Publishing Co., New York.

Mead, Margaret. 1956. *New Lives for Old.* William Morrow and Co., New York.

————. 1963. *Sex and Temperament.* William Morrow and Co., New York.

————. 1967. *Male and Female.* William Morrow and Co., New York.

————. 1978. "A Proposal: We Need Taboos on Sex at Work." *Redbook,* April 1978.

Millett, Kate. 1969. *Sexual Politics.* Doubleday and Co., New York.

Money, John, and Anke A. Ehrhardt. 1972. *Man & Woman; Boy & Girl.* Johns Hopkins University Press, Baltimore.

Murdock, George P., and Caterina Provost. 1973. "Factors in the Division of Labor by Sex: A Cross-cultural Analysis." *Ethnology,* Vol. 12:203–25.

Nadelson, Carol C. 1981. "Alternative Life-styles and the Mental Health of Children." *American Handbook of Psychiatry,* Vol. 7, Chapter 10.

————. 1981. "Child Psychiatry Perspectives: Women, Work and Children." *Journal of the American Academy of Clinical Psychiatry,* Vol. 3(2):187–202.

————. 1983. "The Psychology of Women." *Canadian Journal of Psychiatry,* Vol. 28, No. 3:210–18.

Notman, Malkah, and Carol Nadelson. 1981. "Changing Views of Femininity and Childbearing." *The Hillside Journal of Clinical Psychiatry,* Vol. 20:863–75.

Oliver, Douglas L. 1955. *A Solomon Island Society: Kinship and Leadership Among the Siuai of Bougainville.* Beacon Press, Boston.

Parsons, Talcott, and Robert F. Bales. 1955. *Family: Socialization and Interaction Process.* Free Press, New York.

Pilbeam, David. 1972. *The Ascent of Man.* Macmillan Publishing Co., New York.

Rhey, Marie. 1959. *The Kuma: Freedom and Conformity in the New Guinea Highlands.* Cambridge University Press, London.

Rich, Adrienne. 1976. *Of Woman Born.* W. W. Norton and Co., New York.

Rosaldo, Michelle Zimbalist, and Louise Lamphere, eds. 1974. *Women, Culture and Society.* Stanford University Press, Stanford, Calif.

Rutter, Michael. 1981. "Social-Emotional Consequences of Day Care for Pre-school Children." *American Journal of Orthopsychiatry*, Vol. 51(1):4–28.

Sanday, Peggy Reeves. 1981. *Female Power and Male Dominance: On the Origins of Sexual Equality*. Cambridge University Press, New York.

———. 1981. "The Socio-cultural Context of Rape: A Cross-cultural Study." *The Journal of Social Issues*, Vol. 37(4)5–27.

Schlegel, Alice, ed. 1977. *Sexual Stratification: A Cross-cultural View*. Columbia University Press, New York.

Shapiro, Judith. 1979. "Cross-cultural Perspectives on Sexual Differentiation." In *Human Sexuality: A Comparative and Developmental Perspective*. University of California Press, Berkeley, Calif.

Slater, Philip. 1955. "Psychological Factors in Role Specialization." Unpublished Ph.D. thesis, Harvard University.

———. 1964. "Parental Role Differentiation." In *The Family: Its Structure and Function*, ed. Rose Laub Coser. St. Martin's Press, New York.

Slocum, Sally. 1975. "Woman the Gatherer: Male Bias in Anthropology." In *Toward an Anthropology of Women*, ed. R. R. Reiter. Monthly Review Press, New York.

Smith-Rosenberg, Carroll. 1972. "The Hysterical Woman: Sex Roles and Role Conflict in 19th Century America." *Social Research*, Vol. 49, No. 4:653–78.

Spradley, James P. 1979. *The Ethnographic Interview*. Holt, Rinehart and Winston, New York.

Stevens, Anthony. 1982. *Archetypes*. William Morrow and Co., New York.

Strathern, Marilyn. 1972. *Women in Between: Female Roles in a Male World*. Seminar Press, New York.

Ulanov, Ann Belford. 1971. *The Feminine in Jungian Psychology and Christian Theology*. Northwestern University Press, Evanston, Ill.

Vetterling-Braggin, Mary, ed. 1982. *Femininity, Masculinity, and Androgeny: A Modern Philosophical Discussion*. Littlefield, Adams and Co., Totowa, N.J.

Wecksler, H. 1957. "Conflicts in Self-perception." Unpublished Ph.D. thesis, Harvard University.

White, Douglas R., Michael Burton, and Lilyan Brudner. 1977. "Entailment Theory and Method: A Cross-cultural Analysis of the Sexual Division of Labor. *Behavior Science Research*, Vol. 12:1–24.

Whiting, Beatrice B., ed. 1963. *Six Cultures: Studies in Child Rearing*. John Wiley and Sons, New York.

———. 1965. "Sex Identity Conflict and Physical Violence: A Comparative Study." *American Anthropologist*, Vol. 67(6) special publication:123–140.

Whiting, John W. M., and Beatrice Whiting. 1975. "Aloofness and Intimacy of Husbands and Wives." *Ethos*, 3:183–207.

Whiting, John W. M., Richard Kluckhohn, and Albert Anthony. 1958. "The Function of Male Initiation Ceremonies at Puberty." In *Readings in Social Psy-*

chology, 3rd ed., eds. Eleanor Maccoby, et al. Henry Holt and Co., New York.

Wilson, Edward O. 1978. *On Human Nature*. Harvard University Press, Cambridge, Mass.

Index

Index

Index

Index

Index

Index

A Note
About the
Author

Born in California, Patricia McBroom has lived on the East
Coast since 1965. She is an anthropologist, having done her
work at the University of Pennsylvania. She is also a journalist,
formerly a science writer for the *Philadelphia Inquirer.* She
teaches at Rutgers University and lives in Princeton, New
Jersey.